Shabaka's Stone: An At the Origin and Continu of the Cosmic Universe

Written by Professor Kaba Hiawatha Kamene

African History is Not Hidden
It is Carved on Shabaka's Stone

Table of Contents

Acknowledgments

I thank my wife Shari, daughters Sasha Madeline and Candace Deana, son Heru and GranManChild KaRes. Your support continues to give me the inspiration for all I achieve.

Duau (Many Thanks) to Neset Bity (Pharaoh) Shabaka for rewriting his ancestor's Theory on the Origin of the Cosmic Universe. I dedicate my book to you, Neset Bity Shabaka, my ancestor, as you did for them, your ancestors.

I thank Professor Drusilla Dunjee Houston whose book, **Wonderful Ethiopians of the Ancient Cushite Empire,** gave me a deeper understanding of the intellectual foundations of the Kushite Kingdom.

I thank Dr. George G. M. James, author of **Stolen Legacy**. His book first introduced me to Shabaka's Stone through the Memphite Theology.

I thank Skippia Alvarez and her family for all they do and continue to do.

I thank Janmarie, Shawn and Sonny Brown. Keep On Keepin' On.

Dua Duau to Brother Reverend Philippe Shock Matthews for his brilliant synthesis of tech skills and African metaphysics.

I thank Sister Stephanie Abena Kaashe for her genius graphic for Shabaka's Stone Cover and Back designs.
Cover Image - The Classic Bust of Neset Bity (Pharaoh) Shabaka inlaid in Shabaka's Stone in the Cosmos

Preview

Somewhere around 710 years before the common era (BCE), Neset Bity (Pharaoh) Shabaka directed his scientists and scholars to rewrite the work of their ancestors titled, "The Memphite Theology." This ancient creation story was written on either papyrus or leather and had been damaged by time and climate. King Shabaka had the Memphite Theology carved on black basalt stone and the story tells a metaphoric drama that outlined the coming into being and continuing process of becoming of the cosmic universe. They enhanced this process by comparing and contrasting the pattern in all living things in the cosmos and on earth. The ancient African scholars who studied and taught biology, made comparisons to the development of the divine human embryo. Other scholars in different subject areas made the same comparisons with this cosmic allegory.

The ancient scholars raised the potential of their consciousness by asking the question that would answer all others, "What existed before existence existed." From this question they expressed their studies using figurative language, explaining their theory of cosmic history. Shabaka's Stone connects the heavens with the earth, as above, so below. As it is was before the beginning began, it was in the beginning, is now, and will always be.

Along this cosmic journey, please know that there will be repetitions of certain concepts. It is done on purpose. There is a pattern in this book like the pattern in the Cosmic Tabernacle. When we sing the musical scale, we sing; do, re, mi fa, so, la, ti and do. We end with "do" like we begin with "do". However, the second (2nd) do is at a higher frequency. Where concepts and ideas are repeated in Shabaka's Stone, take note of the new contexts and meanings. Same idea, but on a higher order thinking skill.

Libation to the Creator and Ancestors

A Thunderous WORD from our Ancestors

When we act without the counsel of our elders, and the invocation of our Creator and Ancestors, we are acting alone. Libation is a ritual that pays respect to those who came before us and created the trail that we continue to blaze. We are because they were. Since they were, we are.

Before we began writing, **Shabaka's Stone: An African Theory on the Origin and Continuing Development of the Cosmic Universe**, we sought and received the advice of our elders. Now, we invoke permission from our Creator and Ancestors to escort us back to the Waters of Nun, a time before time existed; before the beginning began, a place called "The Nun, the Eternal Waters." A space where our Creator and Ancestors were, are and will always be. A place we all will return to one day.

All praise is due our Creator and Ancestors who watch over All in this cosmic reality. Be with us as we return back before the beginning began to project ourselves forward where we "Will". Be our best friend. Be satisfied with our work.

I Pour Libation for Drusilla Dunjee Houston

Drusilla Dunjee Houston's book, **Wonderful Ethiopians of the Ancient Kushite Empire,** stressed the importance of the role played by the people of Kush (Sudan, Ethiopia, Eritrea, Djibouti, Chad, Northern Kenya) in the development of Kemet (Egypt) and the world. She tells us that the Kushites were the Kemites (Egypt). This connection is grounded in understanding the evolution of African consciousness in the Northeast corridor of Africa. **Wonderful Ethiopians** is a work of pure genius. Considering the resources available to Professor Dunjee Houston during her time, her insightful scholarship and analysis gave her the ability to brilliantly interpret early African thought using science as her source. She published her first (1st) volume in 1926.

Drusilla Dunjee Houston was born on January 20, 1876 in Harper's Ferry, West Virginia. She died on February 8, 1941. She was an American writer, historian, educator, journalist, musician, and screenwriter from West Virginia. Drusilla went to finishing school in the North and studied classical piano at the Northwestern Conservatory of Music in Minnesota.

In 1892, Drusilla and her family moved to Oklahoma City in the Oklahoma Territory, where their father was assigned by the Baptists. From 1892 to 1898, Dunjee taught kindergarten and elementary school in Oklahoma City.

In 1899 she married Price Houston. They settled in McAlester, Oklahoma. The state was admitted to the Union in 1908. Drusilla founded McAlester Seminary for Girls, leading it for 12 years. She was hired by the Baptists in 1917 to serve as principal of the Oklahoma Baptist College for Girls, and moved to Sapulpa, Oklahoma. She served as principal for six years.

When Drusilla returned to Oklahoma City, she started the Oklahoma Vocational Institute of Fine Arts and Crafts. After 1934, she served as religious director of the Oklahoma Home for Delinquent Boys.

In 1915, Drusilla's brother Roscoe Dunjee, founded the Oklahoma Black Dispatch, the first black newspaper in Oklahoma City. She had joined him in writing for the newspaper even before she returned to the city, serving as a contributing editor and columnist. She became an independent historian. Beginning in 1901, she conducted research into a variety of sources and published a multi-volume history of Africans in their homeland titled, **Wonderful Ethiopians of the Ancient Cushite Empire** (1926). Drusilla Dunjee's work was very influential as part of an early 20th-century effort by African Americans in the United States to document their African ancestors as peoples with a complex, ancient history, culture and civilizations.

Houston was a co-founder of Oklahoma chapters of the YWCA, the Red Cross, and the NAACP, all based in Oklahoma City. She was an early leader of the Oklahoma Federation of Colored Women's Clubs. In 1932, her brother Roscoe Dunjee led several NAACP chapters to come together to form a state organization. She was a co-founder of the Dogan Reading Room of Oklahoma and served as its president." She died of tuberculosis on February 8, 1941, in Phoenix, Arizona.

Professor Drusilla Dunjee Houston wrote, "**Wonderful Ethiopians**," as the first book of a three (3) part series that highlighted the historical and cultural background of the original peoples on the earth. She tracked the movement of this ancient Kushite empire as they inhabited the planet. She presented information that collaborated the fact that the Kemites (Egyptians) were black and belonged to the original African cultural group.

Dr. Peggy Brooks-Bertram has dedicated her research to the life and works of Dr. Drusilla Dunjee Houston. Dr. Brooks-Bertram has edited a book titled, **Wonderful Ethiopians of the Ancient Cushite Empire**, highlighting Dr. Houston's life and work. Dr. Brooks-Bertram also expanded the first (1st) volume's bibliography and sources.

William Leo Hansberry, the noted historian from Howard University, wrote in support of Drusilla Dunjee Houston's key premises, including the conclusion that in view of the remarkable similarities between the basic ideas and concepts as expressed in the Kush-Kemet (Egyptian) inscriptions and in the writings and teachings of the Greek philosophers; it may be reasonably assumed that it was from the African priests, priestesses and teachers with whom the Greeks associated during their travels in Kush-Kemet (Egypt) that they acquired many, if not most, of the philosophical concepts which they, without mentioning their origin, subsequently passed off as their own and for which they have been so long, and so unjustly, renowned. **1**

All praise is due Dr. Drusilla Dunjee Houston for her years dedicated to uncovering the truth about the wonderful Ethiopians of the Kushite Empire.

I pour Libation for George Granville Monah James

I recognize the work of Dr. George G. M. James. His book, **Stolen Legacy**, was the first book I read that introduced me to Shabaka's Stone. In 1978, my mother came home with a xerox copy of **Stolen Legacy.** One of her colleagues sent it to me knowing of my interest in African History and Culture. Each chapter introduced me to concepts I had not studied before. When I got to Chapter Eight, "The Memphite Theology," my mind merged time and space and I walked through an intellectual stargate. It was not so much that the Greek's had plagiarized an African theory, it was the authenticity of Dr. James' cosmic interpretation of the Memphite Text rewritten on Shabaka's Stone that attracted my deepest attention. I was inspired! The comparative metaphor expressed in this cosmic drama. Dr. James' exploration of cosmic culture connected science and spirituality from a philosophical perspective expressed in figurative language.

George Granville Monah James was born on November 9, 1893 in Georgetown, Guyana. He died on June 30, 1956. Dr. James was a Guyanese American historian and author. He is best known for his 1954 book, **Stolen Legacy** which argues that Greek philosophy and religion originated in ancient Kemet (Egypt). Dr. James earned a bachelor's and master's degrees at Durham University in England and gained his doctorate at Columbia University in New York. He was Professor of Logic and Greek at Livingstone College in Salisbury, North Carolina before working at Arkansas A and M College in Pine Bluff, Arkansas. Dr. James died soon after publishing Stolen Legacy in 1954. Dr. James was a Phre-Mason (Freemason) in its truest African original sense and was associated with Prince Hall Freemasonry.

In his book, James claims that, among other things, the ancient Greeks were not the original authors of Greek philosophy, which he argues was mainly based on ideas and concepts that were borrowed without acknowledgement, or indeed stolen, from the ancient Kush-Kemet (Egyptians). He argues that Alexander the Great invaded and captured the Royal Libraries and relocated them at a place in the Delta that he named after himself, Alexandria. Dr. James introduced evidence that Aristotle's ideas came from books stolen from Kush-Kemet, and that he established his school within the library. Stolen Legacy draws on the writings of freemasonry to support its claim that Greco-Roman mystery religion originates from a Kush-Kemet Educational System.

Dr. James recognized Greek sources such as Herodotus who described the cultural debt of Greece to Egypt. He also mentions prominent Greek philosophers such as Pythagoras and Plato who are said to have studied in Kush-Kemet. He credited Democritus's use of the term "atom" (indivisible particle) to the Kush-Kemet Neter, "Atum," who symbolizes the creative word, who names the Creator's cosmic creations. **2**

Stolen Legacy has strongly influenced the Afrocentric school of history including leading scholars such as John Henrik Clarke, William Leo Hansberry, Asa G. Hilliard, Yosef Ben-Jochannan, Chiekh Anta Diop, Theophile Obenga and Molefi Asante.

All Praise is due Dr. James for his lifelong search for Ma'atian truth.

Each of our lives is not only connected throughout time and space, but each of our lives is connected to all life everywhere in the cosmos. We live in an eternal existence that is neither created (life) nor destroyed (death). Cosmic life exists. All forms of life are connected in the time-space continuum. In this continuum, time is eternal, and space is everywhere, and when we perform libation, there is a thunderous call from the heavens, the Creator and Ancestors claim, "One of Us Calls to Us! Let us respond through the caller." **3**

Drs. Drusilla Dunjee Houston and George G.M. James dedicated their lives to searching truths utilizing a correct method. In Kush-Kemet, this precise science, based in the scientific method was called, "Tep Heseb."

Tep Heseb is a Kush-Kemet (Egyptian) term translated to mean, **An Accurate Reckoning by using a Correct Method**. Tep Heseb is mentioned in the Rhind Mathematical Papyrus. The Rhind Mathematical Papyrus was found at Waset (Thebes) in Kemet (Egypt). It was purchased by A. Henry Rhind and after his death it went to the British Museum. It was written by a scribe named, Ahmose, who states that it is a copy of an older document written during the time of Neset Bity (Pharaoh) Amen-em-het III, an African Neset Bity (Pharaoh) of the Middle Kingdom (2065-1784 BCE); BCE means Before the Common Era. It was written in hieratic characters, on a single papyrus roll measuring 18 feet long and 13 inches wide. The papyrus sheet contains 87 mathematical problems with solutions. **4**

To understand the various types of Kemetic (Egyptian) writings in Africa, it is important to know the four different forms of Kush-Kemet script,
1) **Hieroglyphics** used in formal writings such as temple and tomb inscriptions.

2) **Hieratic** was a more cursive form, both of these forms appear in Kush before the beginning of Kemetic (Egyptian) history.
3) **Demotic**, was for everyday use.
4) **Coptic** was the Kush-Kemet (Egyptian) language used by the Greek writing system (another form of an African script). This last form survives today in the liturgies (ritual writings) and utterances (prayers) of the Kush-Kemet (Egyptian) and Greek Coptic churches. **5**

The scribe Ahmose explained that an **Accurate Reckoning by using the Correct Method** was the entrance into the knowledge of all existing things and all obscure, mystical and unknown secrets. **6**

Like the two hemispheres of the brain, African philosophy combines and blends spirituality with science. There is no way to separate these two concepts. Science deals with matter, finity, light and all things seen. Spirituality expresses space, infinity, darkness, and all things unseen. While they are not the same, they are like the head and tail of a coin. Quantum physics is the inner atomic world (from human skin, in); and the General (Gravity) and Special Laws of Relativity (Electro-Magnetic) represents the outer world (from human skin, out). Humans are the mid-point between these two worlds.

An Atom is to the Human Body as the Human Body is to the Universe.
The Before-Life is to Life as Life is to the After-Life.

In order for us to have a clear understanding of the truest meaning of ancient Kush-Kemet (Egyptian) wisdom, we must think like these ancient people. We should develop our analysis within their cultural common sense, using their history, language, values, interests and principles. Re-image the world in which they lived; physically, mentally, spiritually and soulfully. In order to be able to make an accurate reckoning, we must use the correct method of interpreting the writings and evocations of our ancient Kush-Kemet (Egyptian) African ancestors in relation to the time(history) and space (geography) they lived.

Imagine this comparison; A deaf person is watching a dance trying to interpret the dancer's movements. She cannot hear the music of the dance and has no knowledge of the purpose of the performance in this soundless movement. She may not be able to hear and comprehend what makes the dancer move the way they do in the performance, but she can watch the dance movement and be aware that something is happening. **7**

In this sense, it is challenging to understand and interpret ancient Kush-Kemet (Egypt) without knowing what they knew, why they knew it, and how they came to know it. What was the cultural philosophy expressed when they viewed a cat, owl, bird or dog in terms of the powers given to them by nature? What made them evoke the sounds they made when they saw that member of nature, or the meaning of the mystical systems of the Neteru (symbols of nature)? What did they represent? Without a cultural reference, there will be no relational meaning and purpose to us as the observer. However, we will still be able to view their thought process by nurturing the functions of their natural science because nature is the same today as it was back then. Nature does not change. Nature transforms naturally through a Divine process of becoming.

Chapter 1 – Introduction to Shabaka's Stone

Shabaka's Stone is an astronomical theory carved on a black basalt rectangular stone at the direction of Neset Bity (Pharaoh) Shabaka of the Napatan Dynasty (aka 25th Kush-Kemet Dynasty) about 710 BCE, Before the Common Era. Shabaka rewrote a more ancient version of the metaphoric story in honor of his ancient Kushite ancestors. From the time that this text was first theorized millennia before the Napatan Dynasty, to when King Shabaka rewrote it, to today…Imagine, **more** time elapsed from the time it was first created to the time of King Shabaka…then when Neset Bity King Shabaka rewrote it and today, 2021. That's how ancient these ideas were and are.

Shabaka's Stone is a cosmic roadmap that repeats its success for every creation it creates, as long as the creation follows Nature's way. This roadmap is Ma'at…Truth, Justice, Balance, Morality, Order, Harmony, Righteousness and Reciprocity. What goes around, comes around. You get, what you give, seven (7) times.

A practical exercise is included at the end this book, to demonstrate how the Creator's creation reenact these cosmic beginnings every day in each of our lives.

The Earth's First Human Family – The Twa People of Central and South Africa

To fully understand the philosophical point of reference of the ancient African writers of Shabaka's Stone, we must rescue, research and restore the role that humanity's original people, the Twa-Mbuti of Central and South Africa, played in the early development of African philosophy, science and art.

The organization of the Twa-Mbuti hunter-gatherer societies' family structure provided the foundation for their culture and civilization. The Twa-Mbuti also created the first agricultural democracies. These extended communities governed themselves by organizing councils, they did not have kings and queens. Hunter-gatherer societies, the world's first and most just societies were founded by the Twa-Mbuti approximately 150,000 years ago in Africa.

The foundation of Kush-Kemet's mind reflected Africa's cultural and ecological common sense rooted in a spiritual science. Kemet was the tongue, but Inner Africa was the thought and desire of the Twa-Mbuti. Nature was their teacher. Nature taught them how to think, speak and act. They migrated out from the Great Lakes region. Today, these countries are named, Tanganyika, Uganda, Kenya, Central and South Africa. In this geographical location the African thought process shaped and inspired Kush-Kemet's cultural common sense. The Twa-Mbuti were the first modern humans on the planet. They laid the philosophical groundwork for the other African civilizations in other parts of Africa and eventually around the world. They inhabited every continent on earth. As the Twa traveled along the Hapi (Nile) River, they created societies that would become the Kush and Kush-Kemet cultural nations. They all had the same root that grew from the same tree.

The Twa-Mbuti

The ancestors of the Kemites were the Kushites and the ancestors of the Kushites were the Twa-Mbuti. They are all the same people. The Twa-Mbuti have also been called "Kung," "San," "Khoi," "Anu" "Ba-Twa," "Tangu," and "Mmoetia (Mm-mo-ee-sha)." They have also been derogatorily called, "Pygmy."

The philosophical concept of Spirit was the foundation of Twa-Mbuti Civilization. These first people are the Creator's gift to the world. They are the original ancestors of all humanity. Dr. Oba T'Shaka masterfully demonstrated the importance of these original diminutive humans who grew from 3.8 feet to the giants of the Iture Forest towering 5 feet tall.

Dr. Oba T'Shaka wrote in his book, **The Integration Trap: The Generation Gap: Caused by a Choice Between Two Cultures,**
"The Twa, the world's first people, shaped these principles and practices, which were then transmitted throughout the world, creating African and world cultural unity. The Twa, hunter-gatherer societies' cultural organization provided the foundation and cultural stamp for the societies. The Twa were the founders of agricultural democracies. There were no kings and queens. The civilizations of Nubia and Kemet, where the Twa or Anu founded all of the elements of Kemetic civilization during Nubia's and Kemet's most creative period, the pre-dynastic period." **8**

Dr. T'Shaka continued,
"The Twa-Mbuti were the original people who first peopled every place on earth. The Twa or Anu were founders of the ancient civilizations of Asia, including China, India, the Philippines and Japan." **9**

Dr. T'Shaka reviewed the Twa-Mbuti's first six (6) levels of early development:
1) "Hunter gatherer societies, the world's first, and most just societies founded by the Twa approximately 144,000 years ago provided the foundations for the following societies.
2) Agrarian democracies, the second level of civilization and human societies where there were no Kings and Queens. These democracies were founded approximately 18,000 BCE by the Twa-Mbuti.
3) The civilizations of Nubia (Kush) and Kemet the world's oldest civilization, (Nubia) and the world's greatest ancient classical civilization, Kemet (Egypt) founded approximately 9,000 BCE, by the Twa or Anu people.

4) The civilizations of ancient Asia, including China, India, Japan and Philippines founded by the Twa or Anu people. The earliest Neolithic sites in China date back to approximately 6,000 BCE., the period of the Anu people, the first people in China.

5) The Twa are found among the oldest people in Europe.

6) The first people in America (Paleo-American) are Anu or Twa preceding the Native Americans.

To date, the earliest human skull found in South America (Brazil) dates back to 11,500 years ago. The skeleton is that of a Twa person and this skeleton is 2,000 years older than any skeleton found in the Americas." **10**

The Twa-Mbuti established the dynastic system of governing by their emphasis on the family and extended family. From the person to the family, community and nation. The family was the nucleus of the government. Dr. T'Shaka says,

"The Twa-Mbuti lineage system was based on the family and extended family. Twa-Mbuti hunter-gatherer clans are made up of close family members. They established the African tradition of the family serving as the central unit of the hunting clan. Larger African social organizations including tribes and nations followed the Twa practice of founding the organization of their society in larger lineage and clan organizations." **11**

The Twa-Kush-Kemet cultures and civilizations were conceived, created, developed, improved and revised; before the wisdom became the cornerstone of African philosophical deep thought. This ancient research is now the scholarship used by past and present-day scholars. Educators such as Dr. Drusilla Dunjee Houston, Dr. Cheikh Anta Diop, Dr. Theophile Obenga, Dr. Wade Nobles, Dr. Richard King, Dr. Jacob Carruthers, Dr. Peggy Brooks-Bertram, Dr. Yosef ben Jochannan, and historian Dr. John Henrik Clarke agree that all research concerning Kemet (Egypt) and the rest of Africa must, include Kemet (Egypt) as part of Africa. Kush-Kemet's mind was grounded in Africa's cultural reality. Kemet was the tongue; Inner Africa was the mind. The Great Lakes region included Tanganyika, Uganda, Kenya, Central and South Africa. This region was the brain that shaped and inspired Kush-Kemet's cultural common sense that led to great dynasties who ruled in peace for thousands of years in Africa's northeast corridor.

Shabaka's Stone is a metaphoric theory that discusses what happened before, during and after our cosmic universe came into existence. These theories developed into the events leading up to the creation of the "Un-Numerable Cosmic Systems." One of these texts, "The Memphite Theology," rewritten on, "Shabaka's Stone," tells this astronomical story using figurative language.

Along the Hapi (Nile) Valley, African people depended on their environment and cultural common sense to answer the many questions concerning the origin of ancient beginnings. They anointed and appointed sacred and natural representatives called Neteru, from the mineral, plant, animal and human world. Neteru were ambassadors representing their one creative force. Since no one alive today was present at this first moment of these beginnings, this philosophical scientific story is called a theory. However, present scientific information supports what ancient scholars in Kush-Kemet had speculated on thousands of years ago.

Shabaka's Stone is grounded in African Geography, History, Language and Philosophy
   i) Geography –The places where these philosophies were created.
  ii) History –The time and frame of reference concerning African philosophies.
iii) Language –Communicates philosophy based in their cultural common sense.
iv) Philosophy- Inquires and speculates on the ideas and concepts, in order to extract content materials and answer the fundamental and foundational questions concerning,

- The purpose and significance of life and death,
- Ethics and morality,
- Knowledge and wisdom,
- Being and becoming,
- Myth and reality,
- Science and spirituality

African philosophy allows students to appreciate knowledge, (i.e., art, ethics, science, philosophy and spirituality) from their own cultural common sense and perspective.

Intuition is closely connected to a higher form of knowing knowledge that goes beyond the emotional and passionate sense or feeling. It is a form of immediate knowledge, a means by which knowledge is gained without having to reason or think about it. The right decision is made naturally.

Trans-generational, Inter-generational and Ancestral intuition created a Twa-Kush-Kemet spiritual system grounded in one Creator, being both male and female simultaneously. This Creator threw off parts of himself/herself and manifested his/her image in all things she/he created. All creations were images of the Divine Creator. Each creation had his/her own divine purpose and unique specialty.

In Kush-Kemet, this unique purpose became a symbolic representative embodied in what they named, the "Neter." One of the main Neteru (plural for Neter) was named, "Tehuti," his other names include Djehuti, Thoth and Hermes. He represented knowledge and wisdom. Tehuti embodied science, thought and comprehension. He was the Master Scribe (both Teacher and Student). This philosophy personifies a people's shared set of systematic and cumulative ideas, beliefs and knowledge including the common sense that stems from their environmental culture. All experiences must be consistent with the essence of the people's cultural common sense.

These Kush-Kemet writings, carved on Shabaka's Stone, outlined a well-documented, viable theory concerning the origins and continuing development of the cosmic universe. Starting with the singularity, the one fertilized Atum (atom) who called into being the Superclusters, Clusters, Galaxies, Star Systems, Planets, Moons and all the other cosmic creations. The enduring legacy of these theories is the eternal process of becoming posed by these African scholars. However, their deepest and most original thought was the concept of existence before the beginning began. This was a radical thought that raised conscious thought to the next higher level. This "existence before the beginning began," was potential energy existing in a sleepless watery slumber named "the Nun." The establishment of this thought of the Nun, led to the intellectual development of the first moment of existence, Khepera, initiated by Ptah. Ptah was the conversion of energy at rest (potential energy) into kinetic energy (energy in motion).

The first and original self-created Trinity,
- Nun (water, matter)
- Ptah (conversion of energy, spirit)
- Atum (word, creative intelligence)

They were the philosophical underpinnings and purpose for all and everything in the cosmic universe to come into existence and continue becoming. They called this process of becoming, "Khepera," representing this idea by a dung beetle. Once learned, mastered and lived the students joined the forces of nature. To Africans, nature did not bring us here for a conflict. In fact, nature attempted to teach us how to become one with Ma'at.

Shabaka's Stone is both a primary and secondary source.
- A primary source is a resource told in the first person at the scene of the incident. The primary source was there when the event was taking place.
- A secondary source tells the story in the second person. It recalls what the first person recorded concerning the original incident. The secondary source talks about the primary source.

Shabaka's text is a secondary source because it was a rewritten version of the original Memphite Theology (primary source) created thousands of years earlier and the text's authors improved on their ancestor's scientific theory making Shabaka's Stone both unique and updated.

Primary Sources stand in the present, look at the past, and predict the future. Primary sources provide researchers with first-hand insights into the time period they are studying. These sources give all students an opportunity to make the historical past come alive. They help to understand the continuity of history and geography. Primary sources open the doors of yesterday and permit people, places, things and events of the past connect with those living in the present. However, as today's interpreters, we naturally bring our own perspectives, values, interests, principles and viewpoints when researching these primary sources. Our comprehension and interpretation of these resources are influenced by our own cultural common sense.

Primary sources include advertisements, architectural structures, artwork, books, drawings, cartoons, clothing, diaries, memoirs, documents, flags, emblems, games, inventories, letters, maps, money, music, oral histories, paintings, poetry, recipes, speeches, tombstones, tools, treaties, agreements, signs, wills, etc.

Nana Baffour Amantkwatia (Dr. Asa Hilliard) states that when examining the African past, there is direct and indirect evidence that creates a clear view of the Kush-Kemet worldview. Some of these sources include,

- Sacred texts written in Medu Neter (renamed hieroglyphics by the Greeks); Shabaka's Stone, Pyramid texts, papyri, Coffin texts, etc. monuments: Miru pyramids, tekenu (renamed obelisks by the Greeks), stelae, carvings, paintings, pottery.
- Eurasian "classical" writers some of whom were eyewitnesses, Greek, Roman, Persian, and others of the East and Far East.
- The ancient and contemporary cultural practices of inner-Africa (religion, family practices, symbolic structures, education, etc.) are very similar to ancient Kush-Kemet. **12**

The Kemetic Origin of the Cosmic Universe is an African theory concerning the events before, during and after the creation of the cosmos. The cosmos is the ordered and arranged parts of the universe. Along the Hapi (Nile) Valley, using its river as life systems, African people looked to the skies, land and water to answer the many questions they had concerning the beginning of beginnings.

The story of cosmic beginnings carved on Shabaka's Stone is a theoretical theology that ancient African scholars in Kush-Kemet (Egypt) speculated about thousands of years ago. The stone outlines a scientific, yet spiritual allegory concerning the origin of the cosmic universe. This wisdom, like the Cosmos, is a forever evolving process of becoming named, "Khepera."

Kush-Kemet Beginnings

Somewhere around 4,245 BCE, Neset Bity (Pharaoh) Narmer-Menefer-Menes, unified Upper (South) and Lower (North) Kush-Kemet creating the Pharaonic city-state at Heka-Ptah. This unification depended on the organization of an irrigation program that drained and controlled the direction of the waters of Hapi (Nile).

Kush-Kemet writings chronicled the regulation of life, the calendar and the Neset Bitiu's (Pharaohs'/plural) messages to distant parts of the kingdom. This knowledge and wisdom would lead to Kush-Kemet (Egyptian) creating the architectural marvel, the monumental Miru (pyramids) complex. Their construction graduated from the use of sun-dried brick and wood to quarried stone.

Pharaonic philosophy grounded in Kush inspiration flourished and reached its peak during the Old Kingdom spanning from the first (1st) to the sixth (6th) Dynasties about 4245 BCE to 2064 BCE. It was a thorough, dynamic, organic method of thinking, speaking and doing. It transformed naturally outward like a plant that is given the proper support and cultivation. The four elements are,

- Carbon/Fire/Sun, Atum-Ra
- Oxygen/Air, Shu
- Hydrogen/Water, Tefnut
- Nitrogen/Minerals/Earth, Geb

Pharaonic Kush-Kemet conceived of a universe before the beginning began, containing all of its uncreated and created creations at rest, waiting to be called into existence. It is a universe which is very different from the universe we can ever know. The Nun was in a truly original state of pre-existence.

The creative original matter, and the creations created from it, by the energetic power of the Creator, are one and the same thing. There is only one-word a "universe". All things in It, and of It; is It and It is in all things. The Creator and the Creator's creations are made of the same substance.

The cosmos came into being through the unity of three in one, the original Trinity; Nun/matter, Ptah/energy and Atum/creative word. These concepts are humanity's attempt at recording a system of philosophy. The origin of the principle of the creative word is found in the doctrine of free speech as a source for ordering and arranging a natural reality. This concept understood that the sun was the cause of life, eternity, strength, resilience and immortality. Ancient African deep thought viewed this complementary relationship between the sun and its creations as inseparable from humanity's destiny on this planet and throughout the cosmic universe.

Neteru (plural for Neter)

Neteru (natures/plural of Neter) were multi-referential. Neteru could change their meaning when acted upon by different positive or negative situations. Situations altered their cases. The Neter/essence could change its form and actions, but the symbol of the Neter or nature would always remain the same. For example, the **sun** was represented many different ways.

1) **Atum**, the third aspect of the Primate of the Essences, also called, "The Self-Created One," who rested upon Ptah and called the other Neteru Nun into Being. It was the voice of the Creator.

2) The **Primal Serpent**, who delineated the boundaries of the cosmic universe.

3) A **Phoenix Bird**, who when thought to be dead, rises again through its own ashes. Another version of night and day.

4) **Khepera**, the Dung Beetle, with a sun disc on its head, perpetually evolved life by rolling its young in dung to bring forth its new life.

5) **Ra**, the sun, Heru (Horus), epitomized the zenith of energy and power. It was the symbol of eternal insight. Ra kept the world in order by impacting nature.

6) **Aten**, the physical manifestation of light, heat and sound energy from the sun, the spiritual force behind all existing physical life.

All of these Neteru represented a different type of resurrection, rebirth, and regeneration. The sun represented each Neter, however, while the symbol and characteristic remained the same, its purpose changed.

Why was the sun so important? Professor William Leo Hansberry who taught at Howard University from 1922 to 1959, concluded that during the life history of humans, the first object to be worshipped was the sun. This celestial body was considered by ancient African scholars to be the source of life on earth. Because of its impact on this planet, it was viewed as the most important influence in the world. In the earliest intellectual phase of human thought, Africans worshipped the sun because of its majesty and mystery (superstition). The sun was the only celestial body that they saw every day and it could be seen and systematically recorded by everybody.

As time passed, African scientists came to realize that humans and their environment were profoundly and positively influenced by the sun's forces and powers of light, heat and sound energy. As Africans studied this star closer, they were able to create a society revolving around the sun and fathom its purpose and function (science). They measured time, invented calendars and developed seasonal patterns. These discoveries made it clear to these ancient scholars that the sun was more than just the source of the earth's light, heat and sound energy. They theorized that the sun was the principal cause of all the forms of life on earth.
13

Besides Atum, the solar Neter, there were earthly and cosmic Neteru. The earthly Neteru were represented by stones, trees, animals, symbolic objects, statues, human beings, etc. The cosmic Neteru were represented by the great forces of the universe, such as, the sky, stars and earth. On the scientific level, African people did not worship the symbolic representative. They recognized the metaphor in the Creator's presence in each Neteru's specialty. They separated the myth from the symbol. Each Neteru were the personifying forces that depicted cities, thoughts and ideas. However, the most important aspect of the Neteru was the balancing effect they had on good and not good. Humans, by their actions, chose the Neter or, nature, of the situation. The purpose of the Neteru was to guide humans through the mazes and challenges in life.

The Neteru are male and female essences. Their co-existence is interdependent and independent on each other. Each is a part of the whole, they are extensions of one another. These Neteru though seemingly diametrically opposed to each other, differ only in degree. They teach us that pairs of complements can be harmonized and balanced. It demonstrates the laws of opposites and complements are identical in nature, but different in the way they manifest themselves on earth and in the cosmos. This is called the principle of polarity.

Gender is manifested in everything and all. Masculine and feminine principles are forever present and active in all phases of existence, on each and every level in life. It was this balance of opposites and complements which brought all and everything into being and continues the process of becoming in the cosmic universe.

It is interesting to note that the identity of the Kemetic "Egg" called "Atum"; and the Atom of today are similar in name, characteristics and attributes. The similarity of their names demonstrates that the Atom of modern science is the identical name of the Kemetic "Egg", the essence of the sun. The Kemetic "Atum", means, "Self-Created Utterance." Atum is the sum of every thing, some thing and no thing. Atum was the combination of positive and negative principles, the Creator or fire characteristic that gave light, heat and sound energy through the rays from the sun.

Shabaka's Stone takes the early African ideas about creation, bringing forward the Essences of Pre-Existing Order and Arrangement. In turn, these Pre-Existing Essences create the Essences of Order and Arrangement.

Shabaka's Stone brings together ancient African ideas about creation into a holistic philosophical system about the truest nature of the cosmic universe. The creation story is simultaneously spiritual (sacred) and physical (scientific), a Sacred Science. The African sacred and scientific world cannot be separated. The reality of creation is a process of continued becoming, the consequence of the union of both the

- The Nun - Idea – Conception - Theory - Thought
- Ptah - Act – Doing – Implementation – Practice
- Atum - Command – Speech – Ordered and Arranged Consciousness

This process of becoming was guided by Ma'at, truth, justice, righteousness, order, arrangement, reciprocity, harmony and balance. Ancient African scholars saw human reality resulting from thinking and doing; thought and command, theory and practice. The essence of the Creator is revealed as will (thought) and intent (command). The symbol for thought is the heart and command is the tongue. Heart and tongue become the physical and spiritual qualities of thought/will and command/intent.

The heart conceives the idea of the cosmic universe and the tongue concretely makes the idea a reality by giving commands to name and proclaim each and every idea, this call brings them into existence.

To name and proclaim in the metaphor means, to say loud and intelligibly in order to bring into existence. What is proclaimed comes out of pre-existence and takes shape at the very moment of the unique Atumic utterance (naming).

From the time of Pharaonic Kemet (Egypt) the spoken word has been honored and held in the highest esteem. From times past, there have been African civilizations grounded in the powerful creative word.

Medu Neter (hieroglyphics), presents evidence that ancient Kush-Kemet (Egypt) was a civilization grounded in the mighty and mystical word. To call someone by name, proclaim existence of, is to reveal a human being's existence, who is from this village or that community group, from this family having these ancestors. The aim is to place the individual in space (geography) and time (history), and at the same time, give that person his/her identity. To name is to beget, to call up a genealogy, and to create a life's history. It was Atum who called into being the cosmos' life history. This metaphor was carved on Shabaka's Stone.

Shabaka's Stone consists of four (4) parts, one (1) historical statement, and three (3) spiritually scientific philosophies (read from top to bottom),
1) History/Geography of Text – Top two (2) Horizontal Lines
2) Philosophy #1 - Primate of the Essences (Left Vertical Lines)
3) Philosophy #2 - Essences of Pre-Existing Order and Arrangement (Middle Vertical Lines)
4) Philosophy #3 - Essences of Order and Arrangement (Right Vertical Lines)

Shabaka's Stone was originally conceived, studied and taught in temples thousands of years ago. The pharaonic political system governed Qustal, in Kush fifteen (15) generations before the 1st dynasty of Kemet. Kush's huge geographic location included the countries called Abyssinia (Ethiopia) and Nubia (present day Sudan), including Djibouti, Eritrea and Somalia. Wisdom was passed down from dynasty to dynasty, family to family, elder to younger until it finally reached the dynastic families of ancient Kush and finally in Kush-Kemet (Egypt). Thousands of years later, during the Napatan 25th Dynasty, approximately 710 BCE, a Neset Bity (Pharaoh) named Shabaka, rewrote the original Memphite theology. He said it had become worm-eaten and was too important a document to be allowed to perish. He said it housed sacred scientific wisdom of his ancient ancestors. The Memphite theology dates back before the Old Kingdom (2780-2260 BCE). It was copied onto a large black granite tablet. Shabaka's Stone is somewhat damaged and is now located in the British Museum #498.

Shabaka's Stone took the early African ideas about creation and placed them into a symbolic system which revealed the divine laws of nature. It utilized the figurative language of metaphors and myths to tell a spiritual, scientific, philosophical story.

Myth connects the invisible world with the visible world. Myth is the form in which the experience of a people becomes conscious. Myth provides the **meta**physical (unseen) truth about the **physical** (seen) reality. The creation story considered the principles of life and the order and arrangement of the cosmic universe.

From this perspective, Shabaka's text,
a) Perceived the Creator as one Spirit, both male and female, united in self-satisfaction called "Mer" (bliss).
b) Viewed holistically, conceptual ideas as the fundamental, founding principle of the world's organization.

In analyzing Shabaka's Stone through this symbolism and supreme thought, two concepts emerge:
1) It outlined the steps describing what existed before existence existed, how the cosmic universe came into being for the first time (Big Bang) and continued becoming ordered and arranged.
2) It provided a series of symbols to describe the origin and development of life on earth leading up to humans and human consciousness.

This symbolic system reveals the cosmically inspired, divine laws of nature. The Neteru or essences represent certain qualities associated with creation. Neteru are intangible essences or principles of life within nature. Each Neter was a unique representation of the one Creator. The ancient African scholars used concepts of humans, animals, plants, minerals and combinations of the four, to explain the spiritual essences of life on earth and beyond. They used "Medu Neter', or what the Greeks named, "Hieroglyphics," to depict these pictorial entities. For instance, the symbol representing the idea of a Neter was a banner or flag (4).

Multiple Neteru were represented by multiple banners or flags (4444444). Flags and banners represent a person, place, event or thing, including a sports team or college. The Neteru (Natures) were brought to life by giving them physical attributes. Linguistically, this is called "Personification." They were depicted as half-human (material) and half-Creator (spirit). They told a "Natural" human story. These stories were the world's first recorded "Dramas". They represented an aspect of life that had humans in life's situations with positive and negative essences or personalities interacting with them, and at times through them. A very important aspect of these dramas was the results that occurred when the human chose which Neter or personality to follow. Each human possesses all of the Neteru.

The theory of the Nun makes it possible for life to potentially pre-exist in matter and reveal itself as a creative force activated by the energy conversion called Ptah. Once energized, Ptah evoked the word, Atum, the creative intelligence. Atum defined and called into being the main characters of the origins of the cosmic universe,

- Nun – "The Matter"
- Ptah – "The Energy"
- Atum – "The Creative Word"
- Ma'at – "The Path"
- Tehuti – "The Wisdom"

- Khepera – "The Process of Becoming"

It is clear from Shabaka's Stone that the Kush-Kemet (Egyptian) philosophers of Memphis and Nubia had conceived the idea of a cosmic universe made up of numerous phenomena, filled with diverse beings, human, animal, plant and mineral. The Neteru lived celestially, aquatically, terrestrially, luminously and spiritually. While they were different from each other, their characters were intuitively regulated by a rational order, a principle that followed the path named Ma'at.

Ma'at is the primordial principle which gives order to all values, interests and principles including the waging of war by the Neset Bity (Pharaoh). She is part of the cosmic order; the truth and justice that allows the Neset Bity (Pharaoh) to protect the country from disorder, famine and misery. All men and women living in society must conform to Ma'at, the supreme virtue, path, guide, measure and purpose of all human activity. Ma'at represents the human attempt at the perfection of morality.

These Neteru are the basis of Kush-Kemet Philosophy. Nun represents the notion of functioning matter. Nun is the essence of all things and created the passage from,
- Non-being to being
- Before to after
- The unconscious to conscious wisdom

Atum, names, designates, classifies, orders and commands the creative word, bringing everything and all into being. Ma'at is order, arrangement, truth, justice, balance, harmony, ethics, respect and reciprocity. Tehuti teaches and encourages men and women in society to think, speak and do Ma'at according to the laws of nature. This nature contains within it, the entire traditional, transformational and transcendental word (virtue).

In our time, one of the fundamental explanations of the origin of the cosmic universe is matter (Nun) and energy (Ptah). Today, matter is chemistry and energy is physics. Chemistry asks the question, "What is Matter?" Physics asks the question, "What makes matter move?" Through Tep Heseb the correct answer is obtained by using the correct method. The entire cosmic universe is made up of either Matter or Energy. Energy makes Matter move. Energy shapes matter through the process of becoming (Khepera).

Kush-Kemet Philosophy

All civilizations have theories as to how their universe came into being. One of the oldest recorded stories was created and implemented in ancient Kush-Kemet (Egypt). Their interpretations envisioned spirituality (energy), science (wisdom) and philosophy (thought) as part of the same ancient thought system, grounded and given meaning in their cultural common sense.

Ancient systems of thought and writings include,
- Spiritual beliefs
- Moral stories
- Poems

Kush-Kemet wrote dramas dedicated to
- The glory of beauty
- Power
- Existence existing through eternity
- Metaphysical studies on the divine meaning of life

Subject areas included,
- Astronomy
- Geography
- Medicine
- Mathematics
- Ethics
- Metaphysics
- Dialectics
- Grammar
- Logic/Rhetoric
- Art
- Music
- And many more including combinations of many subjects holistically.

Their philosophy was based on,
Moral Exaltation" (harmony, balance, justice, reciprocity, order, arrangement respect and ethics), **preceding "Intellectual Illumination"** (information, knowledge and wisdom based in intellect, reason and language).

Together, morality (Ma'at) and wisdom (Tehuti) symbiotically brought forward the desire for moral perfection (spiritual energy) and certitude (precise science). No matter how intelligent a person may be, without morality, nothing was gained and very little can be shared, and nothing should ever be repeated.

Higher order thinking skills illuminate thoughts of the,
- Here-then
- Here-now
- Here-after

- Abstract imagination
- Creation of new ideas
- Time
- Space
- Numbers
- The nature of things both earthly, cosmic and universal

This same cultural and psychological structure created the foundations for all civilizations in the ancient African world. Dr. Obenga says that the Twa-Kush-Kemet (Egyptian) texts represent our ancestor's original and authentic philosophical questions on,
- Life and death
- Truth and justice,
- Social order and disorder
- Happiness and sadness
- Eternity, the beyond and the afterlife
- The immensity of the universe
- What existed before the beginning began in the primordial waters of the Nun
- The absolute beginning of the beginning Ptah/Big Bang)
- The creative, original word (Atum)
- The conversion of energy within matter

These ancient African scholars personified scientific principles in the form of
- The Nun, The Beginning, the now, and the forever
- Ptah, the conversion of potential energy into kinetic energy
- Ma'at, the true moral path of life
- Tehuti, knowledge, understanding and wisdom
- Khepera, created, uncreated beings and beings in the process of becoming
- Existence and existing
- Being and becoming
- Something-ness, nothing-ness and everything-ness
- Cosmogenesis **14**

Early Kush-Kemet thought can only be understood within an original African psycho-sensual-cultural common sense called, "An African Personality." There is a cultural similarity of cosmic thought among the Twa, Kushites and Kemites during the Pharaonic Dynasties in the North-East corridor of the Hapi (Nile) valley of Africa.

To fully understand Shabaka's Stone, two concepts are to be considered,

1) Kemetic writings belong to Africa's intellectual and cultural traditions introduced by the inner African Kush nations. African philosophy is a "systematic reflection" on the universe, cosmos, world, nature and man/woman. Science is the precise study of Nature and Nature is the physical manifestation of the Creator. Spirituality is unseen science and science is seen spirituality.
2) The philosophical system, literature and utterances of Twa-Kush and Pharaonic Kemet are identical and belong to the same astronomical, spiritual, philosophical, mythological and educational system differing only by matter of degree.

Philosophy is the exercise of reason in the fields of thought and action. In the days of Pharaonic Kush-Kemet (Egypt), to be a true scribe, the philosopher had to be a scientist, sage, poet, wife, mother, husband, father, citizen, and warrior. African education requires that method (how you teach) be as important as content (what you teach). It is more dangerous to have a lot of information taught with a bad method, than to have little information with the correct method.

These priests and priestesses of the philosophical temples of Kush-Kemet (On, Tehuti, Hiku-Ptah and Waset) had national and international reputations. The writing and monumental architecture of the pyramids and temples blended, combined and synthesized various intellectual disciplines such as literature, math, science, astronomy, medicine, spirituality, painting, drawing, sculpture, carvings, music, games, and leisure activities.

Temples of deep thought were created, developed, and implemented in Pharaonic Kush-Kemet (Egypt). The immortality of the soul of Humanity (Ba) was taught in Kush-Kemet as the foundational principle of education. During life, the Jet (body) was a temple to be honored, educated and respected. The Jet (body) was also a tomb where the ascending spirit lived awaiting its resurrection at death.

Upon death, the temple/body transformed into a sah wrapped mummy, a purgatorial waiting room, anxiously preparing falcon wings to fly from this state of earthbound. In this cocoon-like limbo the falcon resurrects its soul into Amenta, the hidden land, where the Creator and Ancestors reside. Like an earth-bound caterpillar spins and wraps itself into a cocoon to come forward as a flight-bound butterfly; so too was the linen-covered mummy, transformed into Heru, the resurrected falcon. Consciousness of Consciousness and Supreme Wisdom was said to have the power to "Liberate" the soul from the body/tomb.

Knowledge is the accumulation of information and wisdom is the application of knowledge. Wisdom in Ancient Kush-Kemet was considered to be a "Sacred Science". The patron of these Sacred Sciences was called, "Tehuti", husband of Ma'at.

The philosophers conducted experiments that demonstrated various ways of knowing,

- In-sight - Self-Reflective
- Time-sight - Balance-Measure
- Fore-sight - Prophetic-Prudent
- Circu-sight - Well-Rounded-360 degrees
- Hind-sight – Corrective-20/20

The philosopher acts with wisdom. This application is made possible by his/her degree of intellect of the thinker/philosopher/scribe. There are three (3) types of intellect possessed by the philosopher,

1) Clear/Concise - information is easily transmitted
2) Ready – accesses information quickly
3) Large – possesses large amounts of information

Intellect can be used by centering on the topic or associating points of reference to the topic. There are certain characteristics of a sage philosopher. Called a "Jegna," among Africans. He/She must

- Be clear-sighted in the examination of a challenge
- Be strategic in action
- Be knowledgeable of the cultural tradition when studying texts (Tep Heseb)
- Have extensive experience of human existence, in order to unravel complicated questions/challenges
- Have the ability to apply himself/herself to thought and meditation, day and night, in order to remain on the righteous path of Ma'at
- Be constantly dissatisfied with his/her results, he/she must always be in search of the next level. Always, perfecting their craft
- To seek, recognize and apply the better and more concise answers to life's challenges.
- Be a sage that asks for advice and ensures that he/she is asked for his/her advice.
- Have knowledge of the causes of all things natural, social and human.

There were a number of Houses of Kush-Kemetic Wisdom (Libraries). There is difficulty piecing everything together in regard to the full libraries of Kemet, due to the destruction of many libraries by Emperors of Rome. Current research identifies a number of Temples of Wisdom in Kemet (Egypt). They include, but are not limited to; Sais, Bubastis, Tanis, On (Heliopolis), Hiku Ptah (Memphis), Tehuti (Hermopolis), Waset (Thebes/Karnak), Abydos, Komombo, and Dendera.

There was the Temple of Heru, at Edfu, with a large collection of information on science. The library of Tebtunis at Fayum contained literary texts along with religious and scientific writings. There were private libraries in the Ipet at Waset (Grand Lodge at Luxor) and the Ipet-Isut at Karnak. At the library of Dier-El-Medina, the collection included texts pertaining to,

- Heka (Magic-metaphors in nature)- Human Will
- Popular mythological tales
- Psalms
- Literature
- Medicine
- Songs of joy and love

To be a true conscious thought it must be,
1) Consciously aware of its existence as a thought (Conscious of Consciousness)
2) Able to separate the myth from the reality.

Through time, philosophy developed into independent subjects or disciplines; the maths, cosmic, physical and life sciences, the communication arts, and the social sciences. Nature's creations became symbols for the energy of the creator. Metaphysics is the spirit that brings the physics into being. In the same way,

   a)   African scholars taught students Communication Arts (Language, Literature,
        Oratory),
i) Philosophical theorists created a Meta-Language, that decoded nature's symbols (grammar, syntax, structure and comprehension)
ii) They discovered the whole grammatical logic of their language, at the syntactical level that structured the form and expression of language
iii) Scholars and theorists conceptualized and contextualized the grammar observing nature's expression

   b) African scholars taught their students Ma'ati-Ma'ati-kos (Mathematics-Number sense, Numerology, Algebra, Trigonometry, Geometry, Calculus, etc.)
i) Philosophical theorists invented a process of coding and decoding numerical symbols (comprehension) and expressions (application)
ii) They solved spiritual challenges (problems) by utilizing this mathematical logic (coding and decoding)
iii) African Mathemagicians separated the metaphysics of math (symbolism), from the reality of the number (symbol). Such a separation of myth from reality took place in all areas of study.

As centuries passed, African philosophers continued to enhance the answers to the inquiries concerning human life, purpose and destiny. Some of the main concepts that developed included theories concerning,

- The creation of the cosmic universe and the world
- Challenges concerning freedom, citizenship and democracy (demos-people/kratia-power), All Power is with the people
- The immortality of the soul
- The existence of the Creator's creative force
- Knowledge of thoughts, thoughts of knowledge, knowing knowledge (wisdom) and knowing that you know knowledge (consciousness)
- Feelings and actions of humanity
- Beauty
- Goodness, morality and values clarification
- Truth (Ma'at)

In assessing the Kush-Kemet creation theory, the writings of ancient African systems of thought comparatively analyzed,

- spiritual beliefs
- moral concepts
- odes to the glory of beauty
- power
- metaphysical questions on the true meaning of life
- Precise science/Tep Heseb

Ancient African philosophers conceptualized knowledge by developing thought systems grounded in Tep Heseb, coming to an accurate conclusion by using the correct method of study. These subjects included

- astronomy, oceanography and geology
- geography, history, governance, economics and social systems
- science – physical, cosmic, life and the healing arts (medicine)
- math - number sense, number manipulation, algebra, geometry, trigonometry, finite mathematics, and calculus
- respect and ethics
- metaphysics
- dialectics
- logic/rhetoric

The existence of this philosophy demonstrates Kush-Kemet's ascending higher order thinking skills. Their texts represent Africa's original and authentic philosophical speculations on,

- Life and death
- Truth and justice
- Social governance
- Pre-existing order and arrangement
- Existence in eternity

- The beyond and sidereal immensity (star power)
- The emergence of energy within matter
- The beginning before the beginning began, the absolute beginning and its relationship to primordial water
- Ma'at, the true moral path in life
- Created and uncreated beings
- Existence and existing
- Being and becoming
- No Things + Some Things = All Things and Every Things
- Cosmogenesis through Atum's Medu Nefer, the good word, was translated and recorded by Tehuti, the patron of wisdom.

The early Kush-Kemet thought can only be understood within an African psycho-culturally metaphoric common sense. This conceptual allegory is guided by an "African Personality." There is a demonstrated cultural kinship, a common speculative cosmic universe, a deep and similar thought pattern among Pharaonic Kush-Kemet (Dynastic Egypt) and the rest of the African continent. This thought originated with the Twa-Mbuti of Inner Africa.

To fully understand the African texts of the coming into being of the cosmic universe, two truths emerge;

1) Kush-Kemetic philosophical texts belong to Africa's intellectual and cultural common sense; it cannot be compared to the religions of Eurasia because it's spiritual base is the origin of all of the world's religions. African philosophy was and still is a system's analysis "reflecting on the cosmos, world, nature, woman and man." Mathematics is the language of science used to express the known, the unknown and the search for the known (consciousness).

2) The philosophical system, literature and utterances of Africa and Pharaonic Kush-Kemet are identical and belong to the same cosmic, philosophical, metaphysical and mythological educational system as the Twa/Mbuti of Central and South Africa.

Somewhere around 4100 BCE with the Pharaoh Narmer/Menes, the Kush-Kemet Pharaonic system emerged. This nation-state unified the country south to north. This movement followed the direction of Hapi's (Nile) flow and the movement of African people from Qustal in the south, north to Edfu, continuing to Heka-Ptah (Memphis) in the north. In Heka-Ptah (Memphis), Neset Bity (Pharaoh) Menes organized an elaborate geological program for draining and controlling the waters of the Hapi (Nile) River in order to clear the way to build the theocratic capitol of Kush-Kemet in order to build the city called "Heka Ptah, the Spirit of Ptah," named after the hill that rose out of the waters of the Nun.

The writing system inherited from Kush, served to record and regulate the rites, ceremony and calendar. This oral and written scholarship was transmitted to distant lands and laid the foundations for the world's civilizations.

At the same time, Kush-Kemet (Egyptian) civilization created a phenomenal architectural kingdom. They called these constructions, "Miru." The Greeks would later call these structures "Pyramids (Houses of Fire)." The building materials first evolved out of the use of sun-dried bricks, then to wood, and finally to quarried stone. It was during the Old Kingdom that Pharaonic Philosophy reached its peak. This thought process was as rigorous as the mathematics of the miru (pyramids), and as precise as applied science. African deep thought expressed the idea of uncreated and created creations, both female and male in natural harmony and balance. They theorized the cosmos' becoming aware of his/her potential and ordering and arranging all and everything into being.

This pattern of "Coming into Being through the Process of Becoming," repeated itself in every facet of Kush-Kemet society. It is this awareness of self that makes the Pharaonic Thought so dynamic. Their "Medu Nefer-Sacred Speech," was written down and called, "Medu Neter-Sacred Writing."

Ancient Kush-Kemet African Texts

The universe and the Self-Created One are of the same substance, yet distinct in their purpose. The universe, the Nun, and the voice of the Universe, Atum; both existed simultaneously and eternally. The concept of cosmic creation is an original thought; firmly grounded in an African cultural common sense.

Atum, the Creator, did not create his/her works from nothing, or, from a matter which was unknown to him/her. Original matter became diversified in forming all and everything in the cosmic universe. It is through this grand principle of the balance of female and male energies that created and animated all life in the universe. The original three, united, harmonized and animated, created the 1st Trinity, which ordered and arranged the emergence of seven (7) more essences. The origin of the principle of the Word energizes and orders the cosmic reality. Symbolically and symbiotically, seeds and eggs, spermatozoa and ovules, are also part of this solar energy within males and females of all species enshrined in the symbol of eternal immortality, the Ankh.

The word "Nature," can be compared to the Kush-Kemet word, "Neter." Neteru (plural for Neter) are tangible representations of intangible ideas or concepts of the Creator. Each Neter is an individual, divinely unique characteristic of the one and only Creator; and each characteristic of the one Creator is a divine and sacred principle expressed in each and every Neter. The ancient Kush-Kemet scholars used concepts of humans, animals, plants, minerals and combinations of the four; including stones, trees, and symbolic objects to reflect aspects of Nature's manifestations.

Three ferociously protective natures were used to depict two very different concepts. The image of the lion, crocodile and hippopotamus was combined to symbolize Ammit, the Devourer of Evil Heart-Souls, the Guardian of Amenta (heaven). Ammit crouched under the right scale of Ma'atian justice. Tauret was the Protector of pregnant women and babies in gestation. Even the Dung Beetle (Khepera) had a place in the pantheon of Divine Beings of nature.

All Neteru are male and female essences and although they appear to be opposite and independent, they co-exist interdependently. Without one, the other would not and could not exist. In fact, the exist to complement one another. On closer examination, they are extensions of each other. These Neteru differ only by degree. They teach us that pairs of opposites may be balanced; that thesis and antithesis are identical in nature, but different in their polarity. They manifest themselves on earth and in the Cosmos, as above, so below. This concept is known for balance, the principle of harmony, Ma'at.

Such world views are rooted in the same African ecosystems dominated by water; oceans, ponds, streams, but most importantly, all the river systems including Hapi, Niger, Senegal, Tamanrasett, Congo, Senegal, Orange, Limpopo and Zambezi. All things came out of the water. Water reigns supreme and water sources are the power that fertilize the earth and give order and arrangement to daily life in Kush-Kemet agrarian and technological societies. But it is the sun's rays of light, heat and sound energy that animate all things on Geb (earth).

Profound cultural unity among Africans is created when viewing these similar doctrines from a common cultural sense. The Dogon of Mali can be compared to this Twa-Kush-Kemet theory, but also the Bambara of Guinea, the Fali of Cameroon and the Abure of the Ivory Coast. The reference to the primordial waters and Cosmic Egg belong to the same African cultural common sense.

In Twa-Kush-Kemet spiritual philosophy, all components of the present world, stars, earth and sky, the world of the living; and the dwelling place of those who have transitioned into the Creator's Ancestral realm. All the dimensions of human existence had a beginning, a genesis, a commencement, however their spiritual essence existed before their existence existed. The absolute plasma water, the Nun, existed potentially in its own eternal existence. The Nun thrived in its own unique humid, aqueous, endless depths. It was this inseminating, creative water that played a central role in African cosmogonies. These scientifically based metaphors were designed, developed and implemented in North, South, East, West and Central Africa. There is a cultural unity in African thought.

Shabaka's Stone Found

During the late 1700's, the French expeditionary forces, occupied Kemet (Egypt). These forces were directed by Generals Thomas Alexandre Dumas (novelist, Alexander Dumas' Haitian father) and Napoleon Bonaparte. Shabaka's Stone was found a few miles south of Cairo by French soldiers in Napoleon's army. Recognizing the Medu Neter (Hieroglyphic writing), they took it from the local farmers who used it to grind wheat. The French soldiers kept the stone in an army barracks at Alexandria. When the French surrendered to the British in 1801, the black basalt stone was sent to Earl Spencer in England. He donated it to be studied by British Egyptologists in 1805.

Shabaka's Stone is now located in the British Museum registered as number 498. Shabaka's Stone was carved on a rectangular slab of black granite, which measures, 1.13 yards by 1.60 yards or 3.4 feet by 4.8 feet. It consists of two horizontal lines, carved at the top, across the entire width of the stone. These two horizontal lines explains the history of how Neset Bity (Pharaoh) Shabaka and his scientists came upon the worm-eaten document called the "Memphite Theology." It continues explaining that His majesty directed it to be rewritten in the same linguistical style as his ancient ancestors. The metaphoric style used to write the Pyramid Texts of the fifth (5th) Dynasty.

Shabaka's Stone was carved onto the stone because the original, written on papyrus (or leather), was found to be worm eaten and could not be read from beginning to end. An unknown scribe testified,
"This writing was copied out by his majesty (King Shabaka) in the house of his father Ptah – South of his Wall (Memphis), for his majesty found it to be a work of the ancestors which was worm-eaten so that it could not be understood from beginning to end. His majesty copied it anew so that it would become better than it had been before." **15**

Under the two horizontal lines are sixty-two (62) vertical columns. Reading from top to bottom. In addition to numerous gaps and spaces, the middle portion of the text, column twenty-four (24) to forty-seven (47), has been almost completely destroyed because the slab was used to crush grain. Farmers grinded away part of the text through the years.

The text is a work of the Old Kingdom or even earlier; its precise date is not known. The text is a scientific theory, spiritual drama and metaphoric allegory. It contains scientific information supplied by the southern Kushites from inner Africa; today's Chad, Sudan, Ethiopia, Djibouti, Eritrea, Somalia and Northern Kenya. The wisdom expressed in Shabaka's Stone begins with the recognition that spiritual, sensory and physical perceptions are important steps in the scientific method of knowing knowledge.

Dr. George G.M. James believed that the Memphite Theology rewritten on Shabaka's Stone was an African theory on the creation of the cosmic universe. The Memphite text, first written in "Heka Ptah" (Memphis), takes the early African ideas about creation and places them into a symbolic system which reveals the divine laws of nature.

"Out of the eternal waters of the Nun, the Original Immortal Creator at rest, energizing him/herself in the form of Ptah, to bring all the other essences/Neteru into existence by conceiving them in his heart, and articulating them with his tongue, called "Atum," the Creative Conscious Word. **16**

This implies that the Kush-Kemet (Egyptians) revered Ptah, the divine architect, as the animating creator of "all things that live." Memphis became the theocratic capitol of Kush-Kemet (Egypt). The Kush-Kemet (Egyptians) called Memphis "He-ka-Ptah," "House of Ptah." Heka Ptah (Memphis) was known as the seat of Power for the Master Builders of Ptah, the technological blacksmiths. The High Priest of Ptah was called, the Supreme Leader of Craftsmen. This craftsmen's guild was introduced into Kemet (Egypt) from the southland, Nubia (Sudan).

Heka Ptah became Ai-gu-ptos to the Greeks. Ai-gu-ptos became the E-gy-pt of today. The literary style of Shabaka's text utilized the figurative language of myths, allegories and analogies to mask a realistic, scientific, philosophical story. Myth connected the invisible world with the visible world. Myth used figurative language to explain the cultural experience of Kush-Kemet people. Myth enhanced metaphysical truths grounded in the scientific method.

Shabaka's creation theory used natural principles of life, and the order and arrangement in the cosmic universe. From this perspective, the theological framework of Heka Ptah (Memphis) suggests that,
- The Creator is one spirit both male and female simultaneously
- Creative Ideas are the fundamental, founding principles of the world's organization.

Shabaka's Stone explores the following two concepts,
1) The Cosmic Universe was created; ordered and arranged from before its beginning began to its first moment of existence; through the cosmos' process of becoming up to the present day and beyond, looking deep into eternity's future.
2) This text is comprised of a series of esoteric symbols (Neteru) that describe the origin and development of all things in the cosmic universe including the evolution (physical growth) of humans, and the involution (spiritual ascendency) of human consciousness.

Dr. Richard King dates the origin of the metaphoric and metaphysical nature of Shabaka's Stone to a very ancient time, long before the founding of the First Dynasty of Kemet (Egypt). He informs us,

"There exist pre-dynastic records from before the times of dynastic Kemet (4,000 BC). This was the Memphite Theology of the Primate of the Gods, Ptah, who first arose, as a prominent hill within the waters of Nun, as an island in the primeval lake in Khuiland, multidimensional vibrational space. The primeval hill arising from the waters of Nun is a symbolic metaphor for the mythological summary of our ancestors' conscious intellectual experiences as they progressed from the collective unconscious womb of African root hominid consciousness itself. This is an epigenetic upward pull of the superconscious, the ascension of individual/group life force, following an earlier descent of light through space into matter and gravitational condensation of Black nanodiamond interstellar laden gas clouds into protostars. It represents the involution of spirit down into matter and the evolution of matter back into spirit in the great cycle of divine manifestation as seen in the sublime vision of Abydos." **17**

This downward spiraling involuting spirit of light is the metaphor for Lucifer (Luz=light) who falls from heaven (fallen angel) to earth. Light falling to earth is a scientific fact not a religious devil. This descending light is the involutionary solar birth on earth. This is explained in the third (3rd) philosophy of the text when Shu (air/male) separates Nut (sky/female) from Geb (earth/male). This separation allowed Nut to give birth to the sun, creating the cycle of life on Geb (earth).

The scientists and scholars of this Napatan dynasty under the leadership of Neset Bity (Pharaoh) Shabaka believed that it housed the wisdom of their ancient ancestors. It is obvious that the Kemetic philosophers of Heka Ptah (Memphis) had developed the idea of a cosmos made up of numerous organic beings, from human, animal, plant, mineral, living within the celestial, aquatic, terrestrial and luminous (spiritual) worlds. Although they may have differed from each other, they were all guided by the same divine order and arrangement called "Ma'at." They each had a purpose in the Cosmos' Great Divine Architectural Design.

Dr. George G.M James divided the Shabaka's Stone into 4 sections.
- One (1) historical statement - The Discovery, History and Description of the Memphite Text
- Three (3) philosophical theories pertaining to Kush-Kemet (Egyptian) cosmology.

i- The Primate of the Essences
ii- The Essences of Pre-Existing Order and Arrangement
iii-The Essences of Order and Arrangement

Shabaka's Stone is the source of modern scientific knowledge. The text provides great possibilities for modern scientific research. **18**

The first (1ˢᵗ) philosophy of the Shabaka's Stone structures the early African ideas about the creation of the Cosmos. The Nun was the Eternal Temple of Immortal Life. The Nun existed before existence existed and before the beginning began. At some divine time, Ptah (original energy system), the first primordial hill, rose out of the Nun (Matter/Universe). Atum, creative thought ascended out of the Nun, through Ptah and sat on Ptah's shoulders to call all things into being. This trinity brought forward, the second (2ⁿᵈ) philosophy, the Essences of Pre-Existing Order and Arrangement. In turn, these Pre-Existing Essences, called forward the third (3ʳᵈ) philosophy, the Essences of Order and Arrangement.

Shabaka's Stone discusses ancient African ideas about creation in a broader, inclusive philosophical context developing a Sacred Science that highlighted the nature of the cosmos, the ordered and arranged part of the immeasurable universe. The underlying law was that organic beings in this creation story were simultaneously spiritual (sacred) and physical (science) living entities. Knowledge (truth) and Wisdom (Tep Heseb) was a sacred science.

Tep Heseb is a Kush-Kemetic (Egyptian) term that can be translated to mean, "An Accurate Reckoning by using a Correct Method." Tep Heseb was mentioned in the Rhind Mathematical Papyrus. The scribe Ahmose explained that an accurate reckoning using the correct method was the entrance into the knowledge of all existing things and all obscure, mystical and unknown secrets." **19**

Like the bridge between the two hemispheres of the brain called the "Corpus Callosum", African philosophy unites spirituality with science. There is no way to separate these two concepts. Science deals with matter, finity, light and all things revealed. Spirituality expresses space, infinity, darkness and all things hidden. While they are not the same, they are two sides of the same coin.

Quantum physics is the inner atomic world (from human skin, in); and the General (Gravity) and Special (Electro-Magnetic) Laws of Relativity represent the outer world (from human skin, out). Humans are the bridge between the outer and inner worlds. Human life is the masterpiece of the universe.

An **atom** in the **body** is to the **human**, as the **human** is to the **Universe**.
The **before-life** is to **life**, as **life** is to the **after-life**.

We live in an eternal existence that is neither created (life) nor destroyed (death). Existence exists, because existence has always existed, even before the beginning began, existence existed. Each life is connected to all life. All forms of life are connected together in the time-space continuum. In this continuum, time is eternal, and space is everywhere.

The truest meaning of ancient Kush-Kemet (Egyptian) wisdom will come when we think like the Kush-Kemet people. To reimagine a civilization framed within the times they lived; physically, mentally, spiritually and soulfully.

The reality of creation is the consequence of imagining three things existing simultaneously,
1) The original Trinity; Nun, Ptah and Atum
2) The unification of the "Idea" (Nun-thought-conception-theory-mind) with the "Act" (Ptah-doing-implementation-practice)
3) This unification creates Atum, the "Word" (Command-Tongue). This process of becoming was guided by Ma'at, truth, justice, reciprocity, balance, righteousness, order, arrangement and cosmic harmony.

Ancient African scholars saw human reality resulting from thinking, speaking and doing. The essence of the Creator is revealed as will/heart/thought and intent/tongue/command. The symbol for thought was the heart and command represented by the tongue. Heart and tongue are the personified aspects for the spiritual qualities of thought/will and command/intent.
- Heart was the thought, mind, and intentions of the Creator,
- Tongue was the word, the voice, expression and speech of the Creator
- Heart/Tongue was the word made flesh, the coming into being and the process of becoming of eternal life.

These inquiries and speculations were created, developed, improved and revised; then taught again in Africa before they ever left Africa. This ancient research is now the foundation of the scholarship used by present-day scholars.

Shabaka's Stone was conceived and taught thousands of years before the first (1st) Dynasty of Ancient Kush-Kemet (Egypt). From Kush, this allegory was passed down from elder to younger, family to family, dynasty to dynasty, until it finally reached the dynastic families of ancient Kush-Kemet (Egypt). Thousands of years later, approximately 710 BCE. during the Napatan sixth (6th)/Twenty-Fifth (25th) Dynasty of Kush-Kemet (Egypt), the Memphite Theology was copied onto a large granite tablet by order of Neset Bity (Pharaoh) Shabaka who professed it housed the wisdom of his ancient ancestors. This tablet which is somewhat damaged is now located in the British Museum.

Shabaka's Stone took the early African ideas about creation and placed them into a multi-leveled system of symbols that revealed the divine laws of nature. It utilized the language of myths to tell a realistic, philosophical story. Myth connects the invisible world with the visible world. Myth is the form in which the experience of a people becomes conscious and as such can be viewed as a carefully constructed symbolic foundation for the metaphoric expression of thought. Myth provides us with the metaphysical truth about a physical reality. The creation story was a speculation about the principles of life and the order and arrangement of the cosmic universe. From this perspective, we see that the text at Memphis,

- Believed that the Creator was One Spirit: both male and female.
- Viewed symbolic metaphors as the fundamental, founding principles of expression representing the world's organization through cosmic events.

The "Neteru" or "Essences" represented certain qualities associated with nature. Neteru are intangible essences or principles of life that represent different aspects of nature. Each Neter was the representation of the Creator. The ancient African scholars used physical concepts of human, animals, plants, minerals and combinations of the four, to explain the spiritual Essences of life on earth and beyond. They used "Medu Neter', or what the Greeks called, "Hieroglyphics," to depict these pictorial characteristics.

To get a sense of how much time elapsed between when the Memphite Theology was originally written, and the time it was rewritten in the 6th Napatan Dynasty of Kush/25th Dynasty of Kemet (Egypt), compared to when it was rewritten in 710 BCE and today (2021), consider this timeline.

More time passed between the original writing of the Memphite Theology in Kush-Kemet about 4,100 BCE and the rewriting of it by Neset Bity (Pharaoh) Shabaka in 710 BCE; then when Shabaka rewrote it (710 BCE) and today in 2021 ACE. A difference of about 1,079 years (give or take)!

When the scholars of the Napatan Dynasty rewrote the great works of their ancestors, they wanted to restore Kush-Kemet's great and enduring legacy. This theory on the origin and development of the cosmic universe was rewritten in order to comprehend the significance of life, morality, knowledge, wisdom, being and becoming in the past, present and future. It was through African consciousness that African people appreciated art, ethics, science, philosophy and spirituality from a point of reference based in their unique original cultural common sense.

Intuition is directly connected to a higher form of knowing knowledge that goes beyond the emotional, passionate sense or feeling. Intuition is the very definition of "Tep Heseb," an accurate reckoning by using a correct method. It is this form of immediate innate knowledge, that wisdom is gained without reasoning or having to think about it. It is intuitive instinct. Instinct is a characteristic of the plant/animal world. Animals obey the laws of nature because nature directly guides them. They hunt, eat, mate and live by nature's command. But, when humanity rose to a higher conscious level, they were given the ability to challenge nature. Human beings could tell the natural order "No!" This is also called free will.

Free will was a gift, but also a challenge. In making decisions on their own, and not because of nature's instinct, humanity was able to achieve higher order thinking skills that led to deeper consciousness called "intuitive instinct." This type of consciousness is a unique form of nature's consciousness. Making intuitive decisions that natural instinct would make. Intuition was a dynamic gift given only to humanity. It gave them the unique ability to not only obey nature naturally, but at higher levels of consciousness. This enabled them to, become "One" with nature, opening up the "Immortal Portal" of becoming conscious of their consciousness. Human beings became the Creator while having a human experience and permitting them to know that they knew, knowledge, and could act on it. This action in light of Nature's command was considered the highest form of wisdom. It was a sacred science.

Science and ancestral intuition created a Kush-Kemet spiritual system grounded in the belief in one Creator. This one Creator threw off pieces of him/herself and manifested his/her image in all that she/he created. Each creation had their own specialty and unique gift (smell in dog, agility in cat, sight in bird, hearing in hares) that became a heraldic emblem, identifying characteristics that became embodied in what Kush-Kemites (Egyptians) named, the "Neter."

Tehuti was represented by an Ibis Bird (cousin to the stork). He was a metaphor for intellect, reason and language; he represented knowledge, thought, wisdom and comprehension. This wisdom constructed a people's shared set of systematic and cumulative ideas, beliefs and knowledge including their cultural common sense that stems from their ecological and climatic worldview.

Shabaka's Stone outlines a well-documented, viable scientific theory concerning the origins of the cosmic universe, beginning before the beginning began, continuing with the Neter, Ptah, converting energy at rest, in the waters of Nun, into energy in motion. This moment of energy conversion in science is called the "Big Bang." From here, over billions and billions of years, this single Black Dot (Black Hole) throws off Superclusters, Clusters, Galaxies, Star Systems, Planets, Moons and all the other celestial bodies like meteors, asteroids, etc. The magnificent legacy of the text was the "eternal process of becoming," presented by these African scholars. They called this process, "Khepera," symbolized by the Dung Beetle.

The characteristics and attributes of Nun (water, matter), Ptah (energy, animating force) and Atum (word, creative intelligence) are the philosophical underpinnings for all and everything in the cosmic universe. Wisdom joins humans when humans join forces with Nature. To Africans, humans did not fight nature, they knew that Nature could not be conquered. Through the ascension of consciousness, they "became" Nature.

Shabaka's Stone is a Primary Source. Primary Sources stand in the present, look at the past, and supply information that allows for the prediction of the future. Primary sources provide students with first-hand insights into the time period they are studying. These sources give students an opportunity to make history come alive. They help them understand the continuity of geography (space) and history (time). It opens the portal of yesterday and permits people, places, things and events of the past to connect with those living in the present. However, today's investigators naturally bring their own personal values, interests, principles and viewpoints to our interpretation of these primary sources. Also, their comprehension and translation of these resources are influenced by their own cultural common sense.

Shabaka's Stone is an African allegory concerning cosmic events. Along the Hapi (Nile) Valley, African people looked to their environment and used their cultural common sense to answer the many questions they had concerning the origin of ancient universal beginnings. They anointed and appointed sacred representatives (Neteru) from the mineral, plant, animal and human world to represent their one Creator.

Shabaka's Stone is an ancient scientific text that outlines a viable, working theory concerning the origin of the cosmic universe and the development of the human brain and the emergence of African philosophical, scientific, and spiritual wisdom and knowledge. This wisdom, like the cosmos was perceived to be a forever evolving process of becoming.

The waters of the Nun (matter) was the universe, it existed before the beginning began and continues to exist to this day. The theory made it possible for life to potentially pre-exist in matter (the Nun), but only reveal itself as an energized creative force (Ptah) through creative intelligence (Atum). Ma'at was a complex, moral and superior form taken by the Nun. Ma'at the primordial path of truth, justice, harmony, balance, reciprocity (what goes around, comes around), proper behavior, order and arrangement. Ma'at, thinks, speaks, acts justice. Ma'at acts in accordance with Nature and gives order and arrangement to all of the Creator's creations.

This original Trinity initiated the process of becoming from,
- non-being to being
- before the beginning to after
- the unconscious to the awakening of thought, reason, and language.

The word (Atum) named, designated, classified, ordered, commanded and brought everything and all into existence. The entire cosmic universe is made up of either matter or energy. Energy makes matter move.

Enough of the writing on Shabaka's Stone remained intact in order to reveal one of the most important texts relating to the physical and spiritual birth and development of the cosmic universe.

Shabaka's Stone states, "For the very great one is Ptah, who gave (life) to all the Neteru…through his heart and through his tongue…Thus all the Neteru were born…For every word of the Neter came about through what the heart desired and the tongue commanded. Thus, it is said of Ptah: He who made all and created the Neteru…Thus Ptah was satisfied after he had made all things." This implies that the Kush-Kemet (Egyptians) revered Ptah, as a divine architect, as the creator of "all things."

Shabaka's text utilized the language of myths to tell a realistic, scientific and philosophical story. Myth connected the invisible world with its visible complement. Myth is the form of expression in which the experience of a people becomes conscious. Myth is a symbolic explanation for the people's abstract thought. Myth utilizes the people's cultural common sense. Myth manifests metaphysical truths relating to a physical truth relating to a physical reality. The creation story was a speculation about the principles of life and the order and arrangement of the cosmic universe.

Knowing that you "know" is a sacred science. The sacred and scientific world expressed in Shabaka's Stone cannot be separated.

What is proclaimed, comes out of total existence, the Nun; and takes shape at the moment of Atumic utterance. This is the metaphoric expression of a scientific theory. The coming into being represented the fusion of hydrogen atoms that created larger and more complex molecules, that eventually create all things that exist in in the cosmos.

From before the time of Pharaonic Kush-Kemet, the spoken word had been very important and venerated as what bonds the visible with the invisible worlds on every level. Civilization was created by a powerful creative word. In Kush-Kemet, to call someone by name is to recognize a person from this village or that cultural group, from this family, having these ancestors. The aim is to situate the individual in space (geography) and time (history), and at the same time, give that person a sense of being, place and purpose. To name is to beget, to call up a genealogy, and to create a conscious life history.

Shabaka's Stone structures the early African ideas about creation. Shabaka's text consists of four (4) parts one (1) historical statement and three 3 spiritually scientific philosophies,
- History/Geography of Text- It explains how Neset Bity (Pharaoh) Shabaka came to possess the Memphite Theology, and how he directed his scientists to rewrite it.
- Philosophy #1 - Primate of the Essences- Tells the story of the original Trinity who existed before the beginning began and how the cosmos was created and continued becoming.

- Philosophy #2 - Essences of Pre-Existing Order and Arrangement-Explains the eight uncreated characteristics that define the attributes of the cosmic universe.
- Philosophy #3 - Essences of Order and Arrangement- Explores the development of the billions of atoms, elements and molecules that would lead to the creation of superclusters, clusters, galaxies, stars, earth and all the life that evolved over billions of years leading up to the birth of bacteria, plants, fish, amphibians, reptiles and mammals.

The essence of life is a paradoxical contradiction that manifests himself and herself in every field of human knowledge and endeavor. It is the paradoxical union, yet, at the same time a harmonious synthesis of opposites and complements. This synthesis, balance and harmony of opposites was called, Ma'at.

The purpose of life unites opposing Neteru/essences. There are three forms of essences.

1) **Theoretical Essence/Neter** – Relating to **Scientific Thought**. It provides consistency to thought and speech– Nun-Matter

2) **Practical Essence/Neter** – Relating to **Moral Action**. It gives purpose to action – Ptah – Energy

3) **Aesthetic Essence/Neter**– Relating to **Feelings, Sensations and Emotions**. It inspires the Cosmic Universe towards artistic expression. It shapes the personality of the society as a whole. Atum is the Creative and Dynamic Word.

- The unexplainable initial principle, the Nun, the foundation of the whole universe and place where the cosmos would emerge.
- Atum, emerges from the Nun, creative, luminous, intelligent; Atum springs from raw, unorganized, primordial matter. Its ability to move is brought forward by "Ptah", the energizer and animator. Ptah is the grand architect of the cosmic universe.
- The Advent of the Cosmic Order: Atum names eight (8) uncreated creations in a state of unordered and unarranged essences. Atum transforms into Atum-Khepera and names four (4) pairs of ordered and arranged essences.

Overview of the Metaphor of Shabaka's Stone

1st Philosophy – Primate of the Essences
Before the Beginning Began and the Coming into Being for the 1st Time - Khepera Sep Tepy

Neteru

Nun-The Primordial Matter (Eternal Waters)

Ptah-The Conversion of Potential Energy (At Rest) into Kinetic Energy (Motion)

Atum-Creative Intelligence-the Divine Utterance Calling All and Everything into Existence

See Appendix # 2 - The Primate of the Essences

2nd Philosophy – Essences of Pre-Existing Order and Arrangement
Atum Names the Uncreated Creations
Nun, Ptah and Atum name the uncreated creations who always existed in the waters of the Nun but had no names.
Neteru
1a) Nun - Matter - Male
1b) Nunet – Space – Female
2a) Huh – Infinity – Male
2b) Huhet – Finity – Female
3a) Kuk – Darkness – Male
3b) Kuket – Light – Female
4a) Amen – Hidden – Male
4b) Amenet – Revealed – Female
See Appendix # 3 - Essences of Pre-Existing Order and Arrangement

3rd Philosophy – Essences of Order and Arrangement
The Ordered and Arranged Eternal and Immense Cosmic Universe
Nun, Ptah and Atum transform Atum into Atum-Khepera and create
Neteru
1a) Shu – Air/Atmosphere – Male
1b) Tefnut – Moisture/Hydrosphere-Female
The Advent of the Terrestrial and Celestial Order
2a) Geb – Earth/Lithosphere – Male
2b) Nut – Sky/Carbon – Female

The Birth of Organic Life – Botanical/Zoological/Biological
3a) Ausar – Fertile Seed – Male
3b) Aset – Fertile Womb - Determination/Will – Female
4a) Seten – Destroyer/Sterile – Male
4b) Nebetet – Oracle Reader/Visionary – Female
5)Asar and Aset give birth to Heru – the Righteous Inheritor – the Sun, representing both male and female humanity
See Appendix # 4 - Essences of Order and Arrangement

More than 2,500 years before the Christian era (4,500 years ago), the Pharaonic Kush-Kemet (Dynastic Egyptians) grappled with the question of questions. The question of origins, of understanding the world they lived in within the cosmic universe. Their thinking was exceptionally brilliant. Shabaka's Stone represents an early attempt, during the long history of homo-sapiens-sapiens, to speculate on the origin of all and everything. It explained life on (Geb) earth and the primordial phenomena in Nature. At its most important level, it offered the Human family, the opportunity to become a super-natural, extra-ordinary Divine human.

The concept of the Nun explains all dimensions of human existence. The process had an existence before it began, and a birth from its first moment of being and an unending, eternal journey of immortality. But first, this creation had to wake up from its sleepless slumber, energize and call the Creator's creations into active being and eternal becoming.

The Primate of the Essence
Before the Beginning Began
Nun brings forward Ptah Who calls Atum into Being
This Unity of Three is the Original Trinity
The Nun-The Primordial **Matter** (Eternal Waters)
Ptah-The **Conversion** of Potential Energy (at Rest) into Kinetic Energy (in Motion)
Atum-Creative Intelligence-the Divine Utterance Naming All and Everything, Bringing Them into Existence

Shabaka Stone's fundamental explanation for the origin and development of the cosmic universe is the unity of matter (Nun), conversion of energy (Ptah) and the creative word (Atum); one becoming three and three reuniting back into the One. In so doing, they become the first (1st) Trinity. The entire universe is made up of either matter or energy. Energy makes matter move. Ptah converts potential energy (energy at rest) into kinetic energy (energy in motion). Kinetic comes from the Greek word kinetikos, from the verb kinien meaning to move. Kinematics are the properties and characteristics of an object in motion.

Energy moves matter through Khepera (the process of becoming). Khepera, the Dung Beetle, represents the ability to transform and grow orderly and consistently. The cosmos was brought into being for the first time, during a moment called, Khepera Sep Tepy (The Coming into Being for the First Time). This big bang brought forward Atum, the creative, dynamic, and living word. This Atumic utterance was a rhythmic vibration that created the very first cosmic frequency.

The Nun is the matter from where Ptah (energy) and Atum (creative word) came. The Nun, Ptah and Atum are three aspects of the same original substance. After Ptah came forward from the Nun, Atum is animated and sits atop Ptah and orders and arranges the many millions and billions of atoms, elements and molecules in the cosmic universe. Atum arises and evokes the creative word, and achieves the process of becoming, Khepera.

Atum has also been compared to the Eye of Heru. This circular symbol represented the divine light imprisoned in matter, awaiting spiritual liberation from its restraints. She was the serpent who swallowed her tail creating the symbol of eternity. It is said that the Eye is the seat of the Soul and is all-powerful, because it possesses in itself, the means for its own salvation. The way life is lived liberates and emancipates humanity's Heart-Soul after death.

The Eye of Heru invokes and evokes the means of the perception of light in all its forms, from the physical light of the sun's shine to the moon's reflection of the sun's light to the spiritual light of knowledge, understanding and wisdom. The inner illumination of the awakened spirit, depicted by the Uraeus (Cobra), is the magnificent symbol of all the powers related to this triple conception. Atum sits atop Ptah and calls all and everything into existence within the waters of Nun.

Scientifically speaking, before the beginning of the cosmos began, this eternal space was spread out over a large area of electromagnetic fields, gravity, strong and weak forces. This diverse, infinite, immense, immortal place was a ancient form of hydrogen.

This eternal cosmic memory suggests that the universe always existed in infinite density (The Nun). The universe was made up of free atoms, elements and particles, in disorder and disarrangement. There was no gravity in the beginning of the cosmic universe, only a hydrogen-plasma-water-matter which in its nature was unique and knew it had the potential to replicate her/himself. To do this, a process of becoming (Khepera) had to be spirituality energized within the Nun by (Ptah). This Ptahian spirit was thought, desired and spoke by Atum into being and this made the word become flesh, and created the pre-existing boundaries preparing to organize and arrange the atoms, elements and molecules in the universe (the Nun).

The cosmos within the universe expanded, one after another, the superclusters, clusters, galaxies and stars distanced themselves one from another. This process of complimentary separation continues to this day and will continue through the billions of years to come.

The ancient theorists studied this forever reappearing, natural scientific process. African scholars believed that life and all and everything that existed prior to this life, was determined by how atoms (Atum) were fused and combined. These atoms, because of the carbon atom (cosmic glue), created molecules that continued the process of becoming leading to unique combinations that lead to intra-universal, inter-supercluster, inter-cluster, inter-galactic, inter-solargistic and inter-planetary life. Let's take a deep dive in the eternal waters of the Nun.

The Nun – The Eternal Waters of Immortality

Before the beginning began, before existence existed, before all the fundamental atoms and elements, before movement and creative intelligence, there was only the Nun, an eternal presence called many things, plasma, ether, water, and hydrogen. The Nun had no beginning, and it has no end. The characteristics of the Nun pre-existed potentially within the Nun. These eight (8) characteristics came in both female and male complementary forms. They were matter and space, infinity and finity, dark and light, hidden and revealed.

The Nun was the one place where the many would emerge as the entities that would become the cosmic universe. Nun was the immortal totality of knowable consciousness. The cosmic universe was created by what came out of the eight (8) uncreated creations (characteristics). Ancient Kush-Kemet scholars called them the Neteru Nun. The uncreated creations are the attributes and characteristics of all things that always pre-existed at rest within the Nun. However, they did not exist, because they had not been named by Atum. Once named, they came into existence.

The Nun was the original seed-womb of thought and command. Kush-Kemet (Egyptians) thought nature to be in sync with the cosmic order, constantly renewing, regenerating and resurrecting itself, just as the sun rises by day and sets at night. There was a pattern in the cosmic tabernacle.

Shabaka's Stone represents an ancient attempt to explain the origin of matter and energy, organic life on earth and the primordial phenomenon in Nature as the cornerstone to understand how science and spirituality manifests in Nature.

Many thousands of years ago, the pharaonic Kush-Kemet (Egyptians) contemplated the question of questions: the question of origins, understanding the world, the cosmos, before its beginning, how did it begin and how does it continue to become. Their thinking was extra-ordinary and super-natural. It went beyond the beyond and found root in the unexplainable spirit and they created a precise science that was able to offer concrete explanations verifying the spirit's presence in all and everything.

This concept of the Nun was an ocean that contained all the raw materials that had the potential of becoming the cosmos. The first mother egg (universe) had a feminine gender, and the first male seed (panspermia within the universe) had a male gender. Together, they were the breath of life at the pre-existence of the cosmic universe.

Matter and form, the essence of the Kush-Kemet Nun is uncreated and eternal. The original substance of Nun is matter; an ethereal water also called plasma. All natural beings of physics (movement) are made of matter engaged in harmonized motion, tuned into a natural cosmic frequency. The Nun is like a fluid ether, not the water (H2O) that we know today. This liquid air or hydrogen plasma is the source of all creation. The greatest mystery of the coming into being is the passage of life from the invisible into the visible, the word made flesh. It is the one who calls forth the many who reside from within the one. The theory of Nun makes it possible for life to pre-exist in matter and only reveal itself as a creative intelligent force called Atum.

Nun or pre-existing matter is living within itself. Anxiously awaiting the moment of activation. It potentially contains the whole universe, existing only in thought. Everything in the tiny acorn will become the mighty oak tree and everything the great oak tree becomes was in the tiny acorn seed, before its beginning began. The eight Neteru, the uncreated creations come in the form of eternal essences or pure ideas. They are matter, space, infinity, finity, light, darkness, the seen and unseen.

Nun is matter and potential form, the essence of the Kush-Kemet Nun is uncreated and eternal. The origin of Nun is matter; it is a pure form containing all and everything. All objects of physics (movement) are made of matter engaged in balancing the motion of beings in action. The Nun's pre-existing matter is living within itself. Nun potentially contains the whole cosmic universe in gestation. The Nun has within him/her, the potential for her/his own evolution toward the present world's actualization. This pre-existing matter contained all the essences of the future beings that one day would be called into existence. This primordial matter, the Nun was elevated to the level of divinity. Each principle's explanation emanated from the Nun reflected an essence/Neter.

The Nun is more like a fluid ether, an invisible form of moisture, but not the water that we know of today, H2O. This liquid hydrogen plasma is the essence of the rest of creation. The greatest mystery of the coming into being is the passage of life from the invisible into the visible. It is the one who calls forth the many. The many who reside in the one. The theory of Nun makes it possible for life to pre-exist in matter and only reveal itself as a creatively intelligent force (Ra-Atum-Khepera).

When we look at the philosophical allegory of ancient Kush-Kemet we see that these ancient scholars paved the way for the concepts currently being taught in universities (microcosmic "universe cities") today. They theorized that before the beginning began there was only a plasma a hydrogen matter (Nun). Within this Matter, there existed the potential for everything and all. Potential energy is energy at rest. When potential energy is activated, it is called kinetic energy. The ancient Kush-Kemet (Egyptians) called this energy conversion, Ptah. Ma'at was the path used to activate and energize Ptah. Tehuti was the wisdom on the path of Ma'at.

Panspermia
The Male Cosmic Energy that Fertilizes the Universal Womb
and Co-Exists in the Creation of the Cosmic Universe

Before the beginning began, **Thought** in the Universe's Mind created **Desire** in Her Heart-Soul, **Desire** spoke **Word** in His Heart, and **Word** made **Flesh**. **Flesh** brought all and everything into **Being** and started the Process of the Cosmos' becoming in the universe. The Creator's first thought, before the beginning began was,

"**I want to know Me**. **I want to think, see, hear, smell, taste, and feel, but I cannot because I am spiritual energy in potential rest in my eternal space. I want to be, and continue to become so that I will know that I am who I** am. I am the Creator who will know that I am the Creator, but the only way to know is to come through physical form and have a human experience, in order to involve and have a spiritual inspirience, then, I know who I am. I am who am.

The Creator decided to create creations in His/Her image that She/He could live to achieve His/Her desire; "**To Know Self.**" To do that, the Creator began as a feminine womb self-impregnated by the male seed in the deepest blackness of the darkest region of the universe.

Think of a vast ocean. Within these endless waters, there is a force that separates the ocean into drops of water. Each drop of water is made up of the ocean and the ocean is present in each drop. The force that separates the universal ocean, the feminine wombed egg, into drops of water is called the masculine seeds, panspermia. The "Act" of creating drops of water gives each drop a "Special Purpose". This purpose is uniquely designated to perform a "specific task," and each specific task is an individual organic soul. The force that keeps all drops of water connected within the great ocean is "Spirit". The ocean is the universal spirit, macro-ka also called the Macro-cosmos, and each drop of water is the Individual Spirit-Micro-Ka also called the Micro-cosmos. **20**

Panspermia is an ancient Greek word, "pan" meaning "all" and "spermia" meaning "seed." Panspermia is the hypothesis that life exists throughout the universe because the universal womb was impregnated by internal, inseminating cosmic space seeds. Panspermia theorizes that life rode to Earth from interstellar space spreading the seeds of life within an interstellar space full of nanodiamonds and the astro-bio-chemicals of life. As humankind developed their intelligence, reasoning and linguistic skills, their consciousness ascended. Life arose within the nature of cosmic consciousness. Life and consciousness extend beyond the boundaries of space (geography) and time (history). Our own earthly life and consciousness arose within them; and each of us has the ability to fuse space and time into the all-encompassing space-time continuum.
See Appendix #5 – Cosmic Panspermia

The cosmic universe is filled with different forms of melanated matter; cosmic, earth and organic. Dr. Richard King tells us,
"Black matter is in the form of interstellar gas clouds laden with these luminous jewels of black nanodiamonds, which are the literal genetic seeds from which stars are born. They arise from the same high-energy primordial shock and flux that populated all of creation. There is a crucial connection between the Black, or dark matter that structures much of the unseen universe and the subtle living dark matter that structures our very bodies, brains, and nervous systems. The study of higher mathematics, physics, and chemistry, which observes such cosmic melanin macrocosmic phenomena, should be a wake-up call that a similar higher science is

required to study carbon/melanin related to microcosmic phenomena in living biosystems on planet Earth."[21]

Following the Big Bang of creation, the universe began to become. It expanded in implosions of pure energy. In time, the cosmic universe cooled down into condensation of early subatomic particles, leading to the first atom, hydrogen. This continuing process formed stars, that were mostly hydrogen atoms, helium atoms are two (2) nuclear fused hydrogen atoms. Dr. King says,

The interstellar material of the Milky Way galaxy contains in a huge state vast interstellar gas clouds composed of hydrogen (70%) and helium (28%), with a small component of solid particles and interstellar, or cosmic dust. In addition to the element carbon, there is found in interstellar expanses the elements oxygen, nitrogen, nickel, sulfur, aluminum, iron and others, along with many different organic and inorganic molecules. [22]

The continued expansion of the cosmos allowed panspermia to fertilize the cosmic womb, Dr. King continues,

"The process of cosmic forces created a nuclear state that fused the nuclei of hydrogen atoms together to produce helium atoms. The helium then continued to fuse, producing atoms of progressively higher atomic number, nuclei with more protons and neutrons and fusion, where internal heat gradually increased and transformed the structure of gas particles. It is out of this flux of "mother" gas clouds that the "father" carbon atom arose. This is a vast simplification of a complex process, but the point is that the critical end product of black nanodiamonds is carbon. Temperature, pressure and composition/molecular precursors in the solar nebula would favor the condensation of carbonaceous compounds, which are called nanodiamonds. Diamond formation is favored by an abundance of atomic hydrogen and low carbon rations." [23]

See Appendix #6 - Human Panspermia

Stars are Cosmic Diamonds conceived and born from "Nanodiamonds." Dr. King explained further,

"Nanodiamonds are a common by-product of star formation and are formed in stellar systems and ejected from a supernova carbon star explosion. Nanodiamonds are a solid crystalline form of mostly carbon atoms that are extremely small in size. Nanodiamonds and interstellar gas clouds play a critical role in the formation of stars and creation of biogenetic molecules of melanin in the interstellar clouds of many galaxies and continues in the same way in our solar system, perhaps since the solar system was created. It is through the interstellar gas clouds that these black biogenetic surfaces, sometimes transported on the larger surfaces of traveling comets along with amino acids, moved through the stellar abyss and throughout the innumerable solar systems, seeding the surface of planets like our Earth. It is these Black matter melanin seeds from the stellar expanses that provide the biogenetic spark of life." [24]

These black matter melanin seeds are panspermia. These womb and seeds are cosmic DNA that contain all intellect, reasoning and language.

Today's human mind is filled with billions of years of emotional, intense active memories of the whole spectrum of one's blood line genetic ancestors. For each person born in 2020, it took 1,048,576 ancestors (18th Great-Grandparents) to get us here. **25**

These million plus ancestral lineage has experienced every type of human emotion and experience, Dr. King assures,

"These experiences form an ocean of incredible human experiences that range from heaven to hell, from the heights of love, romance, and creative genius through the lows of fear, jealousy and post-traumatic stress disorder. This great storehouse of collective memory even includes our fragmented memories of exposure to ecological catastrophes." **26**

Panspermia concentrates on how life began and on methods that distribute life in the universe. These pre-biological building-blocks of organic life originated in space, became incorporated in the solar nebula from which planets condensed, and were further and continuously, distributed to planetary surfaces where life then emerged.

The chemistry of life may have begun shortly after the Big Bang, twelve (12) to fourteen (14) billion years ago, during a habitable time when the universe was only ten (10) to seventeen (17) million years old. Though the presence of life is confirmed only on our Earth, extraterrestrial life is not only possible, but probable.

There could be as many as forty (40) billion Earth-sized planets orbiting in the habitable zones of sun-like stars and red dwarf stars within the Milky Way Galaxy. Eleven (11) billion planets may be orbiting sun-like stars.

The "Panspermia" hypothesis suggests life began on Earth when the "seeds" of life, already present in the universe, arrived here from our sun's sky (Nut). This process was ordered and arranged by Ma'at.

Ma'at – The Feathered Woman – The Cosmic Path - Tehuti's Wife

Ma'at is represented by an Ostrich's feather. She is the near weightlessness of balance, harmony, truth, justice, righteousness, order, arrangement and reciprocity. She lives an honorable life and honestly pursues liberty. Ma'at is the primordial essential principle which gives meaning to all values. Ma'at balances cosmic order and arrangement. She is truth and justice that allows the divine human in the form of the Neset Bity (Pharaoh) to protect the country from disorder, pre-existing order, famine and misery. All life must conform to justice and truth represented by Ma'at, the supreme virtue, the guide and measure of all organic activity.

- Ma'at is the order and balance out of which everything and all was named and brought into existence. The basis of Pharaonic philosophy is the primordial structure of the cosmos, and the development of the knowledge of self in harmony with each person's divine duty.
- Ma'at represents the notion of moral perfection within all living things.
- Ma'at is order, truth, justice, balance, righteousness, reciprocity and ethics.
- Ma'at invites men and women in society to do, speak, think, act, transcend and transform their unique lives according to true, harmonious, balanced laws grounded in nature. This nature contains the traditional, transcendental, and absolute virtue that is expressed in Kush-Kemet mentality.
- Ma'at colors all the myths, morality and life of ancient Kush-Kemet.
- The divine essences and human beings live by, through and for Ma'at.
- Ma'at is all notions of equilibrium and peace.
- Ma'at represents accuracy, honesty, fairness, faithfulness, rectitude.
- Ma'at is Judge Supreme in jurisprudence.
- Ma'at is authenticity, legitimacy, integrity and legality.
- Ma'at is the major harmonic symbol in music.
- Ma'at is the individual type of consciousness that each person carries in his/her heart. That is why the heart is weighed against the ostrich feather of Ma'at at the Kemetic Judgment scene at death.
- Ma'at is the motivating force and path in life.
- Ma'at moves and directs existence.
- Ma'at is the path towards cosmic consciousness.
- Ma'at is a best friend forever
- Ma'at is the counterpart of Tehuti
- Tehuti is the Nature of knowledge, understanding and wisdom

Tehuti – Patron of Wisdom – Ma'at's Counterpart
- Tehuti is Ma'at's mate. He is represented by an Ibis bird. A cousin to the stork
- In the beginning, while everything and all was being ordered and arranged, Tehuti supplied the knowledge and applied the wisdom that maintained Ma'at's path
- Tehuti is the writer of the cosmos' divine plan
- Tehuti is the author, student, teacher and scribe of life
- As Ma'at's male counterpart, Tehuti represents wisdom on the path
- Tehuti is the cosmic encyclopedia containing the eternal wisdom of the universe
- Ancient Africans in Kush-Kemet made an analogy between harmonious governance, and society according to ethical principles in a balanced notion of the cosmos

- The duality of good and not good are seen as two sides of the same idea
- The wrong road, the opposite of Ma'at in ancient writings, is known as "Isfet (Ish-fet)"
- Isfet represents the deviation from Nature's course
- Isfet does not walk the righteous path of Ma'at because Tehuti is absent

Morality is the cornerstone to the truest sense of intelligence. No matter how "intelligent" you may be, if you are not ethical and respectful you are not truly intelligent. Moral Exaltation (Ma'at) precedes Intellectual Illumination (Tehuti).

Ptah – The Primordial Hill - Conversion of Potential Energy into Kinetic Energy

Ptah is symbolized by a primordial hill. Ptah is energy conversion. It is also the spirit of creation. The existence of spirituality is complementary with the existence of matter. Spirit is pure energy, and matter is energy's pure physical form. Ptah is the vital life force which moves everything and all.

The second aspect of Creation, "Ptah," converts the energy at rest (potential energy), within Nun, into energy in motion (kinetic energy). The divine essence, Ptah (energy conversion), is the pure form that is the cause of the movement of matter (Nun) and the cosmos' process of becoming called "Khepera". Ptah's divine purpose is to make the essences (Neteru) go from potentiality to actuality, energy at rest to energy in motion. All and everything that had potential, visualized order and arrangement, then actualized, (brought into being) the cosmic universe. This same process of coming into being still continues today in the same manner.

- Ptah was represented by a hill.
- Ptah is energy conversion.
- Ptah is the animating spirit.
- The existence of Ptah's spiritual energy complements the existence of Nun's potential matter.
- Spirit is pure energy, and matter is energy's pure physical form. This life or vital force is the essential force which moves everything and all and is seen as ever-manifesting matter.
- When the inert mass of primordial matter felt the desire of the primordial spirit; matter began to move, and the seed/womb life systems which were to constitute the future world, were formed.
- Matter without form is in its potentiality (The Nun), matter with form has been energized (Ptah).
- The Word (Atum) is made Flesh (the calling into being).

Atum – The Self-Created Word

The circle is formed by the serpent swallowing her tail. This is the most fundamental mystical symbol of ancient and traditional Africa, signifying infinity, continuity and the void (space). Atum, the creative word gives names to all things in the cosmic universe. Atum represented the Eye of Heru. The Eye symbolized the divine light imprisoned in matter, which must be liberated. Thus, the eye is the seat of the soul and is all-powerful, because it possesses in itself, the means for its own liberation. The Eye evokes the perception of light in all its forms from the physical shine of the sun and light of the moon, to the spiritual light of knowledge and inner illumination of the awakened spirit.

Before the beginning began, before all the fundamental elements, before Atum, the Creative Word or the Creator of the Creator, Ptah; there was only the Nun, an endless, eternal, immortal material spiritual water. The Nun was immeasurable vapor, plasma, water, aqueous and vital; the unique all and everything. The Nun was the singular one, place of the plural, the many from where all things emerge; all of the elements that will form the cosmic universe, the totality of knowable reality. The cosmic universe was created by coming out of the Creator and her/his eight (8) uncreated creations. They emerged out of the energized agitation initiated by Ptah in the waters of the Nun.

The Nun has no beginning, and it has no end. It is where matter, spirit and the word move together developing their cosmic identity. The Nun lives within the innermost center of its mysterious sacred algebra, the search for the unknown and geometry, theorems of the known. The Nun will bring Ptah forward and Atum will rise through Nun, climb atop Ptah and call all and everything into existence. Ptah starts the cosmic clock and Atum tells the time.

Beyond this metaphorical view of all that is and exists, be aware of the fundamental unity of all the elements in the universe living independently and interdependently. The Nun is the womb-seed of thought and command. Pharaonic Kush-Kemet (Egyptians) taught that Nature was order and arrangement on earth. Nature constantly renewed itself, as the sun which rises and sets each day, and why the world is livable even though the sun is absent at night.

Before the Universe came into being, there was the Nun. Nun was alone, original, primordial, absolute and eternal. Nun's waters lived in the depths of where matter had always existed; a matter which would come into being through and by itself, a matter conscious of itself and ready to create. The original matter, under the form of inaugural water, was seen by Kush-Kemet as a vital principle, the principle of principles, the archetype of the universe, the pre-existing, the already existing, and that which would exist in the future and for all time and space.

Shabaka's Stone represents a human attempt to speculate on the origin of matter and energy, and to explain life on earth and in the cosmos. These scholars viewed Nature as a distinct yet connected part of human advancement.

More than 2,500 years BCE, pharaonic Kush-Kemet (Egyptians) researched the question of questions; the question of origins, of understanding the world, and the cosmos. They asked, "What existed before existence existed? What existed before the beginning began?

Before the birth of the Divine human and all the Universe, Neteru/ essences, sky, earth, life, death and all their meanings; there was neither Creator-God nor Nothingness only the Nun. The Nun resembled nothing now known or made.

The Nun was a deep, absolute water, already containing all the raw materials which would be named by Atum.

- Atum is the Spoken Word
- Atum is Creative Utterance

The creation of the cosmos came out of this original water, Nun. Ptah precedes the third aspect of the Creator who emerges from this same water. The creative word, Atum gains consciousness of itself in this primordial pre-existing state and begin naming all things in the universe. Those named by Atum will become the cosmos, the ordered and arranged part of the universe.

The first egg, the Mother egg has a feminine gender in ancient Kush-Kemet (Egypt). It contains the breath of life at the pre-dawn of the cosmic universe. The phenomenon of creation was seen by ancient Kush-Kemet as the purpose for the existence of existing. Atum was the voice of the Creator whose existence came from Nun, the radical principle of all principles, the unfounded foundation for all foundations. Atum manifested the primordial word.

Everything and All comes forth from the Nun, the primordial cosmic ocean, and the eternal and infinite source. At the time of the inundation (flood) the country was transformed into a sea where Hapi (Nile) re-enacts the creation story. When the floodwaters receded, the land left behind recalled the appearance of the first earth, Ptah and the process of "Coming into Being."

The divine essence, Ptah (energy conversion), is the pure form that is the ultimate cause of the movement of matter and its evolution. Ptah's goal was to energize the essences (Neteru) from potential (rest) to kinetic (motion) by bringing Atum forward. All things that had potential were ordered and arranged by Atum. When actualized, the cosmic universe came into being; and still continues today.

A Multi-Referential Comparison of the Pattern in the Tabernacle Embodied in the
1st Philosophy of Shabaka's Stone titled,
"The Primate of the Essence- Nun, Ptah and Atum"

The pattern in the tabernacle repeats its cycle in all living things. Matter, energy and the creative word manifests in the cosmos, earth and organic life. Although different in their own way, their characteristics and responsibilities remain the same. As above, so below.

Matter-The Waters of Nun

Cosmic Universal Matter
- The abyssal, bottomless, topless never-ending waters of plasma.
- The original cosmic matter.
- The unstructured matter, electrons, protons and neutrons with no order or arrangement.

Earthly Matter
- The one original ocean on earth
- The many oceans, rivers, lakes, streams and water systems on earth

Organic Matter
- Feminine amniotic fluids ("Amen"iotic-living fertile waters) and the
- Masculine semen (s"emen") liquids carry life into existence
- Amen being the male hidden waters and Amenet being the female revealed waters
- The five (5) major liquid systems of organic life include blood, phlegm, hormones, mucus and plasma. These liquid systems are called into being by 4 words (4 amino acids "adenine," "guanine," "cytosine," and "thymine.") uttered by the earthly Creator, DNA.
- Deoxyribonucleic acid (DNA) is the cell's hereditary material and contains instructions for development, growth and reproduction. DNA is made up of four chemical (nitrogen) bases:
- Purines
  adenine and guanine
- Pyrimidines
  cytosine and thymine

Energy-The Energy Conversion of Ptah

Conversion of Cosmic Energy
- Cosmic Energy at rest into Cosmic Energy in Motion
- Shaper of waveicle behavior (waves + particles)
- Universal geometric shapes throughout the cosmos interacting with gravitational force fields
- Panspermia – Cosmic space seeds that self-impregnate the Cosmic egg womb

Conversion of Earthly Energy
- Conversion of energy in the core of the Earth
- Ptah, the original hill (continent) that rises up out of Earth's ocean, called Pangaea
- The continent of Africa is the land mass at the top of the hill

Conversion of Organic Energy
- DNA and RNA - Reproduction and genetics
- Organic convergence of energy
- Mitosis and Meiosis (cell division) in organic life
- Hominid development from Australopithecine to Homo Lines leading to human beings
- The process of becoming represented by frogs (metamorphosis) and snakes (resurrection)

The Creative Word of Atum

Cosmic Creative Word
- Cosmic Utterance of Atum (Atom)
- Atum (Atoms) develop the many atoms, elements and molecules
- Light, Heat and Sound Waves, Vibrations and Frequencies
- Star light that creates life on planets

Earthly Creative Word
- Evolutionary process
- Atoms, Elements, Molecules
- Earth (Nitrogen), Air (Oxygen), Water (Hydrogen) and Fire (Carbon).
- Light, heat and sound in relation to photovoltaics and agriculture

Organic Creative Word
- Consciousness of Organic Matter

- The Process of Becoming from Zygote (Blastula) - Protozoon (Single Cell in early waters)
- The union of two cells constitute the beginning of the development in unique organic patterns
- DNA and RNA ordering and arranging life - The 4 major chemicals of life (adenine, guanine, cytosine, and thymine)
- The four (4) major elements of life – Earth, Air, Water and Fire

The waters of the Nun, every thing and no thing, is a vast ocean of eternity where all things are in equilibrium, harmony and balance. In that first moment, when the beginning began, everything was activated in the waters of the Nun.

As energy continued the process of becoming, Atum, the creative word, called the cosmos into being. This unification of the original trinity is what science calls a "singularity," with Atum as the verbal expression of the cosmos.

This metaphor of Khepera Sep Tepy, the first philosophy of Shabaka's Stone can be scientifically expressed by astrophysics today. Drs. Neil deGrasse Tyson and Donald Goldsmith speak of the early cosmos when it came into being for the first time,

"Some 14 billion years ago, at the beginning of time, all the space and all the matter and all the energy of the known universe fit within a pinhead. The universe was then so hot that the basic forces of nature, which collectively describe the universe, were merged into a single, unified force, the time before which all of our theories of matter and space lose their meaning - black holes spontaneously formed, disappeared, and formed again out of the energy contained within the unified force field… During this epoch, phenomena described by Einstein's general theory of relativity (the modern theory of gravity) and quantum mechanics (the description of matter on its smallest scales) were indistinguishable." 28

Universe = Nun = 100% of All, Every Thing and No Thing

4% of the Universe is **Ordinary Matter** - The stuff from which the ordered and arranged cosmos was created.

23% of the Universe is **Dark Matter** – The Nun when named, remains in pre-existing order and arrangement

73% of the Universe is **Dark Energy** - Ptah, the animating energy always in motion, constantly activating Dark Matter to become Ordinary Matter

Dr. Tyson describes this cosmic phenomenon,

"Dark matter of today can be compared to ether; a weightless, transparent medium through which light moves. **29**

The Nun existed before the beginning began. And then the first time occurred. It was called, "Khepera Sep Tepy, the Coming into Being for the First Time." The outcome of this first time was named "Ptah." But the universe had an existence before the beginning began. At a specific moment, time began, with beings beginning to search for the Creator within. Dr. Tyson expresses this idea in scientific terms,
   Every one of our body's atoms is traceable to the big bang and to the thermonuclear furnaces within high-mass stars. We are not simply in the universe; we are part of it. We are born from it. One might even say that the universe has empowered us, here in our small corner of the cosmos, to figure itself out." **30**

To figure itself out, "is the realization that each of us is the Creator having a human experience.
   Matter and energy existed in balance and harmony within the eternal universal waters of the Nun. Matter is chemistry and energy is physics. Chemistry answers the question, "What is matter?" and physics answers the question, "What makes matter move?" The moment matter moved for the first time, Khepera Sep Tepy, Ptah came into existence and Atum followed. Atum names the Creator's uncreated creations, the four (4) pairs, who act as the identifiable attributes and characteristics of the cosmic universe. These eight essences or "Neteru," are matter, space, infinity, finity, darkness, light, the hidden and revealed. As the cosmic universe cooled, the four great natural forces of the universe were created, electromagnetism, gravity, the strong and weak forces. Dr. Tyson says,
   "Physics describes how matter, energy, space, and time behave and interact with one another. The interplay of these characters in our cosmic drama underlies all biological and chemical phenomena. Hence, everything fundamental and familiar

to us earthlings begin with, and rests upon the laws of physics. When we apply these laws to astronomical settings, we deal with astrophysics. **31**

The fusion of Nun, Ptah and Atum, the three into one, the original Trinity was the initiator of the cosmic universe. It is through the matter of Nun, the converting energy of Ptah and the creative voice of Atum, that the cosmos was ordered and arranged. Dr. Tyson continues,

"When the universe cooled, somewhat hotter than a blast furnace, the lower electrons moved slowly enough to get snatched from the cosmic soup by the roving nuclei to make complete atoms of hydrogen, helium, and lithium, the three lightest elements...Within just the volume of the cosmos that we can see, a hundred billion of these galaxies formed, each containing hundreds of billions of stars that undergo thermonuclear fusion in their cores...After seven (7) or eight (8) billion years of such enrichment, an undistinguished star (our Sun) was born in an undistinguished region (the Orion arm) of an undistinguished galaxy (Milky Way) in an undistinguished part of the universe, (the outskirts of the Virgo cluster). The gas cloud from which the Sun formed contained a sufficient supply of heavy elements to spawn a few planets, thousands of asteroids, and billions of comets. During the formation of this star system, matter condensed and accreted out of the parent cloud of gas while circling the Sun." **32**

The first philosophy of Shabaka's Stone discusses the events that initiated the cosmic universe coming into being and continued the process of becoming. In the second philosophy, "The Essences of Pre-Existing Order and Arrangement," Atum joins with Khepera and calls into being the four (4) pairs of Neteru Nun, the eight (8) uncreated creations.

Chapter 3 - Philosophy #2 - The Essences/Neteru of Pre-Existing Order and Arrangement

When Atum, the Voice of the Original Trinity, Called into Being and Named the Eight (8) Neteru Nun The Uncreated Creations

Before life could come into existence in the cosmic universe, African scholars believed that certain philosophical concepts had to be recognized in the human mind, to allow humanity's consciousness to fully comprehend the two worlds of the heavens and the earth,

Science-Matter-**Nun**
Spiritual- Conversion of Energy-**Ptah**
Spiritual Science –As above, so below-The Creative Word-**Atum**

Ptah was not energy itself, it was the initiator, ignitor, the activating spark of life. Within the eternal matter of water, animated energy, the creative conscious voice, Atum. The synthesis of this trinity initiated the calling into being of eight (8) concepts that had always existed at rest in the Nun. Atum named four (4) pairs of male frogs and female snakes. The Kemetic scholars called them the "Neteru Nun," the "Uncreated Creations" living at rest in the waters of Nun.

These scientific principles expressed by philosophical characteristics allowed early African scholars to consider the ability to think the unthinkable, hear the inaudible, smell the scentless, see the unseen, taste the inedible and feel the untouchable. These uncreated creations became the bridge between the spiritual and physical worlds. They remained in the waters of the Nun representing eight (8) characteristics of life; matter, space, infinity, finity, darkness, light, the hidden and the revealed. These ten (10) essences connected the seen scientific matter to the unseen spiritual energy in the cosmic universe. The figurative language used in Shabaka's Stone described abstract spiritual principles that were expressed through precise science.

In the 1st philosophy, the Primate of the Essence, Nun had no name. It was important for the trinity to come into existence that would allow Atum to give Nun a name, making it possible for the Creator to know her/himself. While the Nun contained the whole universe in potential gestation, Ptah moved matter creating Atum in order to call into existence eight (8) eternal essences or pure ideas. These ideas were not created, they always existed, but were inactive (potential) in the unnamed universe (the Nun). The eight (8) Neteru, were visually depicted as being uncreated by not having navels (belly buttons), therefore, they did not come from a birth by mother. They were not connected to mother's womb by an umbilical cord. Nun (matter), Nunet (space), Huh (infinity), Huhet (finity),

Kuk (darkness), Kuket (light), Amen (hidden) and Amenet, (revealed) are the attributes and characteristics that define all things in the universe. These eight (8) abstract attributes and characteristics concretized spirituality, which was science.

These eight uncreated characteristics of the cosmos are,

1) Nun (Male)–Matter/Water- This Nun is the same Nun from the Primate of the Essences, however, now Nun has been named by Atum, and brought into being. Before the beginning began, Nun was nameless. However, once named, Nun took physical form and was recognized as matter/water. The Nun was the place where everything and all lived. The Nun was the original and ancient place of places. Nun represented the moisture of the rain, and the wetness of all the rivers and oceans of the cosmic universe. He was the deluges and floods of Eternal Springs. He was the "Matter" of the cosmic fact.

2) Nunet (Female)-Space/Counter Heavens. She was where the superclusters, clusters, and galaxies first appeared, the stars commenced to shine, and the air began to breathe. Nunet permitted the sky to be. Nunet was the space between all and everything.

3) Huh (Male)-Infinity. He was countless, limitless, without boundaries and sure to endure forever in eternity. Huh was immeasurable.

4) Huhet (Female)-Finity-She was destined to limit and be the boundaries for everything and all things that would come to be in the cosmic universe. She could be counted, measured and numbered. She was exactitude and kept all things in order and arrangement.

5) Kuk (Male)-Darkness-He was the unknown, the ignorant. He was the source from whence all light drew her strength. Kuk was the sunless shadows of dark unknown nights. Kuk was the dark black from where his mate, Kuket, the light shone bright.

6) Kuket (Female)-Light- She brought the glowing intelligence of the light of day into existence. She shone the fiery rays of knowledge, where her wisdom prevailed.

7) Amen (Male)-The Unseen- He was hidden, the concealed one, invisible to the eye. He was named by Atum to remain unseen, unheard, and untouchable, without smell or taste, but, forever present. He was the spirit of his mate, Amenet's science.

8) Amenet (Female)-The Seen-She was the revealed one, visible to the eye. Through her all-seeing eye, the cosmic universe thinks, sees, hears, touches, smells and tastes. It is through Amenet's eye that human

spirituality experiences her invisible mate, Amen. She was the science of his spirit.

These four (4) pairs symbolically represented by frogs and snakes remained in the waters of Nun. Theoretically, there were metaphoric reasons why frogs and snakes were the Neteru chosen to be the representatives, heraldic emblems of the uncreated creations.

Snakes were females. Nunet, Huhet, Kuket and Amenet symbolize the principle of resurrection. Snakes have the ability to shed their skin and start anew. This natural process appeared to have the attributes of coming back to life (new skin), after death (old skin). The snakes shedding skin is called, "Molting." When it is time to molt, the snake's color becomes dull as the worn-out skin separates from the lower layers, and its eyes cloud over until it is almost blind. A new outer skin is already growing under the old one. Eventually, the old skin splits, and the snake wriggles out of it with its new skin. The snake is now back to its proper color and has bright new spectacles over her eyes. The old skin is left behind like a past-life as she moves forward with a new skin towards her new resurrected life.

Frogs were males. Nun, Huh, Kuk and Amen describe the metamorphosis of life. They are equally at home on land (amphibian/reptiles/mammals) as in the water (fish). Frogs spend the first few weeks of their lives as a legless, fish-like tadpole which looks like a spermatozoon and nothing like a frog. But then it begins to transform. The frog goes through the story of how organic life came to be. Frogs explain in about 14 weeks, what it took humans to become over billions of years. The growing of legs shows the importance of life systems attaining mobility; the loss of the tail describes, upright walking and balance, the dawn of thinking and the attainment of self-consciousness. Chapter 7, Ontogeny Recapitulates Phylogeny continues this metaphoric concept.

The eight (8) essences/Neteru, plus Ptah and Atum add up to the number ten (10); like the world's base ten (10) numerical system.
Drs. Tyson and Goldsmith, in their book, "Cosmos," makes this observation,
"At the time when the universe was just a fraction of a second old, a ferocious trillion degrees hot, and aglow with an unimaginable brilliance, its main agenda was expansion. With every passing moment, the universe got bigger as more space came into existence from nothing, not easy to imagine, but here, evidence speaks louder than common sense. As the universe expanded, it grew cooler and dimmer. For hundreds of millennia, matter and energy (co-habited in a kind of thick soup in which speedy electrons continually scattered photons of light to and fro. 33

Shabaka's Stone records the first moment of time called, "Khepera Sep Tepy," meaning, "Coming into Being for the First Time." From this big bang moment on, space Nunet began to expand out from its singularity. To do this, Atum developed and shaped the various aspects of the Nun. Nunet pushed matter out to infinity by way of the nature of its own finite boundaries. The Nun was darkness, but as it expanded out, it created light from within the dark. While dark, all and everything was unseen, but in the light, all could be seen. The mystical aspects of the unseen were revealed.

Science theorizes that the creation and development of the universe came in stages. Dr. Tyson says,

"Matter in large regions of the universe had already begun to coalesce. Where matter accumulates, gravity grows stronger, enabling more and more matter to gather. Those matter-rich regions seeded the formation of superclusters, while other regions remained empty. The photons that lasted scattered off electrons within the coalescing regions developing a different, slightly cooler spectrum as they climbed out of the strengthening gravity field, which robbed them of a bit of energy."**34**

As the cosmos continued the process of becoming, the eight (8) attributes continued to order and arrange the dark material aspects (dark matter) of the universe by the animating forces of energy in motion (dark energy). As eons of time passed, the eight (8) characteristics, the Neteru Nun, refined, shaped and reshaped the stuff of the universe by fusing hydrogen atoms into more complex atoms like helium and lithium, etc., forming them into simple and complex molecules. Drs. Tyson and Goldsmith say,

"Continuing onward with what is now laboratory-confirmed physics, the universe was hot enough for photons to spontaneously convert their energy into matter-antimatter particle pairs, which immediately thereafter annihilated each other, returning their energy back to photon. For reasons unknown, this symmetry between matter and antimatter had been "broken" at the previous force splitting, which led to a slight excess of matter over antimatter. The asymmetry was small but crucial for the future evolution of the universe: for every 1 billion antimatter particles, 1 billion + 1 matter particles were born." **35**

Khepera Sep Tepy representing the first moment of existence immediately began formulating the pre-existing plan for the further development of the cosmos. In science, it took millions and millions of earth years to implement this plan. The process continued, by fusing two (2) hydrogen atoms that became one (1) helium atom, three (3) hydrogen created 0ne (1) lithium, etc. Dr. Tyson states,

"From 380,000 years after the big bang until about 200 million years later, matter continued to gather itself together, but nothing shone in the universe, whose first stars were yet to be born. During this Cosmic Dark Age, the universe contained only what it had made during its first few minutes – hydrogen and helium, with traces of lithium." **36**

Over billions of years, cosmic forces moved at infinite speeds through endless space. These forces were organized at the centers of superclusters, clusters and galaxies called black holes. Black holes have a magnetic attraction that captures everything in its environment, including light. It was scientifically natural for major creative events to occur from this point. It was only a matter of space and time. Drs. Tyson and Goldsmith explain the birth of cosmic black holes.

"One of the natural results of gravity at work was the formation of supermassive black holes, each with a mass millions or billions of times the mass of our Sun." 37

Kuk was the darkest place where Kuket, the light, was animated. Light lives in the dark. In balance, the dark and light, as well as the other Neteru Nun, the uncreated creations, continued the process of setting the boundaries for the ordering and arranging of the cosmic universe. The authors of Shabaka's Stone ventured into the deepest recesses of consciousness by contemplating what existed before existence existed. What existed before the beginning began. Something had to exist. In what state did it exist? Their answer was, all things existed in potential energy, energy at rest. From this metaphor to the science of today, Dr. Neil deGrasse Tyson says,

"During the first half million years after the big bang, a mere moment in the 14-billion-year sweep of cosmic history, matter in the universe had already begun to coalesce into the blobs that would become clusters and superclusters of galaxies. But the cosmos was expanding all along and would double in size during its next half million years. So, the universe responds to two competing effects: gravity wants to make stuff coagulate, but the expansion wants to dilute it. If you do the math, you rapidly deduce that the gravity from ordinary matter could not win this battle, by itself. It needed the help of dark matter, without which we would be living-actually, not living-in a universe with no structure-no clusters, no galaxies, no stars, no planets, no people." 38

On earth, centrifugal force repulses outward from the center but attracts back inward towards the center. Centrifugal force is harmonized by centripetal force, the force that attracts inward, but repulses outward. The delicate balance of these forces in physics assists in life on earth.

The Neteru Nun were intellectual characteristics, yet scientific emblems of the boundaries of the creation of the cosmos. The cosmos is,
- Matter that takes up space and space that separates Matter
- Infinite as the Heavens and Finite as the Earth
- Dark as a Black Hole and Light as the Stars
- Hidden in the spirit and revealed in the science

When the original African theorists proposed the outcomes of their research, they said that the process of cosmic beginnings came through the expansion of the universe (infinity). But they also theorized that as the cosmos was expanding, it was contracting (finity) by nature of the law of polarity, all things came into existence by the harmony of the complements. When citing the science of dark and light, Dr. Tyson says,

"The cosmos we now know, has both a light and a dark side. The light side embraces all familiar heavenly objects, the stars, which group by the billions into galaxies, as well as the planets and smaller cosmic debris that may not produce visible light but do emit other forms of electromagnetic radiation, such as infrared or radio waves." **39**

After the 1st moment occurred, the expanding contractions continued. Infinity created a place for finity to exist, the darkness was where the brightest stars shone. Dr. Tyson continues,

"We have discovered that the dark side of the universe embraces the puzzling dark matter, detected only by its gravitational influence on visible matter but otherwise of completely unknown form and composition. A modest amount of this dark matter may be ordinary matter that remains invisible because it produces no detectable radiation. But, the great bulk of the dark matter must consist of non-ordinary matter, whose nature continues to elude us, except for its gravitational force on matter we can see." **40**

Once Atum named the four (4) pairs of Essences of Pre-Existing Order and Arrangement, the cosmos developed very quickly, by geometric progressions. Nun (matter) and Nunet (space) expanded their reach outward, while pulling inward at the same time, these two opposing forces continued the development of the cosmic universe. When the figurative language of Shabaka's Stone is compared to the scientific principles of today's creation stories, the precise science is recognized in the allegorical story.

From a scientific perspective, Drs. Tyson and Goldsmith say,

"During the early days of the universe, the cosmos expanded rapidly. It evolved into a cosmic soup. It was a starter for all concentrations of matter and energy that would later emerge. Without this head start, the rapidly expanding universe would have prevented gravity from ever gathering matter to build the familiar structures we take for granted in the universe today. In tracing the growth of structure from times soon after the big bang, we gain some insight from two key epochs we have already met, the "era of inflation," when the universe expanded at an astounding rate, and the "time of decoupling," about 380,000 years after the big bang, when the cosmic background radiation ceased to interact with matter. The inflationary model of the universe asserts that when the universe was young, the prevailing energy field went through a phase transition, one of several that would have occurred during these early times. This particular episode not only catapulted the early, rapid expansion but also imbued the cosmos with a specific fluctuating pattern of high- and low-density regions. These fluctuations then froze into the expanding fabric of space, creating a kind of blueprint for where galaxies would ultimately form. We can assign our origins, and the beginnings of all structure to the fluctuations on a sub-nuclear scale that arose during the inflationary era. **41**

The Essences of Pre-Existing Order and Arrangement was the second (2nd) philosophy. The third (3rd) philosophy witnessed Atum join with Khepera and continue the process of becoming. Atum-Khepera gives birth to the Essences of Order and Arrangement. These Neteru, would eventually bring into existence the universe's ultimate masterpiece…Earth's Human Family.

Chapter 4 - Philosophy #3 – The Essences of Order and Arrangement

When Atum joins with Khepera,
Atum-Khepera calls forward Shu (air) and Tefnut (moisture)
who give birth to Nut (sky) and Geb (earth)
who give birth to Aset (Mother), Asar (Father), Neb-het-tet (Oracle) and
Seten (Incompletion)
Aset and Asar give birth to Heru (Resurrection)

This third (3rd) philosophy is a natural extension of the first and second philosophies. Although it has its own respective Neteru, characteristics and personalities; it follows the story's pattern of cosmic beginnings. The story of the creation of life in our solar system and Earth continued with Atum-Khepera, naming the atoms, elements and molecules that would create the air, moisture, sky, earth and all things that existed on and walked upon the land.

Khepera is the beetle who comes forth from the flood of Hapi (Nile) pushing a ball of dung containing her fertilized eggs. Under the rays of the sun, the eggs in this ball of dung burst forth with new lives as if they generated themselves from the purged substances of nature. Since thousands of these beetles emerge from these balls in fertile waters, the beetle is synonymous with the natural genesis of creativity. Khepera, the process of becoming, joins with Atum, creative utterance; and transforms into Atum-Khepera. These Neteru gave birth to all cosmic and living things; superclusters, clusters, galaxies, stars, planets, bacteria, plants, fish, amphibians, reptiles and mammals, including the human race in Africa.

In reference to earth's elemental essences, in the first moment after self-creation, the one, Atum-Khepera produces two, Shu-male-air and Tefnut-female-moisture. The unity of Shu and Tefnut (air and moisture), under the guidance of Atum Khepera (the process of becoming that initiates nuclear fusion), gave birth to the next two elements Geb-male-earth, and Nut-female-sky. This metaphor can be explained scientifically,

Our planet's ozone layer, which is located in the stratosphere, is about 9 to 18 miles above the earth's surface. The ozone layer protects all life from the sun's harmful ultraviolet radiation. It acts like an invisible shield against harmful UV-B and UV-C rays, which have been linked to skin and eye damage, a reduction in the productivity and quality of crops, and changes in various biological functions for different species. Due to human activity and pollution, some atmospheric ozone has been depleted. Naturally occurring events and processes such as volcanic eruptions can also affect ozone levels.

Shabaka's Stone continues the history of life in the cosmos and planet Earth. Nut (sky) and Geb (earth) are in a lover's embrace (the act of reproduction) when Shu (air) separates Nut (sky) from Geb (earth). Nut (sky) then allows for the emission of rays (waveicles) of light, heat and sound energy that bring life to earth. Nut (Sky) swallows the Sun (Ra) at night and gives birth to the Sun (Ra) at dawn. While in a lover's embrace, Nut (sky) was impregnated by this union with Geb (earth). He (Shu/air) separated her (Nut/sky) from him (Geb/earth). This separation provided space between the sky and earth for everything to come into being on Geb (earth). When the sky was raised from the earth, the sun's light, heat and sound energy rays were sent to the earth to create organic life. The sun's rays were like the ship and spirit/energy was the captain of the ship. The cycle of life was created on earth because of the sun's rays and the world became alive.

The Essences of Order and Arrangement continue the earthly process. Geb and Nut then gave birth to Asar, Aset, Seten, and Nebhetet. Asar and Aset gave birth to Heru, who represented all living things, including the botanical and animal life on earth (Geb), including the human race in Africa. This third philosophy described what science teaches today regarding the creation of the earth.

There are five (5) philosophical underpinnings to be understood by Shabaka's Stone:
1) Water is the source of all and everything (The Nun)
2) Creation was accomplished by the unity of creative principles, Nun, Ptah and Atum; the unity of mind
    (Ptah) with creative intelligence (Atum) within cosmic water (the Nun). All divine creations came into
    being by the thinking of the mind (Ptah), the desire in the Heart (Ma'at) and the commanding of the
    tongue (Atum) in the deep eternal waters of the Nun.
3) Atum was the intermediary essence/Neter in creation. She/He was the sun or fire essence.
4) The Law of Polarity (twinness/opposites/complements) directs the life of the cosmic universe.
5) Philosophy came from the creation of the Essences of Pre-Existing Order and Arrangement. **42**

The philosophical allegory of ancient Kush-Kemet used by these ancient scholars paved the way for the cosmic concepts currently being taught in universities (Universe Cities) today. They theorized that in the beginning there was only a watery Matter (Nun). Within this matter, there rested the potential energy in everything and all. When activated, potential energy became active, kinetic energy. The ancient African Kemites (Egyptians) called this conversion process, Ptah. On earth, Ptah, (Pangaea, the original continent), rose out of Nun (earth's one ocean) as a mighty hill on the path of Ma'at. Tehuti was the wisdom that kept Ptah's nature on the righteous path and kept creation in the process of becoming (Khepera). Atum was the organized and arranged life on Geb (earth).

Scientifically, this Kheperarian process of becoming contained a powerful electromagnetic field, a reminder of the beginnings of the universe, indicating that the universe began within a state of infinite density (matter). It was made up of free atoms, elements and particles, not in any particular order or arrangement. There was no gravitation in the beginning of the cosmic universe, only a matter unique and waiting to be replicated. The cosmic universe expanded and one after the other, the superclusters, clusters and galaxies distanced themselves one from another. This process continues to this day and will continue for many more millions of years.

The ancient African theorists who created the metaphor of the Essences of Order and Arrangement understood their study of the natural scientific principles of existence, was determined by how atoms, elements and molecules were combined and recombined. These molecules created by these unique combinations lead to intra-universal, inter-supercluster, inter-cluster, inter-galactic, inter-solar and inter-planetary life. However, before life could come to exist in the cosmic universe, certain philosophical concepts had to be created in the human mind, to allow the mind to fully comprehend the Atumic Creative Word that balances the two worlds of the Material-Nun-Water and the Spiritual-Ptah-Energy.

Philosophy means the "love of wisdom." "Philo" is love and "Sophia" is wisdom. It is the exercise of reason through intellect, language, thought and action. The result of this exercise is the conception of the rewards and challenges of life in the world. To be a true scribe in Pharaonic Kush-Kemet (Egypt), the philosopher had to be a scientist, teacher, sage, poet, benefactor, husband/wife, mother/father and warrior. Education demanded that methodology of study was very important in the educational process. These priests and priestesses of Kush-Kemet's educational temples had world-wide reputations. Writing and monumental architecture (pyramids, temples, etc.) synthesized literature, math, science, astronomy, medicine, religion, painting, drawing, sculpture, carvings, music, games, to identify some of the areas of study. Leisure activities were created, developed, implemented and enjoyed in Pharaonic Kush-Kemet (Egypt).

The immortality of the soul of Humanity (Ba) was taught in Shabaka's Stone. The sciences co-existed with spiritual philosophy but had to wait to be called into being by the word. Knowledge is the accumulation of information, and wisdom is the application of knowledge. Wisdom in Ancient Kush-Kemet was identified as a Spiritual Science. The patron of wisdom, "Tehuti", husband of Ma'at, guided Africans along the path of righteousness and harmony. Spirituality is Unseen Science, and Science is Seen Spirituality.

Shabaka's Stone brings together ancient African ideas about creation into a broad philosophical system about the nature and purpose of the cosmic universe. The concept of being in the creation story is simultaneously spiritual (sacred) and material (scientific). Shabaka's Stone expressed a science of the soul using figurative language. The African sacred and scientific world was completely united.

The reality of creation is the consequence of the **Idea** (Nun-Thought-Conception-Theory) and the **Act** (Ptah-Doing-Implementation-Practice-Command) bringing forth the **Word** (Atum-Creative Utterance).

This process of becoming was guided by the code of Ma'at; truth, justice, righteousness, harmony, reciprocity, order, arrangement and balance. Ancient African scholars saw human reality resulting from thinking and doing; thought and command, theory and practice. The essence of the Creator is revealed as **Will** (thought) and **Intent** (command). The symbol of thought is the heart, and the tongue represents command. Heart and tongue become the material aspects for the spiritual qualities of thought/will and command/intent. The Heart conceives the idea of the cosmic universe and the tongue concretely makes the idea a reality by giving commands to name and proclaim the idea's existence.

To name and proclaim is to say loud and intelligibly in order to bring into existence. What is proclaimed comes out of non-existence, takes shape and has effect at the very moment of utterance (naming). In its truest spiritual essence, the cosmic universe is unknowable; however, it is imaginable in the precise science developed by the human mind.

Shabaka's Stone revealed a high science that has not yet been matched in today's intellectual world. The foundational principles are grounded in the ongoing effort to balance science with spirituality. It is theorized that electromagnetic plasma is comprised of electrically conducted hydrogen gases. As plasma crosses existing magnetic fields, it generates tremendous new electrical currents; this motion translates into electricity. Magnetism is a feminine energy and electricity is a male energy. As much as one-tenth of all energy now being released from the stars (nuclear energy), is converted into electricity.

Electricity creates and enhances magnetism; magnetism enhances and creates electricity. Electricity lives for, through and because of magnetism. Magnetism lives for, through and because of electricity. Human/animal life inhales oxygen from plants and exhales carbon dioxide. Plants get carbon dioxide from human/animal and releases oxygen. Like electricity and magnetism, biological and botanical entities live in symbiotic harmony with each other.

The universe was a place filled with uniform hydrogen plasma. This plasma was free, unorganized and unarranged, contained in a state of pre-existing order and arrangement. When ordered and arranged, they were held in Mills and Yang Fields that contain electrons, protons, and neutrons. It is reasonable to imagine that this plasma had the potential for motion and energy. These electrical currents and magnetic fields flowed through the universe like the essences of energy with flashes of lightening. At some appointed time, one of these flashes ignited (Ptah) for the first time (Khepera Sep Tepy) and started the process of becoming.

After the cosmic universe came into being, there was an ordering and arranging of these electrons, protons and neutrons held within these Mills and Yang Fields. This initial action that converted energy at rest into energy in motion, created the superclusters. Superclusters created clusters, Clusters exploded and brought forward galaxies. Galaxies formed stars and star systems gave birth to planets and other celestial bodies. Our sun's light, heat and sound energy, created organic life on our planet. At each stage, the inward flowing electrical currents, and the background magnetic fields had an impact within the plasma. This gave way for further contraction and extraction of the superclusters, clusters, galaxies and stars. Order and arrangement came into being through the natural processes of electromagnetism, gravity the strong and weak forces in the cosmos.

Gravity created regions of the cosmic universe that contained matter. These regions attracted other regions that contained less matter. As more and more matter gathered together, a uniform balance of matter, imploded and exploded forming smaller, but denser balances of matter (Nun), with large spaces (Nunet) between them. These regions gradually broke up into superclusters, clusters, galaxies, and finally star systems, planets and all things that make up the cosmos. The cosmos is the ordered and arranged parts of the universe. The waste matter of one cycle's release of gravitational energy, became the raw materials for the next creative life cycle.

Comparing this scientific theory with Shabaka's Stone, we see that the result of this electromagnetic and gravitational stage of evolution is the product of a complex and ordered system of entities, ranging from superclusters to clusters to galaxies to stars to planets; each pouring out concentrated electrical currents and magnetic fields.

The following three (3) excerpts demonstrate the idea that the writers of these philosophical spiritual texts believed in One Creator and He/She created all and everything by throwing off aspects of Her/Himself.

In the Book of Knowing the Evolution of Ra, "Neb-er-Tcher," records the following story of creation and the birth of earthly Neteru. The text states, "**I** am she/he who evolved him/her under the form of the essence, Khepera. **I,** the evolver of the evolutions and developments which came forth from my mouth. No heaven existed, and no earth, and no terrestrial animal, or reptiles had come into being. **I** formed them out of the inert mass of watery matter. **I** found no place whereon to stand...**I** was alone, and the Essences Shu (air) and Tefnut (moisture) had not gone from me; there existed none other who worked with me. **I** laid the foundation for all things by my will, and all things evolved themselves from there. I united myself to my shadow and set forth Shu (air) and Tefnut (moisture) out of myself thus from being one I became three, and Shu and Tefnut gave birth to Nut (sky) and Geb (earth) and Nut gave birth to Asar, Aset, Setesh, and Nebhetet. Asar and Aset gave birth to Heru, at one birth, and their children multiply upon this earth." **43**

The importance of Atum naming all of the Creator's creations through the "Word," can be seen among many ancient peoples believing that the calling of a person's name was regarded as an act of creation; and the refusal to invoke the name of a person, place or thing was equivalent to them not existing.

In the text titled, Ra's Description of His Description, the scribe states,
"Thus, said Ra, the Lord of All, Lord of the Utmost Limits (Universe), after He had come into being, **I** am the One who came into being as Khepera. He who comes into being and brings into being. When **I** came into being, being itself came into being. All beings came into being after **I** came into being. Many were the beings that came forth from the commands of my mouth. Heaven had not yet come into being. Nor had earth come into being. Nor had the ground been created or the things which creep and crawl upon it. **I** raised up beings in the primordial waters (Nun) as inert things. **I** found no place on which to stand. **I** formed it from the desire in my heart; **I** laid the foundation through Ma'at. **I** created forms of every kind. Many were the forms which issued forth from the commands of my mouth. Not yet had **I** established Shu, the power and principle of air. Nor sent forth Tefnut the power and principle of moisture. There existed no one who acted together with me. **I** conceived it in my own heart. And there came into being a vast number of forms of divine beings as forms of offspring and forms of their offspring. **I** came forth from among the plants which **I** created, and **I** created all things which creep and crawl and all that exists among them. Then by the power and principles of light and air and the power and principle of moisture, heaven and earth were brought into being, and by earth and heaven Asar, Aset, Neb-Het-Tet, Set and Heru were brought into being from the womb, one after another, and they gave birth to the multitudes in this land." **44**

The seeing of the eyes, hearing of the ears and the breathing of the nose are communicated to the heart and mind, and the heart and mind cause all perceptions to be perceived. What the heart and mind think, and wish is spoken by the tongue. The action of the arms and hands, the motion of the legs, the movement of every member of the body, according to the command which is conceived by the heart and mind and commanded by the tongue, create the usefulness and action of everything.

Every word of the Creator came into being through what the heart desired, the mind thought, and the tongue commanded. By means of the word, all faculties and qualities were shaped and created which furnished all food and yielded all nourishment.

It is said of Ptah (Ra) then, "He is He who made all and created the divine powers. He is Ta-tenen (the risen land) who produced the divine powers and from whom everything came forth, food and provisions divine offerings and every good thing. Thus, it was recognized and understood that He is the mightiest of all divine powers. And after he/she had created all things and all the divine utterances. Ptah was pleased and rested." **45**

The Grand Unified Theory unifies the outer world with the inner world, the world of the stars with the world of the atoms. Dr. Gabriel A. Oyibo, a brilliant mathematician has created the "God Almighty Grand Unified Theory." His "Theory of Everything" unites all things in the waters of Nun, which is hydrogen or as he has named it "Africogen." Dr. Oyibo compares GAGUT with the Shabaka Stone, he says,

"The Shabaka Stone, named after a Pharaoh Shabaka of Egypt, is a stone on which the Ancient Africans' creation theory was carved. The theory states the Creator created the universe using a fundamental building block called the Atum, (Hydrogen or Africogen). The Greeks mis-defined and misspelled Atum as Atom. The theory is depicted by Roaring Water Waves (called God's Word by the "holy" books and the Big Bang by science as decoded by GAGUT) with Atum emanating out of the Waves." **46**

Atum is similar to the black hole, the singularity that exists in the center of the cosmic universe, as well as each galaxy. The magnetic pull of black holes order and arrange all things that happen anywhere near their event horizon (the point of no return). The event horizon is that area on the edge of the entry point of the black hole. Once you get to a certain point, it is like going over a cliff. Dr. Tyson said,
"Every giant galaxy harbors a supermassive black hole, which could have served as a gravitational seed around which the other matter collected or may have been manufactured later by matter streaming down from outer regions of the galaxy…Some galaxies begin their lives as quasars. To be a quasar, which is the visible center of a galaxy. The system has to have not only a massive, hungry black hole but also an ample supply of in-falling gas. Once the supermassive black hole has gulped down all the available food, leaving uneaten stars and gas in distant, safe orbits, the quasar simply shuts off." **47**

The black holes are not only the centers of galaxies, but black holes are also related to every other black hole throughout the cosmos. Super-Sized black holes vibrate on the same cosmic frequency. Black holes are like cosmic motherboards vibrating throughout the universe.

"The energy of the orbits of all the stars and gas clouds ultimately compose a galaxy that pales when compared with what made the black hole. Without supermassive black holes lurking below, galaxies as we know them might have never formed. The once luminous but now invisible black hole that lies at the center of each giant galaxy provides a hidden link, the physical explanation for the agglomeration of matter into a complex system of billions of stars in orbit around a common center…Most of a galaxy's stars were born within relatively loose "associations." The more compact regions of star-birth remain identifiable "star clusters," within which member stars orbit the cluster's center, tracing their paths through space in a cosmic ballet choreographed by the forces of gravity from all the other stars within the cluster, even as the clusters themselves move on enormous trajectories around the galactic center, safe from the destructive power of the central black hole." **48**

Shabaka's third (3rd) philosophy speaks of the law of complements joining two opposing forces in order to continue the process of becoming. Science describes a similar process when discussing the thermonuclear fusion of the nuclei of atoms. Dr. Tyson said,

"At this magic temperature, some of the protons (which are simply naked hydrogen atoms, shorn of the electron that orbits them) move fast enough to overcome their mutual repulsion. Their high speeds allow the protons to approach one another close enough for the "strong nuclear force" to make them bond. This force, which operates only at extremely short distances, binds together the protons and neutrons in all nuclei. The mass that disappears during this fusion, turns into energy, in a balance described by Einstein's famous equation. The energy embodies in mass (always in an amount equal to the mass times the square of the speed of light) can be converted into other forms of energy, such as additional kinetic energy (energy in motion) of the fast-moving particles that emerge from nuclear fusion reactions." **49**

As the new energy produced by nuclear fusion diffuses outward, the gas gets hotter and begins to glow. Then, at the star's surface, the energy formerly locked in individual nuclei escapes into space in the form of photons, generated by the gas as the energy released through fusion heats it to thousands of degrees and in time "a star is born." Thermonuclear fusion within stars creates dozens of elements in their cores. The process (Khepera) starts with hydrogen (the Nun) and proceeding to Atum calling into being helium, carbon, nitrogen, oxygen, neon, magnesium, silicon, calcium, and so on, all the way to iron.

The earthly version of Shabaka's Stone claims that Atum-Khepera named all and everything into existence. Dr. Tyson explained the early evolution of organic life on earth emanating from the stars,

"The greatest gift to the cosmos from these supernovae consists of all the elements other than hydrogen and helium – elements capable of forming life on the planets. Protista, a kingdom or large grouping that comprises mostly single-celled organisms such as the protozoa, simple algae and fungi, slime molds, and bacteria. We on earth live on the product of countless stars that exploded billions of years ago, in epochs of Milky Way history long before our Sun and its planets, condensing within the dark and dusty recesses of an interstellar cloud-itself endowed with chemical enrichment furnished from previous generations of high-mass stars." **50**

There are distinct similarities and differences between an element and an atom. They are made up of the same "stuff." Imagine going to an ice cream store. They have 30 different flavors of ice cream. Flavors are the elements. The smallest amount of ice cream the store will sell is a scoop. The scoop is an atom. A molecule is when two or more scoops of ice cream are put together. If a molecule has more than one flavor of ice cream, it is called a compound.

In summary:
-Element - a basic substance that can't be simplified (hydrogen, oxygen, gold, etc.)
-Atom - the smallest amount of an element
-Molecule - two or more atoms that are chemically joined together (H_2O_2, H_2O, $C_6H_{12}O_6$, etc.)
-Compound - a substance that contains more than one element (H_2O, $C_6H_{12}O_6$, etc.)

Hydrogen #1 (1H)

The word hydrogen is derived from the Greek words, **Hydro** and **Gene**, which means "**water forming**," because when hydrogen burns, it combines with oxygen to form water. Hydrogen is a colorless, odorless gas. When hydrogen burns, it combines with oxygen producing water.

Hydrogen is the simplest of all the elements and the simplest atom. It is the only atom that exists. All other atoms are multiples of hydrogen. Its nucleus is composed of only a single electron. This is the reason that hydrogen is also the lightest of all the elements.

Hydrogen is the most abundant element in the universe. Stars are composed mostly of hydrogen, and it is the fusion of hydrogen atoms into helium atoms that release the energy that makes stars shine.

All atoms on the Periodic Table of Elements are the result of the fusion of the only atom (Atum) that exists, the hydrogen atom. Hydrogen is the natural starting point for thermonuclear fusion. At about 20 million degrees Fahrenheit, hydrogen fuses two of itself (self-impregnating in the waters of Nun), to form helium, the next heaviest element, with two (2) hydrogen atoms. When you fuse two (2) hydrogen atoms together, you create a helium atom. After converting hydrogen into helium, the core of our massive star continues fusing hydrogen atoms into lithium, beryllium, boron, carbon, then carbon to nitrogen to oxygen, and so forth up to ninety-second (92nd) hydrogen atom we call "iron."

Helium #2 (2He)

The word "Helium" comes from **Helios**, the Greek sun god. Before the beginning began, before existence existed, all was in the water/matter of Nun. The conversion of energy (Ptah), in union with matter, initiated the ordering and arranging of organic life on our planet. Atum, a solid tiny singularity of infinitesimal size was at the center of our sun and planet alike. The same way our sun was born in our galaxy, the earth was created from our sun. Dr. Tyson notes,

"The planetary core plays an essential role in the formation process: First came the core, and then came the gas, attracted by the solid core. Thus, all planet formation requires that a large lump of solid matter must form first. Astro-biology ranks among the most speculative of sciences, but astro-biologists can already assert with confidence that life elsewhere in the universe, intelligent or otherwise, will surely look at least as exotic as some of Earth's own life forms...The remarkable diversity of life on Earth, and (we may presume) elsewhere in the universe, arises from the cosmic abundance of carbon and the countless number of molecules (simple and complex) made from it; more varieties of carbon-based molecules exist than of all the other molecules combined." **51**

Whatever life exists in the cosmos, because of the importance of the assimilation of the carbon atom, all living things are born in the black. The metaphor expresses the process of organic life on earth in the Asarian Drama. When Asar appears green, he represents botanical (chlorophyll) life. When Asar appears black, he symbolizes animal and human (melanin) life. Plants were born to be green and humans were born to be black, indigo and brown. With the importance of carbon in organic life; and with the assurance that if there is life in the cosmos, extra-earth (extraterrestrial) life would also be pigmented. When six (6) hydrogen atoms or three (3) helium atoms are fused, the carbon atom (Atum) is created.

Carbon #6 (6C)

Dr. Tyson says,
"Carbon is created quite readily in high-mass stars that have converted their core supply of hydrogen into helium. Helium, when brought to over two hundred million degrees Fahrenheit, will form the very simple reaction.

6H = 2He + 2He + 2He = 1C + Energy

You will notice that the three helium atoms provide the required total of six neutrons, six protons and six electrons to create carbon. Stars that undergo this reaction are in their red giant phase. Carbon atoms comprise one-fourth of all the atoms in the universe that are not hydrogen or helium. If life exists elsewhere in the universe, then it is carbon-based as well. **52**

Carbon is the reason for life on earth. Organic life came into existence when the carbon atom, acting as cosmic glue, began to bind with other atoms, organizing millions of molecules. Dr. John G. Jackson tells us,

"As the heavier elements of the interior of the earth lost heat through volcanic activity, they contracted; and this caused the outer crust to fall in toward the interior, and to crumple up like the skin of a baked apple; and the ridges and depressions thus formed were the first mountains and valleys. The battle between land and sea began as soon as the world cooled enough to hold an ocean. The struggle has been a long one, but the land steadily gained on the water. Life arose in the sea, but the greatest episodes in the drama of life took place on the land.

The challenge of the origin of life is one of great interest. The world was in existence hundreds of millions of years before it became a suitable place for living things, for life can occur only within a very restricted zone of temperatures. There can be no life in the stars, since they are too hot. In outer space, the intense cold likewise makes life impossible. This life must have originated when the earth developed a temperature that was neither too hot nor too cold, for life cannot survive where it is either roasted or frozen.

Of the one hundred-odd atoms of which the stuff of the universe is composed, only a very few show any affinity for life. Living matter consists mainly of atoms which possess the property of forming large molecules. Atoms of hydrogen (H), for instance, (H2 and H1); or atoms of oxygen may form molecules of oxygen (O2) or ozone (O3); and atoms of hydrogen and oxygen may combine to form molecules of water (H2O) and hydrogen peroxide (H2O2).

But none of these compounds has more than four atoms per molecule, and the nitrogen compounds behave in a similar way. But, if to the atoms of hydrogen, oxygen and nitrogen we add carbon, a most extraordinary thing happens. The atoms of hydrogen, oxygen, nitrogen and carbon combine to form molecules consisting of hundreds, even thousands of atoms. Carbon is of prime importance in the chemistry of life. Life first arose in the warm primeval ocean, beginning with the evolution of chemicals capable of assimilating carbon." **53**

The Pattern in the Tabernacle is applied in the philosophy of Shabaka's Stone. There is a comparison between the role of carbon and the development of life on earth. The text exclaims that everything was at rest within the Nun, the waters of earth. Carbon was like Atum, brought all the elements, atoms and molecules into existence. This organic life ranged from single cell protozoon to the multi-celled human being. The life that arose from the waters was like Atum (organic life) rising out of the Nun (the Ocean), through Ptah the one continent. Khepera, was the process of organic life, Ma'at was the path (organic evolution) and her husband

Tehuti was the consciousness of knowledge, understanding and wisdom that kept evolving.

The many different types of life on Earth (bacteria, plant, animal/human, etc.), and possibly in other places in this vast universe; is made possible by the cosmic abundance of carbon and the countless number of molecules (simple and complex) created by it. There are more varieties of carbon-based molecules than any other molecules on Earth combined. Carbon atoms comprise one-fourth of all the atoms in the universe that are not hydrogen or helium. If life exists elsewhere in the universe, it is probably carbon-based and pigmented from deep indigo to dark brown. The way carbon atoms bond to other atoms suggests that we may expect extraterrestrial life to be similar to our melanated earth. Carbon atoms act like cosmic glue connecting atoms, elements and molecules.

Carbon atoms form the "backbone" for all but the simplest molecules within living organisms, such as proteins and sugars. The matter within every living creature on earth mainly consists of just four chemical elements: hydrogen, oxygen, carbon and nitrogen. All of the other elements together contribute less than one percent of the mass of any living organism.

The elements beyond the big four include small amounts of phosphorus which ranks as the most important, and is essential to most forms of life, together with smaller amounts of sulfur, sodium, magnesium, chlorine, potassium, calcium and iron. Carbon's ability to create complex molecules has made it one of the four most abundant elements, together with hydrogen, oxygen and nitrogen in all forms of life on Earth.

Shabaka's Stone allegorically explains carbon's ability to create simple and complex molecules. For instance, Atum calling into being all and everything emanating from the eight (8) uncreated creations that always existed but were disordered and disarranged. Atum naming everything and all is like carbon attracting and capturing atoms in order to create more complex atoms, elements and molecules bringing them into physical existence and continuing the development of the cosmic universe.

Carbon forms a small fraction of Earth's surface but plays an important part in the development of organic life. The carbon atom also has a pivotal role in structuring life. Carbon atoms create more kinds of molecules than the sum of all non-carbon-containing molecules combined. There is an abundance of carbon atoms in the cosmic universe and these atoms are released in large amounts. Carbon is the reason for Earth's diversity of life.

Dr. Miller says,
"Carbon gets its name from "carbos," the Greek word for "Charcoal". Carbon is found throughout the universe and is one of the most important atoms in Astro-

biology. The main reason for carbon's importance is it readily makes long chains of molecules by linking up with other carbon atoms. These chains form a central core where other elements attach themselves, allowing complex molecules such as DNA to form. Carbon is such an essential part of the DNA molecule that life as we know it on Earth is often referred to as "**carbon-based life**." Any molecule containing carbon is called an "organic molecule," whether it is directly related to some life form or not. Carbon forms molecules so readily that there are more than 2 million known carbon-based organic molecules, one and half times as many compounds as those formed by all of the other elements combined." **54**

There are three (3) types of carbon atoms. Dr. Neil DeGrasse Tyson notes,
"**Carbon** is found naturally in three forms: graphite, diamond, and coal. While all three are composed of nothing but carbon atoms, their atoms are arranged very differently in each substance.
Graphite is so slippery that it is often used as a lubricant. Its carbon atoms are bound in very thin layers, much like a stack of playing cards. The carbon atoms are tightly bonded in two directions, but very weakly connected between layers. A familiar use for graphite is the "lead" in a pencil.
A **diamond**, on the other hand, achieves its remarkable hardness because its carbon atoms are linked in a tight, cubical crystal pattern that is enormously strong, as though the stack of playing cards had all been glued together.
A third form of carbon can be found in **coal**, which contains non-crystalline carbon. Anthracite coal is about eighty (80) percent carbon and bituminous coal contains about forty (40) to fifty (50) percent. The burning of coal and other fuels that contain carbon creates carbon dioxide, a greenhouse gas. A greenhouse gas is one that helps trap the Sun's heat, in much the same way that the glass panels of a greenhouse attract and capture the warmth of the sun inside.
Carbon is a "sticky" element in the sense that it bonds strongly with many different atoms (including itself), and it can be bound in many different ways." **55**

Life on Earth owes its diversity to the chemical properties of this single atom. In short, life is carbon-based. You can prove this to yourself. Take any living thing including the food you eat and leave it in the oven too long. The heat will eventually break the molecular bonds and expose the black charred carbon that remains.

Carbon is created quite readily in high-mass stars that have converted their core supply of hydrogen into helium. The helium, when brought to over two hundred million degrees Fahrenheit, will form the very simple reaction.

Shabaka's Stone creates the analogy of the fusion of hydrogen into helium atoms and helium atoms into carbon atoms. This part of the text brought into existence the third (3rd) philosophy; "The Essences of Order and Arrangement," that eventually created life on Earth.

Drs. Neil deGrasse Tyson and Donald Goldsmith explain,

"The matter within every living creature on Earth mainly consists of just four chemical elements: hydrogen, oxygen, carbon and nitrogen. All of the other elements together contribute less than one percent of the mass of any living organism. The elements beyond the big four include small amounts of phosphorus which ranks as the most important, and is essential to most forms of life, together with still smaller amounts of sulfur, sodium, magnesium, chlorine, potassium, calcium and iron. **56**

There is a relational pattern among the cosmos, earth and human family. Dr. Tyson continues this idea,

"Elements and atoms can be identified in the heavens, as well as on the earth, sometimes there is more of a cosmic connection to the atoms (Atum) than an earthly connection. In fact, our earth is made up of the same stuff of the Universe. This stuff of the earth came from the heavens. As above, so below. Dr. Tyson says,

"The distribution of the elements in life on Earth resembles the composition of the stars far more than that of Earth itself. As a result, life's elements are more cosmically abundant than earthly." **57**

It was not the strongest that survived, or the survival of the fittest. The organisms that survived the epochs of our earth's history were the ones that could, would and did, adapt to the ever-changing conditions in the evolving world (Khepera). With this, necessity became the creator of invention. Nature's challenges made living things adjust to a forever changing environment. Shabaka's third (3rd) philosophy implies the result of Shu (air) separating Nut (sky) from Geb (earth). The creation of oxygen pushed organic life to adjust to this new environment. Those that could not or would not, perished. Dr. Tyson notes,

"Oxygen's appearance in Earth's atmosphere meant that all forms of life had to adapt or die-and that if life had not appeared by that time, it could never do so thereafter, because the would-be organisms would have nothing to eat, for their potential food would have rusted away. To this day, every animal's stomach, including our own, harbor billions of organisms that thrive in the anoxic (blue/red blood) environment that we provide, but would die if exposed to air." **58**

When Kush-Kemet explained that Nut (sky) and Geb (earth) were in a lover's embrace, when Shu (air/oxygen) separated them, they outlined the wisdom that science expresses today? What allowed oxygen to breathe life into organic life on earth? The earth (nitrogen) impregnated the sky, when Shu (air) separated Nut (atmosphere) from Geb (earth). Nut transmits rays (waveicles) of light, heat and sound energy bringing life to earth. She is depicted swallowing the Sun (Ra) at night and giving birth to the Sun (Ra) at dawn. This metaphor can be explained scientifically,

Our planet's ozone layer, which is located in the stratosphere, is about 9 to 18 miles above the earth's surface. The ozone layer protects all life from the sun's harmful ultraviolet radiation. There are three (3) types of UV light.

1) UV-A
2) UV-B
3) UV-C

Ultraviolet A is the waveicle that brings life to earth. However, UV-B and UV-C could be damaging to an unprotected surface. Our ozone layer acts like an invisible shield against harmful UV-B and UV-C rays which have been linked to,

- Skin and eye damage
- Reduction in the productivity and quality of crops
- Changes in various biological functions for different species

Human activity and pollution have led to some depletion in the atmospheric ozone layer. The protective ozone layer can be symbolized by Nut, the sky, in Shabaka's Stone. Naturally occurring events and processes such as volcanic eruptions on earth (Geb) can also affect ozone levels. Shu (air) separates the sky from earth and earth's life cycle begins. Drs. Tyson and Goldsmith emphasize the importance of the ozone layer,

"What made Earth's atmosphere relatively rich in oxygen? Much of it came from tiny organisms floating in the sea, which released oxygen as part of their photosynthesis. Some oxygen would have appeared even in the absence of life, as UV light from sunlight broke apart some of the H_2O molecules at the ocean surfaces, releasing hydrogen and oxygen atoms into the air. Wherever a planet exposes significant amounts of liquid water to starlight, that planet's atmosphere should likewise gain oxygen, slowly but surely, over hundreds of millions or billions of years." **59**

After billions of years of our earth's existence, here we are, the human family, the living consciousness of the cosmos, aware that each human is the Creator having a human experience. It took a simple yet complicated process of becoming, an Atum-Kheperarian process that continues to this day and will continue forever and ever.

Ma'at's Moral Foundations are the Path of Knowledge
Tehuti's Intellectual Consciousness is the Knowledge of the Path
Atumic Consciousness Exists When Moral Exaltation Precedes
Intellectual Illumination

Atum was the synthesis of matter and energy. Atum was the voice of the Creator. Nun was the primordial matter of the universe. Ptah converted energy at rest (potential energy) into energy in motion (energy in motion). This balance initiated the third (3rd) and final member of the original trinity, Atum the organizing creative word. All three were of the same stuff, existing before the beginning began. These three (3) aspects of the one Creator came into existence in order to create the cosmos. The cosmos is the ordered and arranged part of the universe. This ordering and arranging of atoms, elements and molecules was spoken (ordered and arranged) by Atum. The path of these actions was grounded in truth, justice, balance, harmony, reciprocity and morality. This chapter will focus on the many aspects of Atum, the voice of the Creator. Atum was Cosmic consciousness, the thought, desire, heart and tongue of the Creator.

Once activated, Atum called all and everything into being. He/She gave all of the Creator's creations names. Atum's voice (carbon) structured the four amino acids (DNA) that created life on earth.

The universe has a vast, grandiose, terrific, spectacular, multi-formed uniform. The eras of interest to us are the ones that extend, from:

- Matter and Spirit to
- Atum (Atoms), Elements and Molecules to
- Earth, Air, Fire and Water through...
- Bacteria, Plant, Fish, Amphibian, Reptile, Animal including Humans.
- These humans went through a 3-part metamorphosis
- From Barbarian, Savage, Civilized to Cosmic.
- They then transformed into six (6) categories of Human Evolution
  1) Australopithecus Robustus – Robust (thick) Human
  2) Australopithecus Gracile – Graceful (less thick/slenderer) Human
  3) Homo Habilis – Human with Ability (toolmaker)
  4) Homo Erectus – Human who stands Erect
  5) Homo Sapiens - Thinking Human
  6) Homo Sapiens Sapiens – Creative Thinking Human

However, the unfolding of consciousness on earth, begins with this drama of thinking, being and becoming aware of the concretization of the Spirit within the Universe,

- The Place - The surface of the planet earth.
- The Time – "illions of eons" of years ago
- The Task – Develop Stages of Intellectual growth that lead to Grades of Consciousness

In a mind made up of percepts (senses), there is life, but no consciousness, only the unconscious. Life is born perceiving its environment. Percepts are the senses; seeing, hearing, feeling, smelling, tasting and thinking. When percepts are stimulated, the receptual mind creates and joins images reflecting the sensual impact that comes into existence and simple consciousness is born. Animals become conscious on this level. They are aware, awoken to, conscious of all and everything around them.

General vision is very old, but the color sense is relatively new, and the musical sense is still developing today. The development of the human moral sense, "Ma'at", including human attraction, advanced by quantum leaps, once receptual images were formed. Concepts created words. Atum (words) made flesh and self-consciousness was born. Self-consciousness allows humans to develop three specific gifts, intellect, reason and language. These unique qualities, when cultivated to higher order thinking skills create intuitive instinct that unlocks cosmic consciousness. This skill takes the human animal's instinctive sense to its spiritual peak called intuition. Intuitive instinct is the link to the Creator's mind.

These four (4) stages of intellectual growth reflected the life history of humanity. These stages of the intellectual mind also developed, inspired and initiated the four (4) grades of consciousness.

THE FOUR STAGES OF THE INTELLECTUAL MIND

1) The Perceptual Mind - Sense Perception - Percepts
Perception is the ability to recognize and interpret external stimuli. Percepts are senses. This perceptual mind came into existence when the primary quality of the excitability of sensation was established. At this point, the acquisition and mental registration of sense perceptions began. For instance, a sound is heard, or an object is seen, the mind registers the impression, and a perceptual sense is created. If we could go back far enough, we would find among our ancestors a human being whose whole intellect was made up of these simple, but numerous sense perceptions.

However, this human being, possessed the potential for growth. Individually and from generation to generation, humanity accumulated these sense percepts. Finally, a condition was reached making it possible for our ancestors to combine groups of these percepts into what are called "recepts". Recepts are visual images of sense perceptions. The accumulation of percepts continues on a higher plane, and the sensory organs keep converting groups of percepts into recepts. By use and selection, the recepts are improved. The multiple, simple and initial recepts become more complex. The images become clearer and begin the climb to a more ordered and arranged frequency. The next level of intellectual growth creates a word for the image. This word creates the conceptual stage.

Perception is the study of how a living organism becomes aware of objects, events, and relationships in the outside world through her/his senses, ex., thinking (brain), seeing (eyes), hearing (ears), tasting (tongue), smelling (nose), and touching (skin).

The world around us consists of various kinds and levels of physical energy. Our knowledge of the world comes through our sense organs, which react to these energies. Certain wave lengths of electromagnetic energy stimulate our eyes. Our ears sense certain kinds of aural vibrations in the air. Noses and tongues are sensitive to certain types of chemical aromatic stimuli. Sense organs in our skin respond to pressure,
temperature changes, and various stimuli related to pain. The sense organs change the various environmental energies into nervous impulses, and these impulses then go to the brain.

The process of perceptual analysis does not reveal objects and events of the world. We see light and color, but there is no light or color in the electromagnetic waves that stimulate the ear. The brain organizes and interprets nervous impulses from the eyes as light and color, and impulses from the ears as sound. Together, the sense organs and the brain, transform physical energy from environmental stimuli into information about the events around us.

Various factors influence what and how we perceive. Our perceptions are influenced by the many ways our bodies are structured to receive and process stimuli from the environment. Our perceptions also reflect our emotions, needs, expectations and learning.

Certain physical and functional features of the brain determine some aspects of perception. The part of the brain that senses vision has different kinds of cells that respond only under certain frequencies and stimulations. Some of these cells respond only when a light goes off, others respond only when a light goes on; but they stop responding if the light stays on. Such cells are arranged in special ways in the brain, and this fact is related to how we perceive.

Much evidence points to the conclusion that early experience, learning, emotion and motivation are important in defining what and how we perceive the world. Part of this accumulating evidence comes from experiments that compare how persons in different cultures perceive things. The perception of such things as form, color, pain, and touch may differ from culture to culture, depending on habits and customs, and the education of the children.

Learning, emotion, and motivation can have an important effect on perception. Sometimes a severe emotional disturbance can prevent perception completely, like when emotional shock causes individuals to lose their hearing temporarily. We are more likely to perceive those aspects of our environment that are related to our interests. For example, motivation can affect the perceived characteristics of objects. To a very hungry person, food may appear larger or more colorful than usual. **Percepts** exist in the grade of consciousness called the **Unconsciousness**. Bacteria and Plant life are on the Unconscious level.

2) **The Receptual Mind – Image – Recepts**
The receptual (images) mind is created by joining percepts (senses). A recept is a combined image of hundreds perhaps thousands of percepts. Images are drawn from many senses. Each sensory system, such as thinking, seeing, hearing, smelling, tasting or touching, has its own specialized body part. These parts are called recepts impacted by the change of energies from the environment by nervous impulses. The human eye, for example, has two major kinds of receptors, in the retina, the light sensitive part of the eye. These receptors are called rods and cones. Rods respond to light. They allow us to see in dim light. cones respond to color, by the different frequencies of light. Cones enable us to see colors and sharp detail in bright light. The particular ways that receptors are structured and function help determine the perceptual effects related to them. **Recepts** give birth to the next grade of **Simple Consciousness**. All animal life are on this Simple Conscious level.

3) **The Conceptual Mind – Word - Concepts**
The conceptual mind is made up of billions of sense percepts. These percepts are converted into super complex recepts. In order that a recept be transformed into a concept, it is named by Atum. If you have concepts, you have language and communication. If you possess concepts and language, you graduated to the level of self-consciousness. Self-Consciousness and language are two sides of the same coin. Concepts develop higher order thinking skills, that order and arrange the images (recepts) constructed by the ordering and arranging of the senses (percepts). There is a moment in the history of life's mind, when the receptual image, capable of simple consciousness, becomes a conceptual intellect, in possession of language and self-consciousness.

A concept is a named recept. This name is a sign or a signature, called into being to represent, in a concrete way, the abstract concept (word made flesh). The process by which concepts are substituted for recepts, increases the efficiency of the brain for thought. As the introduction of machinery increases the capacity of work for humankind. To replace a great cumbersome recept by a simple sign was almost like replacing actual goods, like wheat, fabrics, hardware, etc., by entries in a ledger.

Consider this comparative analysis from a monetary perspective,
Pennies are the Six (6) Perceptual Senses
Nickels are Receptual Images
Quarters are Conceptual Words
Dollar Bills are Intuitive Instincts

Five (5) pennies are one (1) nickel. Five (5) nickels are one (1) quarter. Four (4) quarters are one (1) dollar. It would be cumbersome to carry twenty-five (25) pennies (percepts). One (1) quarter (concepts) equals 25 pennies (percepts) and five (5) nickels (recepts). We can continue these conversions in many ways; however, knowledge is based in percepts and the continued combining of percepts to higher level recepts (images), gives a conceptual name that takes it to the highest level of intuitive instinct. Intuitive instinct ascends to the realm of cosmic consciousness.

The growth of the human intellect is the growth of the concept. The multiplication of the simpler percepts and recepts; and at the same time, the building up of these into more complex expressions of existence. In acquiring this new and higher form of consciousness, we still continue to develop our receptual and perceptual intelligences. There are three (3) types of intellect; large, concise and ready.

The **large** intellect is one that possesses an above average amount of concepts. The **concise** intellect is clear, defined, ordered and arranged. The **ready** intellect is quick and readily assessable.

Our intellect, today, is made up of a very complex mixture of percepts, recepts and concepts. To meet the needs of this forever unfolding process of becoming, early civilizations developed holistic learning centers that at their height gave the human being intuitive instinct that insightfully introduced the learner into the Creator's mind called cosmic consciousness.

4) The Intuitive Mind - Instinctive Free Will - State of Being.

This is the mind whose highest irreducible element is not a percept, recept or concept; but an intuition, a cosmic common sense, a thought unthought yet known without thinking about it. This is the mind in which sensation and image; unconsciousness, simple consciousness and self-consciousness are created, developed, transmuted, elevated and crowned, "Cosmic Consciousness". Cosmic Consciousness has also been compared to Creator inspired Ancestral Guidance. One within the All and the All within the one.

In staying true to their natural world, ancient peoples in Africa created, enhanced, embellished, nurtured and sustained life for all and everything bounded by their environment. The fourth (4th) and final grade was cosmic consciousness also called Atumic Consciousness.

Consciousness

Consciousness is the distinguishing characteristics of humanity. Consciousness possesses the potential for reflecting on its own state of existence. This reflection includes the ability to be outside of itself and view itself from an objective perspective, all the while knowing, that it is the subject being viewed. Animal consciousness is subjective. Human consciousness is subjective and objective.

The mind of humanity from age to age, seeks to master the facts of the outer world. The development of the human mind can be compared to ivy on a building. As the ivy spreads over and covers the stones on the wall, the twig that secures a hold, strengthens and then puts out another twig. Any twig that does not secure a hold after a time, ceases to grow and eventually dies. The twig never came to realize that survival depended on its ability to attach itself to the building and be able to adapt to its surroundings and environment.

Ninety-nine (99) out of one hundred (100) of our sense impressions and emotions have never been represented in the intellect by concepts (words); therefore, they remain unexpressed and inexpressible except in percepts by roundabout description and suggestion. There exists within the lower animals, images that illustrate this idea. They are acute sense perceptions and strong emotion and passions, such as fear, rage, sensual passion and familial love, and yet they cannot be expressed because they have no system of corresponding sounds. If it were not for our sense perceptions and moral nature, we would be like the other animals. Language expresses the main differences between the higher passionate emotions of Asar and lower angry emotions of Set.

Higher Passion of Asarian Consciousness

- Asar acknowledges, accepts and approves himself
- Possesses personal force, courage and faith
- Possesses empathy and affection
- Leans towards calm, rest, contentment and happiness
- Asar does not conquer nature. He becomes one with nature
- Asar vibrates on the Cosmos' frequency

Lower Anger of Setian Consciousness

- Set seeks acknowledgment, acceptance and approval from others
- Set is ignorance
- Lacks personal force, courage and faith given to him by others
- Lacks sympathy and affection from others

- Set easily turns to rage, anger, fear, unrest, discontent and unhappiness
- He lacks internal peace
- He is prone to the fear of things known
- Set is spiritually paralyzed towards things unknown
- Set separates himself from nature
- He is at war with his own nature
- Set is out of tune with the cosmos

Life on earth, arose out of a world without life. On earth as in the cosmos, Nun, Ptah and Atum creates life. Simple consciousness left the water and climbed onto the land, and its constant process of development evolved into self-consciousness. Humans ascended to cosmic consciousness.

The unfolding of the knowable universe presents to our minds, a series of gradually ascending steps, each separated from the next, by an apparent leap over what seems to be a deep gulf. Having once appeared, there occurred what seems like the bridge between the inorganic and the organic worlds.

When studying the intellectual growth of a child, in every instance, the time of the appearance of a faculty in an infant, corresponds with the stage at which the same faculty appears, in the ascending animal/human world. The longer a human being has been in possession of a given faculty, the more universal that faculty will be in the human race. The longer a race has been in possession of a given faculty; the more firmly that faculty is fixed in each individual of the race who possesses it. In dreams, we pass backward into a pre-human mental life. The intellectual faculties which we possess during our dreams are recepts as distinguished from our daydreams that are concepts.

Recepts in our dream state are impacted by the hormone Melatonin, secreted from our pineal gland in the absence of the sun (night). Concepts are impacted by the hormone Serotonin, secreted from our pineal gland in the presence of the sun (day). The process of consciousness in human history recapitulates (repeats briefly) the process of consciousness in a human being's fetal life.

The Four (4) Grades of Atumic Consciousness

Unconsciousness

- Conception to Birth

Unconsciousness exists within a life system not aware of itself. There is an absence, or loss, not only of consciousness, but consciousness of consciousness. Unconsciousness is unaware of its own existence. For some, it contains information that was once conscious, but now unconscious. Bacteria and plant life are this level of existence.

Simple Consciousness

- Few days after Birth to 18 Months entering into a level of perceptual (sense) and receptual (image) world
- 10 weeks – begins to develop a curiosity and by one (1) year begins to use tools
- 15 Months – organic life has a sense of shame, remorse and the ridiculous

Simple Consciousness is possessed by the more advanced of the animal kingdom. For example, a horse is just as conscious of the things around him/her as the human being is. She/He is also conscious of his/her own limbs and body and she/he knows that these are a part of him/herself.

Simple Consciousness makes its appearance in the human infant within a few days after birth. It is universal in the human family, this original consciousness dates back before the earliest mammals. It is present in all dreams. Simple Consciousness is lost only in deep sleep and coma (unconsciousness).

Self Consciousness

- From 18 months to three years of age, the child passes through the mental stage which lies between these animals and Self-Consciousness.
- During that time, the child's receptual intelligence becomes more advanced.
- The recepts become more complex, constantly developing their process into conceptualism.
- Language is developed to express their receptual images.

A self-conscious human being is not only conscious of trees, rocks, water, his/her body, etc., but he/she is aware that he/she is conscious of the trees, rocks, etc. This human being sees him/herself as a distinct entity apart from all the rest of the universe, but still an important part of the universe. No animal can realize him/herself in that way. By means of self-consciousness, humans who know become capable of treating their own mental states as objects of consciousness.

Self-Consciousness makes its appearance in the human at the average age of about three (3). It is the focal point for the human intellect. This intellect uses concepts to develop its image perceptions, and language to express their meaning. But more importantly, the mind uses higher order perceptions to further enhance and embellish its conceptual framework. Some of the characteristics of Self-Consciousness include:

- judgement
- reason
- comparison/measure
- imagination
- abstraction
- reflection
- generalization
- discrimination, etc.

The Moral/Emotional/Passionate Nature develops:

- love
- reverence
- faith
- awe
- hate
- jealousy
- envy, etc.

Cosmic Consciousness

The philosophy of the birth of cosmic consciousness in the individual is very similar to the birth of self consciousness. The mind becomes overcrowded with concepts and constantly becomes larger, more numerous and more complex. When conditions become favorable; fusion takes place. Nucleically, this union joins complex concepts with moral nature. The result is an intuition, an instinctive free will, leading to the birth of the instinctive intuitional mind. The prime characteristic of cosmic consciousness is the unity of everything and all within the universe. Along with the consciousness of the cosmos, there occurs an intellectual enlightenment or illumination which alone would place the individual on a new plane of existence. It would make her/him almost a member of a new species of animal beyond human. She/He could be called, "Super Sapiens," or "Homo Perfectus," the next level of organic genius. Each human has the seed to give birth to this next higher level of consciousness.

To this is added a state of moral exaltation, an indescribable feeling of elevation, elation, bliss and joyousness. There is a quickening of the moral sense, which is important to the individual attaining the enhanced intellectual power. A human entering into cosmic consciousness belongs to the top layer of the world of self consciousness. She/He does not necessarily have to possess an extraordinary intellect, though he/she must be grounded in universal knowledge. She/He will have good nutritional and preventative health practices, but above all, she/he must have an exalted moral nature, strong sympathies and empathies, a warm caring heart, courage, with strong and earnest spiritual commitments.

All these being granted, and the human being having reached the age necessary to bring him/her to the top of self consciousness ascends into the realm of cosmic consciousness. The super conceptual intellect is intuitively instinct. Cosmic consciousness is developed by a cosmic sense. The higher sense that controls evil thoughts, destroys sin and shame, the sense of good and evil contrasted by each other. This cosmic mind does not labor but is energized by human activity. Some of the other characteristics attained include,

- Sense of External Existence
- Loss of Fear of Death
- Moral Exaltation
- Intellectual Illumination
- Sudden, Instant, Increased Mental Awareness
- Prophetic Stimulation of the Personal Aura (Charm)
- Spiritual Transmutation

Dr. Martin Luther King's last speech on April 3, 1968 in Memphis, Tennessee is an example of a
human being attaining and expressing Atum's cosmic consciousness. Let's compare the characteristics of cosmic consciousness with the last time Dr. King spoke publicly. This is how he ended his "I've been to the mountaintop," Atumic speech.

<u>Characteristic</u>   <u>Dr. King's Atumic Words</u>

- **Sense of External Existence** – "Like anybody, I'd like to live a long life, longevity has its place"
- **Loss of Fear of Death** – "But. I'm not concerned about that now. So, I'm happy tonight, I'm not worried about anything, I'm not fearing any man"
- **Moral Exaltation** – "I just want to do God's will and he's allowed me to go up to the mountain"
- **Intellectual Illumination** – "I've looked over and I've seen the promised land"
- **Sudden, Instant, Increased Mental Awareness** – "I may not get there with you"
- **Prophetic Stimulation of the Personal Aura (Charm)** – "But, I want you to know tonight that we as a people will get to the promised land"

- **Spiritual Transmutation** – "Mine eyes have seen the glory of the coming of the Lord and all...

    Dr. King never finished his speech, he left its completion for us to accomplish"

Moving from Grade to Grade

The movement of self consciousness to cosmic consciousness follows the same intellectual path as the movement taken from simple to self-consciousness. Two things occur on the path toward cosmic consciousness, self-existence and intuition.

1) Knowledge of self-existence transmutes humans who possess Simple-Consciousness to Self Consciousness. She/He becomes aware 'for the first time' that it is a separate entity. They can view themselves objectively.
2) The intuition of this human grows through the world in which she/he sees as apart from him/herself.

This oncoming, new faculty instructs the mind without having to go through the entire process of learning. It acquires enormous increased potentials for accumulating large bodies of knowledge; and then, has the ability to initiate dynamic actions that apply learned materials. When a person who has self consciousness enters into cosmic consciousness, she/he knows without learning from the illumination of certain ideas.

See Appendix #7- Stages of Intellectual Growth and Grades of Consciousness

Atum: The Voice of Consciousness
Atum is the Atom of Today
Atum is the 3rd Aspect of the Scientific Unity of Three
The Original Trinity

Atum was brought forward by a unique moment. It is suggested by ancient African scholars that Atum was the original word that gave everything in the universe a name. Atum was the model or paradigm, by which all and everything came into existence and continues to be ordered and arranged. In Shabaka's Stone, Atum, or Creative Word, calls four (4) pairs of opposite complements into being. Atum names these eight (8) different conceptual receptive perceptions (matter, space, infinity, finity, darkness, light, the seen and the unseen).

The ability to see the unseen is comparable to using functional consciousness through psychological consciousness. This concept is seen in the analysis of what today is called the atom. Ancient African scientists in Kush-Kemet told a masterful story metaphorically. The scientific allegory is called the "Atom".

Atomic power is the continuing unification of the three (3) sub-atomic particles called electrons, protons and neutrons. Because of their opposing, yet complementary natures they demonstrate the Law of Polarity.

- Electrons - the electrical spark of life that lives
- Protons - the magnetic aura that attracts
- Neutrons - the gravitational centering force that harmonizes and balances the Atum (atom)

These three sub-Atumic particles revolve around each other and vibrate at very high speeds, degrees and intensities. They are totally interdependent on each other.

The proton seems to affect a certain influence or magnetic attraction upon the electron, causing the electron to rotate around the nucleus of the atom. This action makes atoms assume certain combinations creating and generating Atum to name or create other atoms, elements and molecules.

When this magnetic proton, unites with the electrifying electron, Atum (the atom) becomes balanced (Neutronized) and a process of becoming (Khepera) occurs. This coming into becoming represents the creation and development of the lives of atoms, elements and molecules.

The electron particle vibrates rapidly under the influence of the proton, located in the nucleus within Atum (the atom). The end result is the birth of a new Atum. This new Atum is composed of a balanced, harmonious union of the complimentary electrifying and magnetic forces of the preceding Atum. When this union is formed, this new Atum, while the same as its seed, is a separate essence, having certain properties, but no longer manifesting the same exact electromagnetic properties of its predecessor.

The nucleus of an Atum (atom) is made up of protons and neutrons, very tightly fit together in the nucleus. Since atoms have the same number of protons and electrons, the number of electrified charges equals the number of magnetic charges. The opposite charges balance each other. Therefore, the whole Atum (atom) has no overall charge These ordered and arranged unions and combinations manifest the varied phenomena of light, heat, electricity, magnetism, attraction, repulsion, chemical affinity, the reverse and inverse of everything and all.

Nothing stands still, everything is in the process of becoming, which leads to growth in the positive direction. There are times when events slow down, stop, and then begin to reverse direction. Eventually, regression is slowed down, stopped, then positive growth is resurrected. Another application of the Ausarian Drama says that everything has a place in the cosmic cycle, life is in a state of constant Kheperarian transformation.

The Cosmic Cycle
Conception to Birth to Growth to Aging to
Death to Decay to Rebirth finally Free at Last... Resurrection

Atum (the atom) orders and arranges life. The process of life harmonizes the environment and the process normally always tries to vibrate toward the positive pole, the pole that tends to construct. While the negative pole tends to take things apart and deconstruct everything and all. However, this process is needed for the constitution and reconstitution of Atum (the atom). Under cosmic supervision, this process is continuing to expand the universe.

Ancient Kush-Kemet scholars defined Atum as Being "Self-Created". They revealed in their writing that Atum was the balance of Matter and Energy. Atum named this cosmic harmony, "Ma'at." Ma'at represented truth, justice, harmony, balance, order, arrangement, morality and reciprocity. The same concepts of Atum and Ma'at apply today.

All elements are made up of tiny particles called, "Atum," the atom. Atum(s) of a given element are alike. Atum(s) of different elements are different. Chemical changes occur when Atum(s) link up (nuclear fusion) or separate (nuclear fission) from one another. Atum(s) are not created or destroyed by this change, they merely transform themselves.

Atumic (Atomic) Shells

Although the electron does not circle the nucleus in solar elliptical orbits; the electron does replicate the same essence as the revolutionary and rotational Law of Polarity. There is no exact path of an electron. The quick moving electrons form a cloud around the nucleus. Today, electrons are arranged into energy levels or what are classified as "Shells". Each electron shell is labelled with a capital letter. Their order by size of shell are,

- K Shell - Holds no more than 2 electrons. These electrons are the closest to the nucleus
  and have the least energy
- L Shell - Holds no more than 8 electrons
- M Shell -Holds no more than 18 electrons
- N Shell –Holds no more than 32 electrons

The number of shells that an Atum(s) has depends on the number of electrons each Atum(s) has. In general, every shell must have its full number of electrons before a new shell starts. If there are more electrons than a shell can hold, a new shell starts. Today, there are one-hundred nine (109) known types of Atum(s)/elements. This means that every type of matter must be made up of one or more of these one-hundred nine (109) kinds of Atum(s)/elements. Of the one hundred and nine (109), Ninety-two (92) elements/Atum(s) are found in Nature, the other seventeen (17) were created by humans in laboratories. Many Atum(s) are found in the solid state. Some are found as gases. Only two (2) Atum(s), mercury and bromine, are found as liquids at room temperature.

All matter is made up of Atum (atoms), all solids, liquids and gases are made up of these tiny particles. Philosophical scientists in ancient Kush-Kemet (Egypt) came to realize through investigation, trial and error, there was one thing, divided into three (3) entities in the universe; Nun (matter), Ptah (energy) and Atum (creative word). They believed that these units of force existed from the microcosmically small Atum(s) to the macrocosmically gigantic stars. The planets revolve around the sun and rotate on their axes. The sun moves around greater central points, and these are believed to move around still greater clusters and so on. The molecules of which the particular kind of matter is composed, are in a state of constant vibration and movement.

Ancient Africans taught that no matter how many Atum(s) were identified, there was only one process of becoming; and this process took on different forms by the nature of the forces around them. Life was meant to unite humans with their nature. Humans were brought into existence to contribute their unique divine gift to the universe, cosmos, supercluster, cluster, galaxy, sun, earth, continent, country, community, family and self. Atum was the word and word was with the Creator and the word was the Creator.

Atum in the Nun

Nebulas are born when the cosmic womb is fertilized by panspermia the cosmic seed. Likewise, human embryos are conceived the same way when the female womb is impregnated by the male spermatozoon. This is actualized through the successive divisions from the one into the many.

The one as the foundation of all existence and knowledge is unknowable to itself. So, it started a path to become conscious of itself. She/He, the primordial essence of polarity, became the original description of the relationship between one to the other one. They became knowable through the images created in the mind through the skillful linguistical talents used in the conceptual analogy or metaphoric allegory. This symbolic story masks a physical reality. From an African-centered perspective, the coming into being for the first time is the initial scission in the functions of life. This separation leads to the concept of Ptah rising out of Nun or, the conversion of potential energy into kinetic energy.

This initial action (conversion of energy) is an ever-present activity continuing the process of becoming. Its origin is still a mystery. Within the myth of Shabaka's Stone, this original activity is described in three (3) metaphysical stages,

- First-the active impulse, the contraction (implosion) within Nun
- Second-the coagulating energy, the expansion (explosion) within Nun
- Third-the moving kinetic energy arises from the successive phases of active impulses and coagulating energies (process of becoming)

The Nun, primordial matter in Kush-Kemet thought, is not in any sense, the same matter we know of today. The universe is a concrete symbol of the abstract mentality of the Cosmos. Humans were intended to be the masterpiece of the universe. Human beings were intended to be the crowning glory of the process of becoming. Humanity was the beginning of the new great cycle of the process of becoming on earth.

Up to the heavens from our earth you will see Nut (sky), ceaselessly drawing energy from Ptah; Nut exists within the innermost areas of Nun, the primordial, infinite, energetic ocean of the universe.

When Shu (air) separates Nut (sky) from Geb (earth), Shu, metaphorically, also separates:

- intelligence from ignorance
- above from below
- attraction from repulsion
- day from night
- infinity from finity
- light from darkness
- water from fire
- consciousness from unconsciousness
- energy from matter
- the hidden and revealed
- up from down
- east from west
- in from out

Atum in Ma'at – The Moral Natural Path Called Into Being

Ma'at is the cosmic vision that gave birth to "The New Mind." It is the complex union of all prior thought (Tehuti) and experience (Khepera), just as self-consciousness is the expression of complex union of all thought and experience.

The human moral nature, Ma'at, includes faculties such as,

- conscience, the temple for consciousness of consciousness
- the abstract
- sense of right and wrong
- parental/sibling love
- brotherly/sisterly love
- romantic love
- platonic love

Humans share the following instincts with the rest of the animal kingdom,

- attraction towards the attractive
- repulsion away from the repulsive
- sensual desire/instinct
- awe
- familial awareness
- reverence
- sense of duty
- responsibility (response to ability)
- accountability (accountable for ability)
- sympathy/empathy
- compassion
- faith

Human nature is not complete without these and others; it is therefore a very complex function, but this process is naturally simple. This human moral nature is rarely present in very young children. It could be absent at puberty and even during adolescence. It is a faculty that is acquired through maturity. The moral nature appears somewhere about 15 years of age.

It is not our eyes and ears, or even our intellect that report the world to us. It is our moral nature, our Heart-Soul that recognizes and records the significant people, places and events that exist in our life. The moral sense is the law of the Supreme High Judge, Ma'at. Her feather of righteousness is what is weighed on the right scale of justice while our Heart-Soul is on the left scale of justice. It is a judgment that is not derived from reason, but by intuitive instinct. The Heart-Soul always tells the truth. Nature's truth knows truth.

Atum in Tehuti – Intellectual Illumination – Knowledge

Knowledge has never been lost and never will be lost. Knowledge can only be forgotten. Its source resides in the conscience, receiving its inspiration from cosmic consciousness. It cannot be disputed or destroyed by false writings or unnatural words. Knowledge and organic life's history are united. They are founded upon the primacy, life and consciousness of Africa's original human race, the Twa-Mbuti. This consciousness maintains the original memory pattern of creation.

The human intellect is made up principally of concepts, just as a forest is made up of trees. These concepts are mental images of sense perceptions. The recognition, registration and recording of these concepts is called memory. When we contrast and compare them between and among themselves, we are reasoning. Reasoning uses the imagination. Imagination is the act of forming mental copies, likenesses and metaphors. Imagination develops the "Power to Negate" (free will). This power of Negation is identified with cerebral thinking and determines the faculty of reasoning and critical thinking. Imagination is the ability to retain an image and then, project it outward like the sun thrusts the planets from him/herself.

Reason, intellect and speech are the gifts given to humanity from nature. No words can come into being, accept as an expression of a concept. A new concept cannot be formed without the simultaneous creation of the reasoning of the intellect.

Intellect and speech complement one another as the hand is to the glove. The life history of the intellect must be accompanied by the life history of language. The life history of language expresses the life history of intellect. Knowledge results from the comparative process of elimination; matter from energy, infinity from finity, dark from light, the hidden from the revealed. Knowledge, the accumulation of information, disengages truth from error, sense from non-sense. All discussions require the utilization of the Law of Polarity, (complements/opposites) also known as the negation of contrary affirmation. All intelligent observations require comparisons (measurement) which compares and contrasts one thing from another. The whole universe is action, a struggle against being at rest, creating Khepera, the process of becoming; a living drama among electricity, magnetism and gravity, the result is order and arrangement.

Moral exaltation inspires intellectual illumination, intellectual illumination experiences moral exaltation. The following two theories closely resemble the Kush-Kemet Ptahian theory in Shabaka's Stone. The universe originated from a single minute primordial atom which exploded and subsequently repeats this process through the expansion of the universe. We still perceive this expansion, in all forms and phases of life and consciousness today.

The nucleus of the universe was an inferno of primordial vapor, seething at unimaginable hot temperatures. This heat was unique, the temperature no longer exists, even in the interior of the stars today. In this type of primordial heat there were no atoms or elements. No thing and every thing was disarranged and disordered.

Before the beginning began, before existence existed, everything was disordered and disarranged, mis-ordered and mis-arranged. There were no atoms, elements or molecules, nothing but hot, seething plasma water. These free trons would eventually form themselves into electrons and protons through the transmutation of neutrons. These free trons existed in a state of pre-existing order and arrangement. They constantly were in a process of becoming. When this cosmic mass began to expand, the temperature began to fall and balance the heat and cold. The free trons at this harmonic temperature began to condense into groups. These groups were comprised of individual things (in this case, trons) brought together into a group of distinct particles, however, they act as a whole. This process was represented in Shabaka's Stone by describing the Essences of Pre-Existing Order and Arrangement.

Atum names and calls into existence the 4 pairs of Neteru, (uncreated creations),
- **A**men-Hidden-Male   **A**menet-Revealed-Female
- **N**un-Matter-Male   **N**unet-Space-Female
- **K**uk-Darkness-Male   **K**uket-Light-Female
- **H**uh-Infinity-Male   **H**uhet-Finity-Female

At this highly charged rate, trons were propelled, centrifugally, from within this tronic state of being, electricity and magnetism was ordered and arranged to attract and repulse,
- Electricity-Repulsion-Male
- Magnetism-Attraction-Female

The centered balancing force was the neutron. This neutron threw off parts of itself (electron), while retaining part of itself, (proton). This is contained within the law of complements. Within this projection, the electron was able to remain within the gravitational magnetism of the nucleus of the atom. As this process continued, more atoms were formed. In time, these atoms became more stable elements, elements became molecules, and the process continues to this day, with the development of our world and the billions of other life forces that humanity's limited perceptions have become conscious of. This all began at that one critical moment in history called by the ancient African scholars, "Khepera Sep Tepy, the Coming into Being for The First Time."

The Ptahian theory contained within Shabaka's Stone explains the complimentary nature of the centrifugal and centripetal forces.

- **Centrifugal (Push out, pull in)** Force is the inertial reaction of a body against a force constraining it to move in a curved path away from the center but naturally attracted back to the center.
- **Centripetal (Push in, pull out)** Force is a force attracting a body toward a center around which it revolves, directed or tended toward a center. However naturally moving away from the center.

These centers while opposite, complement and act symbiotically keeping everything and all in harmony and balance.

Atum – The Hidden Treasure

Atum created life and brought forward creatures in order to be known by them. The poles of life are: "To Be or Not to Be." For example. Hydrogen, a fuel, has a strong affinity, a natural attraction or inclination towards oxygen; a fire for burning, and by these poles in balance, concretizes itself in unity. It is no longer hydrogen or oxygen, it rematerializes itself. By its nature, it seeks to build (Asar) and to destroy (Seten).

The seed selects from within its environment, the energy appropriate for its activity. The same seed produces similar effects on the varieties of a single effect, they became signatures, not of the seed, but of the environment on which it drew. It is this vital abstract environment, the quality of non-sensible energy unknowable in itself, that you must seek to know through the signature. The Path (Ma'at) is a unique gift inspired and shaped by the temper, tone and taste of the person. Atum-Ra is the Sun of Nature. Ra is the consciousness, animation, the energetic intellect of humanity, potentially Divine.

Life is the harmonious coordination of polar forces; energy and matter. In fact, life is very complex and efficient. Life shows, signs and symbols of being divinely self-created, self-ordained and self-sustaining. Its existence is a process measured by infinite time and bounded by eternity. Kush-Kemet depicted the electron as open praying hands, facing upwards; suggesting that the electron flow travels away from the earth, this suggests what modern science suggests about the Sun's system of "Centrifugal" force. The electron is the electricity of the life of the world, the substance of the soul. It is indivisible and irreducible. The electron is like the fin of a whale or the tip of an iceberg. The fin and the tip are the only thing that can be seen, but in no way does it depict the magnitude of what exists under the water.

An oscillator is a circuit which produces or responds to an electromagnetic wave, usually with a range of frequencies. Atum (atoms), elements and molecules are perfect oscillators that respond to light. They absorb, capture and emit this energy at specific vibrations. Even complex organic molecules like melanin exhibit quantum states, once thought to be limited to atoms and molecules. Atum was represented by a snake with its tail in its mouth, signifying its infinite nature. The snake also makes oscillating, wave-like movements across the sand. The Uraeus (cobra) was representative of this eternal movement.

Atum the Carbon Atom-Melanosome Granule-Melanin Molecule-Melanocyte Cell

Melanocytes are neuron-like cells which produce melanin, and numerous proteins, in response to electromagnetic radiation. The production of melanin starts with the conversion of Tyrosine (amino acid) into Indole by the enzyme Tyrosinase. Tyrosinase is a copper containing enzyme which begins the process of the conversion of Tyrosine (amino acid) and stabilizes the order and arrangement of the melanin structure. The life sustaining process includes,

- Amino Acid - The building blocks of protein
- Enzyme - A protein that controls chemical activity
- Nutrient - The chemical needed for growth and energy
- Protein - Needed to build repair and heal tissues

With these basic definitions in mind, let us now look at the role of nutrients and the cycle of life. There are five (5) groups of nutrients. All nutrients work together to keep humans in good health. Life could not go on without these nutrients. However, everything human beings need for life is contained within fruits, vegetables and clean water.

The five nutrients are,
- Carbohydrates
- Fats
- Proteins
- Vitamins
- Minerals

Carbohydrates are the nutrients that supply energy to the body. Fats store the energy in the body and proteins are needed to build and repair cells. Vitamins and Minerals supplement the oxygen needed to be able to develop a healthy well-tuned body.

The body uses proteins in several ways, but the two most important functions are to;
1) build new cells
2) repair damaged cells

The chemical make-up of proteins are comprised of the four major Atum (atoms),
- Carbon
- Hydrogen

- Oxygen
- Nitrogen
- Sometimes Sulphur and Phosphorous.

Proteins are made up of smaller compounds called amino acids. Amino acids can link up in different ways. Human bodies use about twenty (20) different amino acids. The human body produces twelve (12) amino acids, the other eight come from food, including herbs. Once digested, amino acids break away from one another and go to cells in need. These cells convert amino acids back into proteins again.

There are thousands of kinds of proteins. Different cells need different kinds of proteins. These cells customize the type of protein they need. This is a very important process in the manufacturing of melanin. Proteins are giant molecules. They are very complicated in their structure. A single protein molecule may have as many as a thousand amino acids. This is very large for a molecule; however, a protein molecule is so small, the human eye cannot see it. It is the function of melanosomes (melanin granules) to absorb, capture and decode electromagnetic waves. This neural computer is a learning machine.

Melanin is the most important substance in the human body. It is an oxidized form of RNA, ribonucleic acid. RNA is present in all living cells. It is responsible for the characteristics of a species and for the transfer of inherited traits. RNA also enables the body to coordinate the production of proteins needed in cellular repair. Wherever there is cell damage, melanin is seen surrounding the site, functioning as a neurotransmitter in coordination with melanocyte protein production the repair of damaged DNA. DNA is the fundamental component of life tissue, occurring in the nuclei of all cells. Its structure contains the genetic code responsible for the inheritance and traits of chromosomes and genes.

As an enzyme, Tyrosinase, is manufactured in the body like in a factory. It is made, for the specific needs of the organs. We could not live without the creation and implementation of this enzyme.

Atum's Wave Theory

Light Waves

Light is made up of waves. Shadows of ordinary objects like buildings, trees and telegraph poles appear sharply defined, but, when a very fine wire or hair is held between a light source and a screen, it casts no distinct shadow whatsoever, suggesting that light rays have bent around it, just as waves of water ripple around a rock.

A beam of light passing through a round aperture (opening), projects a sharply defined disk upon a screen, but, if the aperture is reduced to the size of a pinhole, then the disk becomes ribbed with alternating concentric bands of light and darkness, somewhat like a conventional bullseye target. This phenomenon is known as diffraction and has been compared with the tendency of ocean waves to bend and diverge when
passing through a narrow mouth of a harbor.

If instead of one pinhole, two pinholes are employed, very close together and side by side, the diffraction patterns merge into a series of parallel strips. Just as two wave systems that meet harmoniously in water, will reinforce each other. A wave will annul itself when this crest of one wave meets the trough of another, the adjacent pinholes, the bright stripes occur where two light waves reinforce each other and the dark stripes where two waves have interfered.

Color Waves

The human eye is sensitive only to the narrow band of radiation that falls between the red and the violet color. A difference of a few one hundred thousandths of a centimeter in wavelength makes the difference between visibility and invisibility. There are other electromagnetic waves of lesser and greater frequency, the gamma rays of radium, radio waves, cosmic, which can be detected in various ways and differ from light only in wavelength. It is evident; therefore, the human eye suppresses most of the light in the world and that what humanity can perceive of the reality around him/her; is also distorted and enfeebled by the limitations of his/her organ of vision. However, sight perception can be enhanced and embellished by the eye's ability to produce melanin.

The following chart offers a view of the limiting sight perceptions of humanity's abilities. But the ancient scholars taught that as above...so below. Even a shadow had a reflection in the sky.

Sight Perceptions Bounded by Humanity's Physical Consciousness
From Highest Frequency to the Lowest Frequency

- Cosmic Rays
- Gamma Rays
- X Rays
- Ultra-Violet
- Violet
- Indigo
- Indigo
- Blue
- Green
- Yellow

- Orange
- Red
- Infra-Red
- Heat Wave
- Spark Discharge
- Radar
- Television
- Short Radio Wave
- Broadcast Wave
- Long Radio Wave

We live in a universe of waves and particles called, "Wave-icles". All matter is made up of these waveicles, our world is waves. A wave electron, called a photon, is a wave of probability that cannot be visualized. They are symbols useful in expressing the mathematical relationship of the microcosm. It is theorized that the speed of this photon in space was equal to traveling at a distance of 186,000 miles per second. This velocity (speed) is theorized to be the top speed in the universe. However, the speed of dark is faster than the speed of light because wherever light goes, darkness is already there.

A physicist named, Max Planck, developed the Quantum Theory. It said that all forms of radiant energy; light, heat, sound and x-ray energy travel through space in separate, discontinuous, but eternally flowing "Quanta".

Light Energy - Bombardment of our eye's optic nerves by light and color quanta.
Heat Energy - Sitting in front of a roaring fire, bombarding our skin by innumerable quanta of radiant
                        heat.
Sound Energy – Listening to music, sound waves impress hearing, impacting our aural frequency.

Each quanta carries a certain amount of energy. This radiant energy is emitted in discontinuous waves, bits or portions. Since the mass of a moving body increases as its motion increases, and since motion is a form of energy, kinetic energy, then the increased mass of a moving body comes from its increased energy.

The energy contained in any particle of matter is equal to the mass of that body. If matter sheds its mass and travels with the speed of light, we call it "radiation" or "energy". If we square this radiation, it could travel to the sun and return in 5.3 seconds.
If energy congeals and becomes inert (moving, acting slowly); if we can ascertain its mass, we call it matter. This energy congealing within matter is

produced by electrical currents and magnetic fields acting together to create electromagnetic waves. The oscillation of electromagnetic charge produces these waveicles. Waveicles are the motions of movement that carry energy from one place to another.

Electrical Currents/Magnetic Fields

A current of electricity is always surrounded by a magnetic field. Magnetic forces induce electrical currents. From this theoretical concept evolved the Kush-Kemet idea that the electromagnetic field acts as the conductor for light waves, radio waves and all other electromagnetic movements in Shu (Space). Electricity and magnetism may be considered the unity of a single force. Except for gravity, nearly all other forces in the material universe are,

- Chemical reactions - chemistry – matter - Nun
- Physical forces - physics – energy - Ptah

Forces hold atoms together in molecules, these cohesive energy systems bind larger particles of matter. Elastic, organic, transformative, determined and destined forces cause bodies to maintain their shape. These forces are of an electromagnetic nature. They invoke the interplay of matter; and all matter is composed of atoms which in turn, are composed of electrical particles. The similarity between gravitational and electromagnetic phenomena are very striking. The planets spin in the gravitational field of the sun like electrons revolve around the electromagnetic field of Atum's (atom's) nucleus. The sun also has a magnetic field along with all of the stars in the cosmos.

A closer look at the electromagnetic system shows that magnets create a certain physical condition in the space around it, which is called a magnetic field. This magnetic field then acts upon the physical matter, making it act in a certain predictable attracting or repulsing fashion. A gravitational field is as much of a physical reality as an electromagnetic field, and its structure is **defined** within the field.

Just as electrical currents are surrounded by magnetic fields; magnetic fields are surrounded by electrical currents. Electricity and magnetism act together, in balance, to produce radiant energy in the form of electromagnetic waves. Oscillation of electromagnetic charges produce electromagnetic waves. Waveicles are motions that carry energy from one place to another.

The Signature of Atum

The Signature of Atum is the balance of complements. The Totem, Neter and Essence are similar examples of Atum's Signature. Intellectually speaking, this signature harmonizes the analogical (right hemisphere) and analytical (left hemisphere) mind, allowing the person in possession of this mind the full, 100 percent capacity to function. On earth, different plants grow because of the same vital power, the sun's light, heat and sound energy. The sun uniquely impacts each seed no matter how different. Each species' seed will offer a selective resistance to this same vital power. This selective unique resistance creates the generations of different plants including fruits, plants, flowers and all living entities that blossom from their proper cultivation.

This selective unique resistance is determined by climate and impacted by weather. The variety of phenomena is the result of a variety of resistances to a single activity, the attraction, capture and assimilation of the sun's light, heat and sound energy. The sun's impact can also be applied to animal life including human beings.

It was the metaphoric directive of the ancient scholars in Africa, particularly in the writings of the ancient Kush-Kemet (Egyptians), to disown the fruit, the physical result, once it was attained. They believed that it was the process of becoming (Khepera) that was the truest reward. It was this spiritual process that fined, refined, ordered, arranged, balanced and harmonized the law of polarity. They taught that the effort and the higher consciousness acquired, was the true goal in life and not the tangible materialized object.

Life lives the eternal principle of "Constant Revolution", becoming a never-ending-process focused on the "Journey", as opposed to the "Destination". Destinations are short range achievements that keep consciousness on the road to the higher development of the journey.

Pre-Existing Order and Arrangement brings into being, the process of order and arrangement. No matter how far back in antiquity we go, these essences are as fixed as the constellations of the heavens. Atum's consciousness expresses itself in two (2) forms,
1) Psychological Consciousness – The Mental Boundaries - Think
2) Functional Consciousness – The Action Boundaries - Do
Psychological consciousness is the physical mentality that concretizes the abstract thought. We utilize this thought process, to ascend to functional consciousness. Functional, in that the thinker is expected to DO an action. Physical consciousness expects the thinker to KNOW a thought. The path of psychological to functional is the balance of Ma'at and Tehuti, grounded in the concept that moral exaltation precedes intellectual illumination. This path allows the learner to lessen the load of cumbersome, confusing and fruitless information, "Take the sense from the non-sense," "Take the best and leave the rest." Along this path, the learner is introduced to Khepera, the process of becoming of everything and all.

Time measures, refines and defines relationships (metaphors). As this measurement of time goes through its process and improves its capabilities to measure functional consciousness, the result is consciousness of consciousness.

The functional nature of your state of consciousness as psychological consciousness is limited by the senses in time and space. This action necessitates separation between matter and energy, infinite and finite, darkness and light, and the seen and unseen.

Atum's Psychological Consciousness

Kush-Kemet (Egypt) developed a holistic educational plan that included, geometry, trigonometry, biology, chemistry, art, dance, song, as well as poetry and all the other subjects we now teach in schools. When Kush-Kemet taught these subjects to the Greeks and Romans, they (Greeks and Romans) understood this knowledge only cerebrally (Psychologically Conscious). These new students could only perceive (Percepts) through material means, essentially reducing curvilinear holistic concepts into linear planes. The Greeks and Romans after dividing matter from energy, learning about each in depth, never united them again. Western civilization separates and never reunites matter with energy, body with spirit. This reunification is at the root of consciousness and is very necessary for all students to truly learn and apply information, knowledge, understanding and wisdom.

Ancient Africans gave some of these esoteric principles names from nature. The following words concretize these principles of the cosmic universe.,

- Attraction
- Repulsion
- Magnetism
- Polarization
- Coagulation
- Exaltation
- Illumination

The following words concretize the vital functions of the body,

- Disintegration
- Assimilation
- Digestion
- Respiration
- Thought
- Sight
- Sound
- Taste
- Touch
- Smell
- Integration
- Segregation

Functional Consciousness

Consciousness constructs the Nun (universe) as one single essence. This harmonious unicity brings forward all and everything, creating multiplicity where consciousness evolves. Consciousness is the only thing that evolves. Psychological consciousness separates, Functional consciousness unifies. Psychological consciousness thinks from the Left Hemisphere of the brain. Functional consciousness executes actions from the Right Hemisphere of the brain.

The subtle matter of the universe begins to concretize itself in the brain and creates an image of the universe and its regions. There is a rigorous succession of evolutionary phases in the concretization of consciousness. The life history of the sun and the planets is like the final concretization of the animal kingdom up to human, then the concretizations of humanity's upward ascending path towards consciousness. This is the pattern in Atum's tabernacle (the Cosmic Holy of Holies).

Functional consciousness possesses a reason to exist. It is the action and execution of creation. The present moment is without limit, but concretization knows a finality. Functional consciousness is action personified. It has a metaphysical basis and a method of consciousness that is appropriate to its foundations.

Functional consciousness is in accord with Nature's way of thinking. Each and every function exists within us. Functional consciousness is easily and readily accessible to us. The function, Neter, essence, principle and signature of Atum form the link between the real and the unreal, the myth from the reality. Human beings, at their holistic best, are a synthesis of all functions. She/He can recognize and know through functional identity. To be and do and know that you are doing. This form of knowing leads to a perception of things as vital processes rather than dead, disconnected facts. Nothing is separated outside of our senses, as a nebula gestates in a universe, a woman's womb gestates a human world. As above...so below.

During a human's life, her/his whole physical life obeys unreasoned impulses (to act without thinking) also called, intuitive instincts. Functional consciousness, innate in humans, leads her/him along a destiny beyond the total control of psychological consciousness. Humans have only one power. The power to negate, also called free will. Negation is the power to say no to Nature, and go against that nature. This gift of free will allowed humans to freely choose to or not to, follow nature. This gift can also be a curse if saying no brings natural detrimental results. This heightened consciousness is enhanced by three characteristics. Each characteristic is defined and identified with a Kush-Kemet Neter,

- Righteousness = Truth = Ma'at

- Rhetoric = Knowledge = Tehuti
- Reciprocity = What goes around, comes around = Khepera

The Neset Bity (Pharaoh) represented the union of the Creator with the created. The Divine Human who knows that she/he is the Creator having a human experience.

The Neteru were formulated by defining and conceptualizing the first phases of the irreducible unity, the cosmic common denominator as the source of all creation, the singularity who gives birth to all and everything.

From these Primate of the Essences, come the Essences of Pre-Existing Order and Arrangement. These essential emanations become what orders and arranges everything and all. Through this one cause of unicity comes all of the effects of multiplicity. They come in pairs, and further develop the creation of the universe, galaxies, and other life systems including the Earth. Shabaka's Stone philosophy presents the concept of "The Law of Polarity." The first four (4) major functions of this law include,

- Scission - Splitting into the like and dislikes within Nun
- Selection - Attraction of like to like, dislike to dislike within Nun
- Harmonization - the Balancing of like and dislike within Nun
- Individualization - Each like and dislike is named and brought into being within the
Nun by Atum

No time exists between the function of scission and the function of selection. The first scission invokes the second Selection. Selection is the faculty of choice by affinity. Affinity is the first form of consciousness. Selection is assured by the nature of the split, which separates, hence distinguishes and creates harmony, the third essential function. It is inseparable from the notion of scission and selection. It is this harmonization which by connecting elements (electricity), attracts and repels (magnetism), further determining and creating the fourth and final function of the Law of Polarity, Individualization. Individualization yields one single unique Neter/essence.

A new unity through which all will polarize, select, harmonize and individualize; only to resurrect again. Individualization is the fruit of the womb/seed of life in all forms. The concept is an attempt by humanity to find the meaning of the metaphoric allegory. At the head of this concept, the ancient Kemetic scholars placed the Neter. This Neter represented the attainment of consciousness as it pertained to this particular Neter.

Shabaka's Stone - The First (1st) Scission - The Ptahian Theory
Scission leads to the separation of the Nun from within to bring forward the energy to convert potential energy into kinetic energy, the fire-heat energy. The

second aspect of the Trinity, Ptah creates Atum, the Self-Created One who calls into being eight (8) conceptual ideas that take the form of frogs and snakes. Frogs represent the eternal metamorphosis of organic life. Snakes represent the immortal resurrection of organic life.

Eight (8) Concepts Concretized and Called into Being by Atum
1) Amen - Unseen
2) Amenet -Seen
3) Nun – Matter
4) Nunet – Space
5) Huh - Infinity
6) Huhet - Finity
7) Kuk - Darkness
8) Kuket - Light

-**Scission** separates the 8 uncreated creations within the sacred waters of the Nun
   - Nun from Amen from Huhet from Kuket from Nunet from Kuk from Amenet from Huh
-**Affinity** joins like to like...
   - Nun with Huh with Kuk with Amen…Nunet with Huhet with Kuket with Amenet
-**Harmonization** balances like and unlike
   - Nun with Nunet…Huh with Huhet…Kuk with Kuket…Amen with Amenet
-**Individualization** names each, and brings them into being
   - Nun…Nunet…Huh…Huhet…Kuk…Kuket…Amen…Amenet
All and everything have come into existence and continue becoming in the waters of Nun.

The Science of the Neter
The Neter Equation measures the Pattern in the Tabernacle
   - The Cosmic Neteru of the Universe = The Biological Neteru of Humanity
   - The Biological Neteru of Humanity = The Botanical Neteru of Plants
   - The Botanical Neteru of Plants = The Geological Neteru of Minerals

There is a pattern in the tabernacle. The names change but the Neteru remain the same. The Neteru are the collective word for the multi-formed essences of the uniform, each is original, primordial and universal. They were not born, they always existed in the Nun, but were at rest. Once energized, the Neteru became alive in rhythm with nature. The Neter comes into being by balancing itself harmoniously with its own particular complement. These natural forms find their metaphoric expressions in the plant, mineral and animal (lower and higher) worlds. The various animal/vegetal forms have each developed and perfected a specific function;

- Sight in the bird
- Smell in the dog
- Agility in the cat
- Hearing in the hare

Humans, though benefitting from the development of these functions, do not possess them in the same special degree of refinement as the animal. Instead, intellectually, humanity continues to vibrate towards her/his ultimate perfection, as the synthesis of all of them. The Ankh became the symbol of eternal life. Life was given to the living as their unique lesson. Once accepted, humans lived by searching for Amen (Unseen Spirit) through Amenet (Seen Matter). Amenet was the symbol that revealed the unseen aspect of her mate Amen. Africans in Kush-Kemet looked into the signature (Unique Medu Script) to know the potential of its spiritual nourishment. Through this process of becoming (Khepera), Atum called into being and gave names to earthbound essences. The Neter looks to inspire, invoke, enhance and embellish consciousness. Each Neter walks the path of truth, Ma'at.

The Kemetic Concept

There is a great need for those who wish to understand ancient Kush-Kemet thought to study the holistic nature of the metaphor. Within the Kush-Kemet version of the origin of the universe, ancient Africans were able to express figuratively, what today's science theorizes. Shabaka's Stone attempts to describe the origin of the first beginnings. They began and ended with the unified field theory in the waters of Nun. Ptah represented the idea of the first electrical spark, with magnetism attracting and repelling like and dislike "Trons". This action was known as the Essences of Pre-Existing Order and Arrangement. These same two philosophies can be superimposed over the development of the earth, with Nun being the first waters Ptah being the original land mass (Pangaea) that emerged from this primordial water. Atum became organic life, or creative intelligence (consciousness) in the waters and on the land.

In Biology, this text described the creation of humanity rising out of water (matter) through energy (spirit). Atum became human consciousness which gave birth to intellect, reason and language (creative utterance). These universal, holistic philosophies overlap within the African metaphor.

Atum Initiates the Coming into Being and the Process of Becoming of Human Life
The Process of Reproduction
NUN = Female Womb...PTAH = Male Sperm...ATUM = Zygote/Blastula
See Appendix # 8 – The Process of Reproduction

Dark Matter – Atum's Cosmic Womb

The primordial water symbolizes a mother's womb. The conception in the divine mind may be thought of as symbolic of the fertilized egg (zygote) which possesses all the genetic traits of the unborn offspring. The emission of the divine word emanating from the mouth of the Creator, Atum is symbolic of the conception of the embryo.

Conception was symbolized by the pictograph of the Ba bird getting trapped in the fishing net, like the spirit gets captured in the body. This mystical symbol of ancient Kush-Kemet signifies the infinite soul, Ba (Bennu Bird) being trapped within finite matter. Spiritual liberation occurred at death symbolically during the "Opening of The Mouth" ceremony, when the soul was released from the mouth we call, "Taking A Last Breath".

Panspermia – Atum's Cosmic Seed

A Spermatozoon (single sperm cell) is formed by a head and a long tail made up of nine treads. A centrosome is
an organelle near the nucleus of a cell which contains the centrioles (in animal cells) and from which the spindle fibers develop in cell division. It is a carrier of a Centriole composed of nine or multiples of nine tubes called, microtubulars. These tubes direct the entire process of the division of the living cell, a division which is in fact a multiplication. It is the action of the sperm that causes the female ovum to contract immediately after the sperm's head penetrates and forms an englobing membrane, thereby, prohibiting the access of any other sperm. The Centrosome then divides, and the Centrioles are carried to the two poles of the ovum. At an impalpable instant, the two pronuclei male and female immediately begin to divide the cell into two new cells, which will also divide into four, and continue to divide.

This process of halving is at the basis of all Pharaonic mathematics, as is confirmed by the famous text carved on the Coffin of Pentamon (Cairo Museum #1160)

- I am One that transforms into Two
- I am Two that transforms into Four
- I am Four that transforms into Eight
- After this, I am One again

Atum Consciousness -To Name - Word made Flesh – The Blastula/Zygote
Atum Speaks - Mitosis in a Blastula/Zygote

The Blastula/Zygote is the fertilized egg. From the moment it comes to be, it begins to divide. It moves into the uterus, attaches itself to the uterine wall and becomes a womb, the Creator's laboratory. Cell division then proceeds at a much faster rate. In forty (40) weeks a Resurrected (Heru), Divine Human (Pharaoh) will be created (Khnum). After fertilization, the zygote is a single cell both female and male in nature. This is the one case when one plus one equals one. Zygote division is called, Mitosis, (Khepera).

At this point, two attached cells are formed. Again, they divide by mitosis and become four attached cells. The cell division continues until a hollow ball of cells is formed. The hollow ball of cells attaches itself to the uterine wall and becomes the womb. This mass of cells is now called an, "Embryo". All of the tissues and organs of the body will form from the cells in the zygote/blastula. Everything that this person will become is contained within the first moment of this womb/seed. Whatever the fruit will be, the seed has already prophesized.

The whole complex human body, with all of its tissues, organs and parts, is made up of hundreds of millions of cells. Each cell is different in structure and function from those belonging to other organs and tissues. However, they all are descended from the one single primordial cell, the singularity, the Nun, Ptah and Atum. Every human being was born from this ancient single trinity. This concept reveals the eternal mystery, the passage from one to two, the first scission of the original unity, which has the immediate consequence of a polarization. This polarization defines two opposing, yet complementary forces, positive and negative, the law of polarity in the flesh. The energy of life (Ptah) makes it possible for Atumic consciousness to call all and everything into being. Scientifically, this process is the organizing and arranging of atoms, elements and molecules in the universe.

Atum Consciousness is the ultimate knowledge, wisdom and understanding of the cosmic universe. It contains all the information that has existed in the past, exists now in the present and will always and forever exist throughout the future. Atumic consciousness is the original word. The word that was in the water. The word that was with the Creator. The word that was the Creator. The Creator is the activation of the three original Neteru, Nun, Ptah and Atum.

Shabaka's Stone
An African Theory on the Origin and Continuing Development of the Cosmic Universe

When we look at the philosophical allegories (stories) of ancient Kush-Kemet (Egypt), we see that these African scholars paved the way for the concepts currently being used and taught in "Universe Cities" today. The difference is in the method of teaching the information. Medu Neter (Hieroglyphics) is a highly developed method of transferring knowledge, using skillfully drawn images evoking conceptual allegories (Metaphoric Analogies) in the human mind. Kush-Kemet theorized that in the beginning, there was only a watery matter, Nun.

Within this matter, there existed the potential for the coming into being of everything and all. This potential energy is energy at rest. Energy can be transformed into another state called, "Kinetic Energy", energy in motion. The ancient scholars called this conversion "Ptah". Ptah rose out of Nun as a mighty hill. Ptah took Nun through the process of becoming. Ma'at was the path for this conversion and Tehuti was the knowledge that kept consciousness on Ma'at's righteous path.

Scientifically speaking, before the beginning began, the universe was spread over a wide electromagnetic field, indicating that the universe began in a state of infinite density. It was made up of free elemental particles, electrons, protons and neutrons, not in any particular order or arrangement. There was no gravitation in the beginning of the universe, only a matter which in its nature was unique and unduplicatable. Thermal balance between radiation and matter was altered, and a period came that was dominated by matter, which was a by-product of radiation. The universe expanded and one after the other, superclusters, clusters, galaxies and star systems distanced themselves from each other. This process of complimentary separation, affinity, harmonization and individualization continues to this day and will continue through the innumerable eons to come. This is the Atumic consciousness that demonstrates that the way the cosmos came into being is the same process that gives birth to human beings. There is a pattern in the tabernacle.

Chapter 6 – DNA-RNA - DeoxiriboNucleic Acid
Atum - The Creator's Voice on Earth

Atum, the Voice of the Creator on earth came in the form of four (4) amino acids called into being by ordering, arranging and assembling the stuff of life. Atum, the four (4) creative words we call DNA are "adenine," "guanine," "cytosine," and "thymine." The word was with the Creator and the Creator was the word. The word was "DNA," **D**eoxyribo**N**ucleic **A**cid which is the ordered and arranged amino acids that brought organic life to planet Earth. Shabaka's Stone symbolizes DNA as Atum calling into being four (4) essences (amino acids) in 2 pairs.

Africans are the only people who have 100 percent (100%) human Homo Sapiens Sapiens DNA, while the European and Asian ethnic stock still have traces of Neanderthal Homo Sapiens DNA in them. Neanderthal DNA affects how keratin filaments develop. As opposed to humans, Neanderthals have more keratin filaments than humans making their skin tougher. This allowed Africans (Grimaldi Man and Woman) to survive in the harsh, cold climate of the Wurm Ice age. Neanderthal skin genes are present in Europeans and Northeast Asians. The rest of the genes are not compatible with human genes and eventually this gene pool will become extinct.

Scientifically, the African woman is the only human being who possess the mitochondrial DNA that has all the variations possible to produce every cultural group on earth. When the DNA of an African woman mutates, all other types of human ethnic stocks and cultures come into existence. This unique original gene is called the "Eve Gene," and is only found in African women.

DNA

Deoxyribonucleic acid (DNA) is the cell's hereditary material and contains each person's divine, unique instructions for development, growth and reproduction. DNA is passed from generation to generation in humans and many other organisms. The same DNA is located in every cell of the human body. DNA is mostly located within chromosomes in the nucleus, but some DNA is also found in the mitochondria. Chromosomes consist of DNA coiled around histones (alkaline proteins).

In Shabaka's Stone, Atum calls into being 4 pairs, just as DNA calls into being 4 amino acids and they are paired Purine and Pyrimidine. And the word made flesh. DNA is made up of the following four chemical (nitrogen) bases:

Purines
  1) adenine
  2) guanine
Pyrimidines
  3) cytosine

4) thymine

The two (2) pairs of chemical (nitrogen) bases are
1) Adenine (Purine) + Thymine (Pyrimidine)
2) Cytosine (Pyrimidine) + Guanine (Purine)

These pairs are called base pairs. The base pairs are held together by a hydrogen bond. One base plus a deoxyribose sugar molecule and a phosphate group creates a nucleotide. Nucleotides are arranged in two long strands and are held together by the sugar-phosphate backbone. The nucleotide strands form a spiral double helix that looks similar to a ladder. The sides of the ladder consist of sugar and phosphate molecules. The middle rungs are formed by the base pairs and the hydrogen bond. Nucleotides are the building blocks of nucleic acids.

The side-by-side arrangement of bases in a particular sequence, unique to each human and other organism, spells out the exact instructions needed to create that person and also gives the person his or her unique phenotype or distinguishing characteristics and traits. DNA endows the human organism with his/her soul. DNA is the physical manifestations of the human soul. Neser Neheh Ali says,

"Genes, the basic physical and functional units of heredity, are composed of DNA sequences. Genes serve as the blueprint for the production of proteins. DNA stands for deoxyribonucleic acid and is the genetic instruction set of all known living animals on earth. It is found in the nucleus (center of the cell) and is shaped like a double helix; picture a rubbery ladder that you can twist 180 degrees and you'll get the idea.
The nDNA double helix is inherited from both human parents through reproduction. nDNA is transcribed (copied) into RNA (Ribonucleic acid) and then RNA is translated into the required proteins. The human body is made of and by proteins created from RNA which was copied from nDNA. How you look (your phenotype by way of proteins) is a result of your bloodline (nDNA) from your ancestors. Forensic anthropologists based their work on this simple fact, regardless of the small percentage of DNA sequences that create these physical traits." 60

Mitochondrial DNA is what connects all humans to the African woman. This gene is in all human beings no matter what their ethnic stock or culture is. Mitochondrial DNA are organelles that are responsible for the cell's energy production (Ptah-energy conversion). Mitochondria contain their own DNA called mitochondrial DNA. Mitochondrial DNA has one chromosome that codes for the specific proteins needed for the metabolic processes that mitochondria perform. Mitochondrial DNA replicates separately from the rest of the cell and is passed down only from the mother. Neser Neheh Ali continues this point,
"There is another source of DNA in humans called "Mitochondrial DNA (mtDNA). Mitochondria are located inside the cell, but, outside the nucleus and

are responsible for generating a cell's chemical energy molecules [Atp=Adenosine Triphosphate]. A notable difference between nDNA and mtDNA is that mtDNA is passed exclusively from "Mother to Child" and bears no genetic input from the father. There is still yet another type of lineage-tracing DNA called Y Chromosome DNA (yDNA). yDNA is passed directly from father to son without genetic input from the mother." **61**

Types of DNA in the Cell
There are two types of DNA in the cell,
1) Autosomal DNA
2) Mitochondrial DNA

Autosomal DNA (also called nuclear DNA) is packaged into 22 paired chromosomes. In each pair of autosomes, one was inherited from the mother and one was inherited from the father. Autosomal DNA is passed down from both the mother and the father and provides clues to a person's ancestry.

RNA
Ribonucleic acid (RNA) is a molecule essential in various biological roles in coding, decoding, equation and expression of genes. RNA and DNA are nucleic acids. Along with lipids, proteins, and carbohydrates, nucleic acids constitute one of the four major macromolecules essential for all known forms of life. Like DNA, RNA is assembled as a chain of nucleotides, but unlike DNA, RNA is found in nature as a single strand folded onto itself, rather than a paired double strand.

Some RNA molecules play an active role within cells. One of these active processes is protein synthesis, a universal function in which RNA molecules direct the synthesis of proteins on ribosomes. This process uses transfer RNA (tRNA) molecules to deliver amino acids to the ribosome, where ribosomal RNA (rRNA) then links amino acids together to form coded proteins.
See Appendix # 9 – DNA/RNA

Evolution of RNA

DNA contains the genetic information that allows all forms of life to function, grow and reproduce. However, it is unclear how long in the four 4-billion-year history of life DNA has performed this function. It has been suggested that the earliest forms of life used RNA as their genetic material. RNA may have acted as the central part of early cell metabolism. It transmits and carries genetic information. This ancient RNA world influenced the evolution of the current genetic code based on four nucleotide bases. Atum uses RNA as Khepera, the concept of the process of becoming, the genetic information that directs, synthesizes and encodes the organism with its power to rejuvenate, regenerate and reproduce itself.

Building blocks of DNA, adenine, guanine, cytosine, thymine and related organic molecules may have been formed extra-terrestrially in outer space.

Complex DNA and RNA organic compounds of life have also been formed in the laboratory under conditions mimicking those found in outer space. They use starting chemicals such as pyrimidine, found in meteorites. Pyrimidine, like polycyclic aromatic hydrocarbons (PAHs), the most carbon-rich chemical found in the universe, may have been formed in red giants or in interstellar cosmic dust and gas clouds. This cosmic Black Womb was impregnated by Panspermia, the male energetic seed that fertilized the universe, creating superclusters, clusters, galaxies, stars, planets and all things in the cosmos.

Panspermia – The Cosmic yDNA
The Male Energy that Fertilized and Co-Created the Cosmic Universe

Before the beginning began, before existence existed, **Thought** in the Universe's Mind created **Desire** in the Heart, **Desire** spoke **Word** in the Heart, and **Word** made **Flesh**. **Flesh** brought all and everything into **Being** and started the process of the cosmos' becoming in the universe. The Creator's first thought before the beginning began was,

"I want to know me. I want to think, see, hear, smell, taste, and feel, but I cannot because I am Spirit. I am in potential rest in my eternal space. I want to be, and continue to become so that I can know that I am who I am. I am the Creator who will know that I am the Creator, but the only way to know is to come through physical form and have a human experience."

The Creator decided to create creations in His-Her image that She-He were destined to achieve His-Her desire, **"To Know Self."** To do that, the Creator began as a Womb-Seed in the Blackness of the Dark Universe.

Think of a vast ocean. Within these eternally endless waters, there is a force that separates the ocean into drops of water. Each drop of water is made up of the ocean and the ocean is present in each drop. The force that separates the universal ocean, the Nun, (**Wombed Egg**) into drops of water is the Creator, Ptah, (**Panspermia**). The "Act" of creating drops of water gives each drop a "Special Purpose". This purpose is uniquely designed to perform a "Specific Task," and each specific task is an individual human soul, the Ba. This act caused Atum to call all things into being, ensuring their continued development. The force that keeps all drops of water connected within the great ocean is "Spirit," the Ka. The Ocean is the universal Spirit (Macro-Ka) also called the Macro-cosmos, and each drop of water is the individual human spirit (Micro-Ka) also called the Micro-cosmos. **62**

Panspermia is an ancient Greek word, "pan" meaning "all" and "spermia" meaning "seed." *Panspermia* hypothesizes that life exists throughout the universe because the universal womb was self-impregnated by cosmic space seeds. Panspermia theorizes that life rode to Earth from interstellar space spreading the seeds of life within an interstellar space full of nanodiamonds and the astral-bio-chemicals of life. Shabaka's Stone discusses this concept metaphorically when Shu (air) separates Nut (sky) from Geb (earth). Nut (sky) begins the cycle of life by swallowing the sun at night and giving birth to the sun at dawn. As humankind developed their intelligence, reasoning and linguistic skills, their consciousness ascended. Life arose within the nature of cosmic consciousness. Life and consciousness extend beyond the boundaries of space (geography) and time (history). Our own earthly life and consciousness arose within them; and each of us has the ability to fuse space and time into the all-encompassing space-time continuum. The cosmic universe is filled with different forms of melanated matter; cosmic, earth and organic. Dr. Richard King tells us,

"Black matter is in the form of interstellar gas clouds laden with these luminous jewels of Black nanodiamonds, which are the literal genetic seeds from which stars are born. They arise from the same high-energy primordial shock and flux that populated all of creation. There is a crucial connection between the dark black matter that structures much of the unseen universe and the subtle living dark matter that structures our very bodies, brains, and nervous systems. The study of higher mathematics, physics, and chemistry, which observes such cosmic melanin macrocosmic phenomena, should encourage the thought that a similar higher science is required to study carbon atom, melanin molecule, melanosome granule and melanocyte cell related to microcosmic phenomena in living biosystems on Earth."[63]

Following the Big Bang of creation, the universe began to come into existence. It expanded in implosions of pure energy. In time it cooled down into condensation of early subatomic particles, leading to the first atom, hydrogen. This continuing process formed stars, that were mostly hydrogen atoms. Dr. King says,
"The interstellar material of the Milky Way galaxy contains in a huge state vast interstellar gas clouds composed of hydrogen (70%) and helium (28%), with a small component of solid particles and interstellar, or cosmic dust. In addition to the element carbon, there is found in interstellar expanses the elements oxygen, nitrogen, nickel, sulfur, aluminum, iron and others, along with many different organic and inorganic molecules." [64]

The continued expansion of the cosmos would allow panspermia to fertilize the cosmos' womb. Dr. King continues,
"The process of cosmic forces created a nuclear fusion state that fused the nuclei of hydrogen atoms together to produce helium atoms. The helium then continued to fuse, producing atoms of progressively higher atomic number, nuclei with more protons and neutrons and fusion, where internal heat gradually increased and transformed the structure of gas particles. It is out of this flux of "mother" gas clouds that the carbon atom arose. This is a vast simplification of a complex process, but the point is that the critical end product of black nanodiamonds is carbon. Temperature, pressure and composition/molecular precursors in the solar nebula would favor the condensation of carbonaceous

compounds, which are called nanodiamonds. Diamond formation is favored by an abundance of atomic hydrogen and low carbon rations." **65**

Stars are cosmic diamonds that are born with nanodiamonds. Dr. King explains,
"Nanodiamonds are a common by-product of star formation and are formed in stellar systems and ejects from a supernova carbon star explosion. Nanodiamonds are one-billionth of something, everything and nothing. Nanodiamonds are a solid crystalline form of mostly carbon atoms that are extremely small in size. A critical role is served by nanodiamonds and interstellar gas clouds in the formation of stars and also in the creation of biogenetic molecules of melanin in the interstellar clouds of many galaxies and continues in the same way in our solar system, perhaps since the solar system was created. It is through the interstellar gas clouds that these black biogenetic surfaces, sometimes transported on the larger surfaces of traveling comets along with amino acids, moved through the stellar abyss and throughout the innumerable solar systems, seeding the surface of planets like our Earth. It is these Black matter melanin seeds from the stellar expanses that provide the biogenetic spark of life." **66**

Today's human mind is filled with billions of years of emotional, intense active memories of the whole spectrum of one's blood line genetic ancestors. Dr. King assures us that,
"These experiences form an ocean of incredible human experiences that range from heaven to hell, from the heights of love, romance, and creative genius through the lows of fear, jealousy and post-traumatic stress syndrome. This great storehouse of collective memory even includes our fragmented memories of exposure to ecological catastrophes." **67**

Panspermia concentrates on how life began and on methods that distribute life in the universe. These organic building-blocks of life originated in cosmic space, they became incorporated in the solar nebula from which planets condensed and were further and continuously distributed to planetary surfaces where life would emerge.

The chemistry of life may have begun shortly after the Big Bang, twelve to thirteen (12-13) billion years ago, during a habitable epoch when the universe was only ten to seventeen (10–17) million years old. Though the presence of life is confirmed only on the earth, extraterrestrial life is not only possible, but probable.

There could be as many as forty (40) billion Earth-sized planets orbiting in the habitable zones of sun-like stars and red dwarf stars within the Milky Way Galaxy. eleven (11) billion of these estimated planets may be orbiting sun-like stars.

The "Panspermia" hypothesis suggests life began on Earth when the "seeds" of life, already present in the universe, arrived here from space. This is the science of

Shabaka's Stone 3rd philosophy, the Essences of Order and Arrangement. The text describes, Shu (air) separating Nut (sky) from Geb (earth). Upon separation, Nut (sky) is pregnant with the sun, Ra, the light, heat and sound energy that created organic life on earth. Once life was conceived, DNA, as Atum ordered and arranged the four (4) amino acids and called life into being and RNA, as Khepera, kept creation in the process of becoming.

Chapter 7 - Ontogeny Recapitulates Phylogeny
An Application of Shabaka's Stone
Atum the Creative Intelligence in the Pattern in the Tabernacle

"Ontogeny Recapitulates Phylogeny," expresses Atum as the calling into being of the pattern in the life cycle among organic life on earth.

- **Ontogeny** - The Life History of an Individual Organism..."Embryology"
- **Recapitulation** - To summarize or repeat briefly
- **Phylogeny** - The Life History of Organic Life on Earth..."Evolution"

Ontogeny Recapitulates Phylogeny is a theory developed by Ernst Haeckel (1834–1919). His concept described a physical, psychological and spiritual hypothesis comparing Ontogeny, which is the embryonic development of an animal/human, with Phylogeny, the physical evolution of organic life's history (culminating with humanity's life history).

Ontogeny is the origin and development of an organism, from the time of fertilization of the egg to birth. Ontogeny is the growth (size change) and morphological development (structural change) of an organism. Ontogeny, Embryology and Developmental Biology are closely related studies and can be used interchangeably.

Phylogeny records the evolutionary history of humanity through the stages of bacteria, single-cell, multiple-cell, plant, fish, amphibian, reptile, mammal, animal and human.

Recapitulation briefly summarizes these two comparative patterns. This theory suggests that humans, during their embryological life in ten (10) months, summarizes briefly what it took organic life to become over billions of years. During mother's ten (10) month pregnancy, human embryology, physically and structurally repeats human evolution. The process goes from the single cell organism through the age of the fishes, amphibians, reptiles and continuing through the age of the mammals. The life history of these two phenomena repeats each other's Kheperarian process of becoming.

Organs and faculties appear in the individual (fetal growth) in the same order in which they appeared in the million-year history of the human race. During human embryology, the fetus retraces not only humanity's development, but it also retraces humanity's mental development (Consciousness). We see that Nun is the unconscious level, Ptah is Simple Consciousness, Atum is Self-Consciousness that eventually ascends into Cosmic Consciousness.

Ancient African people constantly measured and compared like and dislike. They sought to measure and compare what they could physically experience through their senses. Medu Neter was the scriptic way they expressed Mother Nature.

Shabaka's Stone emphasizes the cosmic formation of a pattern in the cosmic universe. The pattern reflects a holistic recurring theme among all living things on earth. Ontogeny Recapitulates Phylogeny is a scientific theory that compares and contrasts the life cycles of all living things on earth. This theory is also called, the Theory of Recapitulation, Biogenetic Law and Embryonic Parallelism. It explores the similar characteristics between embryonic development (ontogeny) and biological evolution (phylogeny). This comparative analysis can also be made between the mental and spiritual evolutionary paths from single-celled life to multiple-celled existence through all the stages of life during the Cambrian Age when life proliferated in the waters and land on earth.

Ontogeny Recapitulating Phylogeny suggests that over three (3) billion years ago, life came to exist in the waters of the Earth. First, starting out as tiny forms of single-celled organisms. Gradually, evolving into plant, to fish, to amphibian, and to reptile; eventually culminating into primate, hominid and human.

Dr. David Attenborough's two (2) part television program on the Smithsonian channel outlined organic life's evolution, from fish, amphibians, reptiles and mammals, to the intellectual consciousness of the human family.

Phylogeny - Earliest Organic Life on Earth (Geb)
Essences of Order and Arrangement
Asar, Aset, Neb-het-tet, Set and Heru
Botany and Biology

Life's beginnings originated from geological events that energized and activated (Ptah) the potential life in earth's water (the Nun). The light, heat and sound wavicles emanating from the rays of the sun (Atum) initiated life in the waters. About three (3) billion years ago, eruptions occurred in the earth's crust, scientifically known as plate tectonics; causing the one continent, Ptah/hill rising from the waters in Nun to divide and drift apart. Science calls this land movement "continental drift". These motions created by heat that builds up in the Earth's interior, continually forced pieces of our planet's crust to slide by, crash into, and ride over one another.

Life began early in earth's history. The oldest definite evidence for life on earth goes back three (3) billion years into the Earth's past.

There are three (3) major branches on the tree of life. Archaea, Bacteria and Eukroyote.

- Archaea (Ar-KAY-ah)
- Bacteria (BAK-teer-ee-ah)
- Eukaryote (Yoo-KAH-ree-oht)

Archaea

The Archaea (Ahr-kay-ah) consists mainly of "extremophiles or thermophiles," who are organisms that live in what we call extremely hot conditions. These temperatures were near or above the boiling point of water, high acidity, or other situations that would kill other forms of life. During this ancient time on earth, it was still very hot, including the water.

Archaea constitutes a domain of single-celled organisms. These microorganisms lack cell nuclei. Archaea cells have unique properties separating them from the other two domains, bacteria and eukaryote. Archaea and bacteria are generally similar in size and shape, although a few archaea have very different shapes. Archaea uses more energy sources than eukaryotes. Salt-tolerant archaea use sunlight as an energy source, and other species of archaea use carbon. Archaea reproduce asexually by binary fission, fragmentation, and budding. Binary fission is asexual reproduction by a separation of the body into two new bodies. This happened in the waters of the Nun, self-impregnating her/himself for the first time, and then throwing off parts of him/herself.

In the process of binary fission, an organism duplicates its genetic material, or deoxyribonucleic acid (DNA), and then divides into two parts (cytokinesis), with each new organism receiving one copy of DNA. The first observed archaea were extremophiles, living in extreme environments, such as hot springs and salt lakes with no other organisms. Archaea live in almost every habitat, including soil, oceans, and marshlands. Archaea are particularly numerous in the oceans, and the archaea in plankton may be one of the most abundant groups of organisms on the planet. Archaea are a major part of life on earth.

Bacteria

Bacteria (Bak-TEER-ee-ah) are a type of biological cell. They constitute a large domain of micro-organisms. Bacteria have a number of shapes, ranging from spheres to rods and spirals. Bacteria were among the first life forms to appear on earth and are present in most of its habitats. Bacteria inhabit soil, water, acidic hot springs, radioactive waste, and the deep biosphere of the earth's crust. Bacteria also live in symbiotic and parasitic relationships with plants and animals. The study of bacteria is known as bacteriology, a branch of microbiology. Nearly all animal life is dependent on bacteria for survival as only bacteria and some archaea possess the genes and enzymes necessary to synthesize vitamin B12 and provide it through the food chain. Archaea and Bacteria belong to the Prokaryote family.

Eukaryote

Eukaryote (Yoo-KAH-ree-oht) are organisms whose cells have a nucleus enclosed within membranes, unlike prokaryotes (Bacteria and Archaea). Eukaryotes belong to the domain Eukaryote. Unlike single-cellular archaea and bacteria, eukaryotes may also be multicellular and include organisms consisting of many cell types forming different kinds of tissue. Animals (including humans) and plants are the most familiar eukaryotes.

Eukaryotes can reproduce both asexually through mitosis and sexually through meiosis and gamete fusion. In mitosis, one cell divides to produce two genetically identical cells. The domain eukaryote makes up one of the domains of life in the three-domain system. The two other domains, bacteria and archaea, are prokaryotes and have none of the above features. Eukaryotes represent a tiny minority of all living things. However, due to their generally much larger size, their collective worldwide biomass is estimated to be about equal to that of prokaryotes. Eukaryotes evolved approximately 1.6 – 2.1 billion years ago.

Fish

There are more than thirty-five thousand (35,000) species of fish. Vertebrates (organisms with a backbone) evolved out of the Invertebrates (organisms without a backbone) during the Cambrian Age. About Five Hundred (500) million years ago fish dominated life in the waters on the earth. The first fish were called, **"Myllokunmingia (my-lo-kun-minj-ee-ah)."**

The species called **"Lampry (Lam-pree),"** had no fins and no mouth. They had a hole in the front of their face that allowed them to eat. By four hundred fifty (450) million years ago, plants, worms and insects inhabited the earth. Four hundred and twenty (420) million years ago, sharks developed a jaw that let them grab food. The species called **"Panayunnanolepis (Pan-ay-un-na-NOH-leh-pis),"** evolved next. They were a fish with bones that had a jaw and four (4) fins.

Amphibians

Amphibians were fish who began to adapt to spending time on dry land. The Vertebrate fishes' fins became limbs that allowed them to move onto the earth. They could push their bodies up from the ground in order to move forward or backward. They remained in shallow waters or thick swamps. Their eyes were on top of their flattened head. The lobe fin fish developed shoulder joints which acted like limbs. Fish still swam, but their fins could also act as limbs allowing them to walk on land. The first vertebrate fish on land became the first group of amphibians to learn how to breathe oxygen from the air, instead of gills in the water.

Salamanders are the largest amphibians still alive today. The original amphibians include frogs, salamanders, and newts. They have moist skin and lay their eggs covered with jelly. The lizard is also called a "Tree Dragon." Their skin is dry and has rough scales.

Reptiles

There are about nine thousand (9,000) species of reptiles. Reptiles evolved from the amphibians. Reptiles began laying their eggs outside of the water. Their first eggs were leathery. Over time, their eggs became hard and water-tight that allowed them to lay eggs on dry land.

Dinosaurs were born and began their development between two-hundred-thirty (230) million years and one-hundred-sixty (160) million years ago. The key to their advancement was the relationship of their legs to their body at the hip which allowed for greater freedom of movement. Finally, their weight rested on their back leg, the best example is the Tyrannosaurus Rex which was the largest animal on earth.

Anteone (AN-tee-own) is the link between the sky dinosaur called, pterodactyl (ter-ah-DAK-tyl), and the birds. Some dinosaurs grew feathers that allowed them to fly. Anchiornis (Ank-ee-OHR-nis) were the first real birds.

About Sixty-Five (65) million years ago, the dinosaurs disappeared from earth. Many amphibians and birds continued to live; however, the mammals were in the background, getting ready to take over the earth.

Mammals

There are over 5,700 species of mammals. Mammals evolved from reptiles. The first mammals came into existence about 195 million years ago. "Hadrocodium" (Had-row-KO-dee-uhm), is the oldest recorded ancestor of all mammals. They were smaller than the top digit on a human pinky finger. Because mammals generate heat from the inside, they are warm-blooded. Since they could see in the dark, and they had a very refined sense of smell, they hunted at night. Reptiles had two bones on either side of their jaw and the third bone was for sound in the ear. In mammals, these three bones shifted from their jaw to their ear, which became the middle ear: hammer, anvil and drum. The heightening of the senses allowed early mammals to survive during and after the age of the dinosaurs. Humans dominate the mammals and are the most numerous.

Other forms of Mammals include,
1) Monothemes were early mammals who laid eggs like reptiles, but their mothers produced milk. Their babies fed off the combination of yolk in egg and milk from their mother.
2) Marsupials/Placentals came into existence about 160 million years ago. Placentals gave birth to live babies (eggs need time to hatch).

One hundred and twenty-five (125) million years ago, Marsupials (Kangaroo-Wallabee) were born. They lived during the dinosaur age. Eventually, Juramaia (Jer-ah-maya/Jurassic Mother), in the form of the Opossum nurtured their young before birth. The mothers carried their baby's body inside their body in the Egg/Womb. The Placenta in the mother's womb brings nutrients to their baby and carries the babies waste out. The main features of the Placentals are,

1) hairy bodies
2) milk
3) live birth

With this explosion of diversity, mammalian life began to specialize. Ten (10) million years ago, there was a global warming effect on the earth. New mammals emerged from the early primate with an opposable thumb on their hands and feet, creating the ability to climb. This gave mammals the chance to get food from the trees.

Forty-seven (47) million years ago, mammalian eyesight greatly improved. Fleshy fruit adapted to the heat and developed color codes that improved mammals' dietary choices, as well as refining their visual color perception. As the plants' seeds were scattered by the wind, plant-life diversified and botanical choices flourished for the mammals. During this period, the earth's climate changed again, and the dryness of the climate made earth's forest dwindle which ushered in the Age of the Mammals.

Ten (10) million years ago a new mammal emerged that had a re-shaped pelvis who walked upright and could create tools. The babies born would have skulls with small bones that would remain separate. The skull changed shape as it left its mother's body and the skull's plates did not fuse until the child was at least two (2) years old.

Humanity began their ascendency to the position of masterpiece of the cosmic universe. However, the human family must thank all of his/her predecessors for the phenomenal gifts they received from them. Through the millions of years of physical evolution, homo sapiens sapiens inherited the best attributes and characteristics from the earlier forms of fish, amphibians, reptiles and early mammals.

- Fish – backbone and jaw
- Amphibians – lungs and limbs
- Reptiles – watertight skin
- Nocturnal mammals – larger brain, sharper senses, manner of birth
- Primates – hands, opposable thumbs, and color vision
- Early Humans – larger brain, intellect, reason and language

The development of humanity's physical body was developed during the Triassic age, the third (3rd) and final age of the Mesozoic era. The Triassic age witnessed the ultimate transformation of the lower animal into the higher animal and finally into human being.

Professor William Leo Hansberry of Howard University, wrote an unpublished manuscript titled, "A Discussion of the Morphological and Physiological Changes that Are Supposed to Have Taken Place in the Transformation of Ape-Like Creatures (pongids) to Human (hominid)."

Professor Hansberry suggested that, sometime in the Triassic Period (248-213 million years ago), there lived in South Africa a group of animals called, "Therapsidae (Ther-ahp-si-day)". These animals presented a blend of primitive reptilian and primitive mammalian characteristics. They lived mainly in the water (fish) but were capable of surviving on land (amphibians). They possessed, like all reptiles and mammals, four (4) limbs, but they were short and mobile, capable of producing motion, but not able to support the weight of the body.

Over time, these animals either voluntarily or involuntarily, took to living on land exclusively. In an attempt to adapt themselves to the new conditions and environments, its organs and limbs began to specialize in order to support the body and carry it clear off the ground. But in doing this, fifty percent (50%) stability was gained, and fifty percent (50%) mobility was lost. This feat was very gradual, but successful. The limbs at first, supported the body only during the act of propelling the body forward, backward, or side-to-side. Its body sunk to the ground when progression was completed. Soon the limbs became strong enough to support the body continuously and hence stability became fixed.

As stability became fixed, the limbs gradually became less mobile. They had been capable of moving in any direction, but now were only able to move in a forward or backward motion. This creature became the ancestor of the quadrupeds or pronograde (four-legged) animals. But not all of the Therapsidae species followed the above course. Some took to climbing, first over objects in their pathway, and then into bushes and up trees. In the climbing process, the animals reached ahead with one or the other of the mobile forelimbs for a new grasp. While doing this, the weight of the body was temporarily shifted to the hind limbs. Simultaneously, the hind-limbs became specialized for supporting the upper body and became stable. The first part of this is called, "The emancipation of the fore/upper-limbs."

This habit of climbing saved the forelimbs their mobility and prevented them from becoming organs of more stability. It also allowed these early mammals to further adapt to human characteristics, such as, the use of tools with the fore/upper limbs that would become arms and hands. These conditions culminated in preventing these mammals from continuing as pronograde (four-legged) animals and gave them the potential to develop into orthograde (two-legged) animals.

Human beings are the masterpiece of the cosmos. Humanity's life history began during the Miocene Period. The Miocene Period began about Twenty-Five (25) million years ago; it was known as the "Period of the Great Ape." During the Miocene, the earth was largely covered with thick, luxurious forests where this primate lived. Two major lines of advanced primates co-existed: ape-tending pongids and human-tending hominids. The ape-tending pongids remained in the trees, while the human-tending hominids periodically walked on the African grasslands.

Somewhere between Fourteen (14) and Four (4) million years ago, it is theorized that humanity's most ancient ancestor moved almost entirely out of the forest and into the open savannah grasslands. In so doing, they became entirely upright, bipedal walkers, a unique development in primate growth. When humanity's ancestors emerged as ground-dwellers, he/she differed from the other tree-dwelling apes by being more willing to venture into this open savannah. This led to his/her dietary change. This change was reflected in the reconstruction of their back teeth. These dietary and habitat changes also led to their new and different choices that caused changes in other parts of their body such as arms, legs, pelvic girdle (lower torso/groin area) and skull. We can see this difference between the ground-dwelling humans and the tree-dwelling apes. These ancestors, while retaining many pongid features, differed from tree-dwelling apes, enough to be considered the first human beings.

During this period, because of the flourishing forests, the ape-tending pongids were superior to the human-tending hominids. The population of apes grew and spread all over central, central-east, central-west and southern Africa. During this early time, human-tending hominids were well down the road to extinction. Pongids eagerly adapted to the forest world while hominids remained stubbornly primitive on the grasslands.

If the Miocene age had lasted longer, the hominids (early humans) might have become extinct, but it did not last. The Miocene Period became the Pliocene period; neither the pongids, nor the hominids had any responsibility for this change, the world's climate altered (just like present-day). At this point, the earth entered a drought millions of years long. As forests dwindled, ape-tending pongids dwindled with them. By accident, human-tending hominid's liabilities during the Miocene period became assets during the Pliocene period. The hominids failure to adapt to the forests allowed them to flourish during the new environmental conditions of the Pliocene. These conditions favored the hominids' primitive characteristics. Humans are primitive and unspecialized primates. However, because of their ground-dwelling lifestyle, humans eventually acquired three (3) very special gifts; intellect, reason and language. These three characteristics, intellect, reason and language separated hominids from pongids and all other animals. We find the first traces of human fossils in the Pliocene period, followed by the Pleistocene period.

Humanity is Born in Africa

The development of the human family in Africa happened over many millions of years. The basic model of humanity is patterned clearly on the African archetype. The abundance of archeological records report that no skeletal remains older than 500,000 years can be found outside of Africa, but multiple records of humanoid remains in Africa date back over four (4) million years.

Human footprints have been found in Africa preserved in a volcanic ash floor dating back millions of years. They are called the, "Laetoli Footprints." The Laetoli footprints are located about thirty (30) miles south of Olduvai (located in Northern Tanzania). Of all the fossil sites in the Rift Valley, Laetoli has always been different than the others. Laetoli was dry then, but today the area is greener. Presently, there are several small lakes in its vicinity and a good deal of vegetation. Laetoli has attracted students of the ancient world for more than forty (40) years because its deposits were believed to be very old. The hominid fossils have been dated to be approximately 3.7 million years old. Laetoli was the first place where an adult Australopithecine tooth was found. What set Laetoli apart from the other sites in the world are footprints that were found there. They confirm that hominids were fully erect walkers three million years before the common era and even possibly earlier.

The central theory of humanity's life history is that all species, living and extinct, are related through descent, to a specific group of common ancestors. In an inter-related branching pattern of descent, relationships between any pair of species may be one of two kinds:
1) Both are descended, at some point, from a common ancestor (pongid and hominid)
2) One species is the ancestor of the next (Australopithecine to Homo Sapiens Sapiens)
Closely related species, those with a recent common ancestry, tend to look more alike than those more remotely related since they will have inherited a larger proportion of characteristics of their common ancestor.

Human history reveals itself in a call and response pattern; Nature signals to living species through her/his continual changes, and the species, if they are to survive, initiate adaptive changes both at the micro and macro level, mediated through the agents of heredity, DNA genes.

Humans belong to the order called, "Primates." The larger group contains the living lemurs and their allies (the lower primates) as well as, the monkeys, apes and us (higher primates). The earliest known primates (before humans) lived alongside the last dinosaur, over 65 million years ago.

Apes and humans, share the same basic structure, but compared to apes, humans are specialized in a number of features,
1) Large and internally reorganized brain
2) Bi-pedal walking modified body skeleton
3) Reduced face and canine teeth
4) Manual dexterity leading to use and manufacture of sophisticated tools.
5) Humans have intellect, reason and language

The acquiring of the ground-dwelling habitat necessitated the transformation of the foot from a prehensile (seizing, grasping) to a supporting organ. Little change took place in the arms and hands. The complete freedom of the hand brought about the further opposability (oppositeness) of the thumb, which became long and opposed to the other fingers, and increasingly useful on that account. The freedom of the hand led to tool-producing and tool-using habits and opened the door to the creation of cultural history.

Ontogeny Recapitulates Phylogeny
Reflected Humanity's Life History

Humanity's mental ascension to consciousness has been divinely planned and steadily fulfilled. From the earliest days of Australopithecus Robustus to modern humanity, there is a gradual evolution of mental strengths and abilities. There are three (3) levels of this intellectual history,

1) **Savage** – No sense of belonging to a particular group, not cultured, living in the wilderness. Living in the lowest stage of development. Fierce and wild mannerisms. Acting on the most primitive emotions. The fight or flight mentality emanating from the **Reptilian (R) Complex**, the most ancient section located at the base of the brain. Possessing a mind preoccupied with a need to survive. Believes by **superstition**.

2) **Barbarian** – Is a higher order savage who belongs to a group, living in a much more structured system of living than the savage. The barbarian created a society, recognizing that nature was the first teacher. They began depending on their feelings located in the 2nd section of the brain that grew out of the R-Complex, called the **Limbic system.** The Limbic system feels life. This part of the brain decides and concludes their life's

outcomes. They organized their spiritual systems around organized superstition, called **religions**.

3) **Civilized** – A civilization is created when the society has spiritualists, scholars and scientists. The scholars and scientists develop the spiritual content and methodology that guides and encourages the upliftment of all the people within the society, with no "isms" that create "schisms." Growing out of the limbic system was the 3rd and largest part of the brain, the **Cerebral Cortex**. The Cerebral Cortex became responsible for thinking creatively. Civilized societies have all the attributes of the savage and the barbarian; however, they take what they learned from superstition and religion; study their findings and apply their wisdom to the upliftment of the entire society grounded in truth, justice, order, arrangement, righteousness, harmony, balance and reciprocity. Ma'at personified. The civilized civilization is made of humane humans who do not have faith or belief, but a knowledge, understanding and wisdom, called **Soul Science**.

With these categories in mind, think of an infant just born. Follow their mental growth from mother's womb to family's arms, from crib to house/school, from life to the grave. There is a similar relationship. The child from birth to about nine (9) years of age are at a pre-reasoning stage in their development. From nine (9) to adult age, a human's reasoning skills lead them to the perfection of humanity's three (3) gifts, intellect, reasoning and language. Once cosmic consciousness is attained, the elder has been inspired and shaped by the principles of Ma'at. This life cycle can be seen through the six (6) forms of human evolution.

The Six (6) Physical Transmutations of the Human Family

Modern humankind was initiated by the Australopithecines who had a massive skeletal structure and a cranium resembling an arrowhead. Australopithecines existed for more than 3.5 million years. This is the age attributed to "Lucy/Ardi" in Central/South Africa. By two and a half (2.5) million years ago, three (3) hominids had existed. Each was born from the preceding ancestor. They were Australopithecus Robustus, Australopithecus Gracile (who had a denser cranium than the former and a more developed bone structure), and Homo Habilis, decidedly more advanced than the former two, with a much denser cranium. These three (3) specimens that represented the very beginning of humankind cannot be found in Europe, Asia, America or anyplace else in the world, because they never left Africa.

These three (3) hominids were followed by Homo Erectus, Homo Sapiens and Homo Sapiens Sapiens. There is an anatomical difference between Homo Sapiens and Homo Sapiens Sapiens. Homo Sapiens, the fifth (5th) species, did not have a frontal lobe in his/her brain, which is the seat of creative intelligence. By the time the sixth (6th) species, Homo Sapiens Sapiens came into existence, his/her brain expanded and housed the frontal lobe that would enable him/her to energize and activate their pineal gland. This led to the free flow of the brain's hormones and cerebral spinal fluid, culminating in the "Claustrum, a special liquid secreted in the brain. This creative intelligence allowed Homo Sapiens Sapiens to develop hunter/gatherer, agricultural and technological civilizations.

The Australopithecine Line

In the beginning, the ancestors of Homo Sapiens Sapiens began their journey being called Australopithecine (Austral=Southern). This name refers to the ancient hominid genus Australopithecus. The first (1st) Robust australopithecine is distinguished by having larger teeth and a more heavily built jaw structure than the next species known as Gracile (graceful) australopithecine.

With the appearance of Australopithecus four (4) or more million years ago, we reach the dawn of humankind. There are certain things we can say about the Australopithecines,
1) They were efficient bi-pedal walkers.
2) Their habitat was largely open savannah and woodland.
3) They lived in hunting/gathering societies

It is also theorized that Australopithecines developed patterns of food sharing that had a profound effect on hominid history since it created a whole new behavior of cooperative economics. Australopithecines were probably herbivorous; the bulk of their nutrition depended on gathering vegetables and fruits. Their environment was largely open savannah. Through the comparisons of Australopithecine skulls, it has been demonstrated beyond all argument that while they had some ape-like features, Australopithecines were not pongid apes, but a hominid in the process of becoming human.

The Homo Line

Homo Habilis

Homo Habilis first appeared in the fossil record about 2 million years ago and seems to have persisted for under half a million years. Homo Habilis means, "Human of Ability." Their artifacts can be found in Kenya, Ethiopia, Uganda and parts of Central and Southern Africa. They were given this name because they were the first tool makers. Making and using tools is clearly one of the main features of humanity. Homo Habilis differed little from Australopithecus Gracile in the teeth, but had a significantly expanded, more dense brain, a less protruding face and a slenderer body skeleton. Homo Habilis actively hunted small and medium sized animals as well as collecting a variety of plant foods and butchering dead or disabled larger animals. The remains of Homo Habilis, like those of

Australopithecus, lived in Africa. Homo Habilis was the first producer of the technological foundations (tool making) of human culture.

Homo Erectus

Homo Erectus first appeared in Africa about 1.7 million years ago. These Africans also migrated to Western and Eastern Asia. Homo Erectus is perhaps the most distinctive of all fossil human species, but essentially modern in its body structure. The brain of erectus was larger, but its teeth were smaller than habilis. Erectus was the earliest form of human to not only use fire as early as 1.4 million years in East Africa), but they also lived in caves, an early concept of a home, as well as in open sites. A more complex stone tool kit appears in Africa at around the same time as fossils of its probable maker, Homo Erectus. These tools are larger and more carefully shaped than tools made by Homo Habilis and were made from a greater variety of stony materials. Many tools were made for butchering, digging and cleaning animal skins. Such tools have been found across Africa, Europe, India, China and South East Asia.

Homo erectus was the first to stand fully erect called, "Bipedalism." Bipedalism is the ability to stand or walk on two legs rather than animals who walk on four "Quadrupedalism". Humans exhibit habitual bipedalism; they stand and walk on two legs all the time. Habitual bipedalism evolved independently in several lineages of vertebrates, including the ancestors of certain lizards and dinosaurs and the ancestors of the birds and humans.

Homo Erectus' height ranged from 3½ feet to 5 feet. She/he was an avid, highly skilled tool maker and was like his/her hominid predecessor, had a black pigmentation. It is believed that the work of Dr. Leakey and other experts have resulted in the triumph of the "Monogenetic" theory of humanity in Africa; they were by necessity melanated before becoming less-melanated in complexion through environmental adaptation at the end of the Wurm glaciation in northern Europe.

After one million years, Homo Erectus was the sole hominid living on the earth, until they became Homo Sapiens, two hundred to one hundred fifty (200-150) thousand years ago. His/her intellectual level represented a quantum leap over her/his ancestors, and he/she was, consequently, was able to efficiently cultivate his/her environmental and economic culture. Although Homo Erectus migrated out of Africa into other parts of the world, the Homo Erectus population was five to ten (5-10) times as high in Africa as elsewhere.

Homo Sapiens

The next Homo species that evolved out of Homo Erectus was Homo Sapiens. Although Homo Erectus shared the same habitat with Homo Sapiens for about one hundred thousand (100,000) years, they died out entirely between thirty to forty (30-40) thousand years ago. The big difference between Homo Erectus and

Homo Sapiens is the presence of the prefrontal lobe in the brain of Homo Sapiens. Homo Sapiens means, "Thinking Human."

Homo Sapiens gave birth to Homo Sapiens Sapiens, "Creative Thinking Human." All modern populations belong to the species Homo Sapiens Sapiens. The oldest Homo Sapiens Sapiens population is found in Africa, dating back to at least one hundred fifty thousand (150,000) years ago and perhaps two hundred thousand (200,000) years ago. No Homo Sapiens Sapiens fossils of comparable antiquity can be found outside of Africa. The accumulation of the best information now makes it very clear that humankind had his/her origin in Africa in all six (6) physical transmutation. This African family peopled and influenced the world from five (5) million years ago to the beginning of the glacial thaw of the Wurm glaciations period that began about ten thousand (10,000) years before the common era.

Homo Sapiens Sapiens

Homo Sapiens Sapiens at this point of evolutionary development, evolved into their physical perfection. Their hands were the right size. The organs worked as they should. The endocrine glands distributed the right amounts of hormones throughout the body to be able to function properly. The skeletal system fortified the body so that the muscular system could stand firm, erect and strong. The respiratory system breathed, while the circulatory system allowed the blood to carry oxygen throughout the body. The digestive system ate, while the excretory system got rid of everything the body could not use constructively. The womb/seed of the human reproductive system recreated other humans and the immune system protected the body from invading enemies. The human body went through a Divine evolutionary process. Everything was in their proper proportions. And the pineal, pituitary and optic thalami gland sat on the throne in the vault of initiation.

African Education – To Educe – To Draw Out from its Potentiality

The African art of scientific Tep Heseb required the scholars and scientists to develop the content of wisdom (what to teach) and the method by which this body of knowledge was to be taught to the students.
To record this eternal library, the higher order thinking skills of Homo Sapiens Sapiens began the concept of teaching their wisdom to the community and children through the development of the Arts and Sciences.

Communication Arts

- **Grammar -** the artistic structure of language,
- **Logic/Rhetoric -** the art of persuasion
- **Dialectic -** the art of reasoning.

-**Communication Arts** also included the study of the performing, creative and language arts

Physical Sciences

- **Ma'ati-Ma'ati-kos/Mathematics** - The Language of Science - Ma'at
- **Science** - Knowledge and Wisdom- Tehuti
- **Technology/Engineering** - Application of Science speaking the language of Ma'ati-Ma'ati-kos (Mathematics) – Ptah

Physical Sciences included a focus on Astronomy, Music, Geometry and Arithmetic

Social Sciences

Life's questions were asked and answered

- **Geography** – **Where** in the cosmos/world? (Space)
- **History** – **When** in the cosmos/world? (Time)
- **Politics** – **How** in the cosmos/world? (Governance)
- **Economics** – **What** in the cosmos/world? (Knowledge of Environment/Supply and Demand)
- **Social** – **Who** in the cosmos/world? (Culture)
- **Spirituality** – **Why** in the cosmos/world? (Purpose)

However, let us return to before the beginning began. If we study the billions of years of human evolution, we can compare it to the ten (10) months of gestation. Everything that this organism would become, started its Ontogenetic journey as a fertilized Black Dot Blastula, living in the cosmic waters of mother's Amniotic waters for forty (40) weeks. This Black Dot, the womb/seed is called the Embryo.

Ontogeny - Embryogenesis

The Beginning of Organic Life in the Womb

Ontogeny is also called Embryogenesis. Ontogeny is the ten (10) month process that can be compared to Phylogeny, the billions of years' life history of organic life on Earth. The species compared include fish (fish), salamander (amphibian), tortoise (reptile), chick (feathered reptile), hog (pronograde mammal), calf (pronograde mammal), rabbit (pronograde mammal) and human (orthograde mammal).
*See Appendix 10 - Ontogeny Recapitulates Phylogeny

From its very beginning, the blastula can be compared to the archaea and bacteria of single-celled life in the waters of Earth's waters of Nun. In all organic life, carbon is the glue that connects the atoms, elements and molecules. All human beings are created within the Blackness of their mother's body. Melanin in the brain, **neuromelanin**; in conjunction with internal melanin called, **eumelanin** initiate life's history in the fertilized egg/seed called the **blastula**.

Melanin in the human brain, called neuromelanin, separated the human animal from the rest of the animal kingdom. From the beginning of a human's embryological development, neuromelanin inspires, shapes and develops direct relationships with the higher order skills of intellect, reason and language. This human embryonic process began in the Great Lakes Region of Africa, the countries of Kenya, Tanganyika, Uganda, Central and South Africa.

Embryogenesis is the original development of the embryo in the mammalian mother's uterus. Immediately after conception, the female egg begins to divide and multiply into a cluster of fetal cells called a "**blastula**." The initial blastula has three distinct layers of cell, the **outermost** level, **ectoderm**, the **middle** layer is the **mesoderm,** and the **inner** layer is the **endoderm**. Each area of the adult human body is rooted in one of these three early layers of fetal cells. Neuromelanin is melanin located in areas of the brain. Neuromelanin is an organizing black molecule that orders and arranges the development of the human being during embryogenesis.

The **ectodermal** layer contains melanin in high concentrations throughout its region. Only 28 hours after conception, the ectoderm has moved into the interior of the blastula and begins to form a neural tube. During embryogenesis, this neural tube develops into the pre-brain and spinal column. The neural tube unfolds into the spinal cord, the end of the tube or the neural crest mid-point develops into the brain, and very importantly the cells along the tube evolve into light-sensitive melanocytes (melanin cells), which eventually develop into all the endocrine glands; pineal, pituitary, adrenal, mast cells, hypothalamus, thyroid, parathyroid, pancreas, and others that will develop into the gastrointestinal tract, lungs, and heart. This initial division occurs prior to the first heartbeat. It is the first step in human life.

All these cells originated out of the melanin-rich ectoderm which captures and absorbs light. This fetal development continues throughout embryogenesis, guiding the development of the embryo from its earliest stages to birth. It is intimately associated with the development of various melanocytes along the neural crest and spinal line. Melanin is in every part of our body, mind, spirit and soul. Melanin is the molecule, but carbon is the atom that initiates the Kheperarian process of becoming. It manifests itself in these areas in various ways.

The neuromelanin tract is believed to be responsible for illuminating the spirit of human beings. The blackness of neuromelanin attracts, captures, absorbs and contains light, heat and sound energy that exists within the human body. The absorption of this energy results in the phenomena of the creation of electrical currents, magnetic fields, gravitational power, strong and weak forces. These photons continually organize the body, mind, spirit and soul into more complex, living energy systems.

The phenomenon of a bio-luminous energy, perhaps a form of biological superconductivity, moving through the physical and subtle body in specific patterns, has been recognized by many cultures from time immemorial and is directly observable to almost anyone who enters the psycho-spiritual disciplines. It is often thought of as the primal energy in our species and directly associated with involutionary spiritual forces. It rises ever upward toward light, heat and sound; like a plant rooted in the earth; always seeking to be united and reunited with the external, eternal light, heat and sound of immortality, represented by the symbol of the Ankh.

This neuromelanin nerve current, the common inheritance of all humanity, both genetically and somatically is rooted in the neuro-dynamics of human consciousness. It is present in embryonic form from the earliest stages of human development. This spiritual animation is perceived as a current of living energy by basic embodiment of the psycho-spiritual process. Melanin unifies all living organisms, bacteria, plant, animal and human. It tends to become localized in the major functional areas of the body. For vertebrates such as mammals and higher primates, it concentrates in the skin, ears, eyes, the central and peripheral nervous system, and the very important glandular systems, i.e., the pineal, pituitary, thyroid, parathyroid, and adrenal glands. It is also found concentrated in all the viscera, liver, arteries, heart, gastrointestinal tract, muscles, and reproductive organs. It is present from the pre-dawn of life throughout the evolutionary adventure on earth (pre-womb to post-tomb).

Ontogeny Recapitulates Phylogeny has also been applied to spiritual development. Research in the late 20th century confirmed that "both biological evolution and the stages in a human's spiritual development follow much the same progression as the billion-year evolutionary stages as suggested in the archaeological and anthropological records. The mental and spiritual advancement of a human being from conception/birth throughout her/his life grows like early mammalian life.

The Seven Characteristics of the Human Soul

1) Ka (From Conception and Birth to 2 years) – The Ages of Enhancing the Senses
2) Ba (Ages 2 Through 6) –The Ages of Acquiring Foundational Knowledge
3) Kaba (Ages 7 through 9) – The Ages of Pre-Reasoning
4) Akhu (Ages 10 through 11) – The Ages of Reasoning
5) Seb (Ages 12 through 14) – The Ages of the Sense of Self-Concept
6) Ptah (Ages 15 through 19) – The Ages of Connecting Higher Order Thinking Skills with Mental Ascension
7) Atmu (Ages 20 through Eldership) – The Ages of Uniting the Seven Souls

In ancient Kush-Kemet, scholars built the "Twin Temples." The "Ipet Isut, Karnak Temple, the Holiest Place." This temple was connected by an avenue of Ram-Headed Sphinxes to the "Ipet, the Holy Place." The Ipet is also called, the "Grand Lodge," at Luxor. This area was the capital of Kush-Kemet for hundreds of years. It was called "Waset, The Place of Authority."

According to R. A. Schwaller DeLubicz, the "Ipet," was built in the direct proportions of the human body. The construction of this temple also demonstrated the mental and spiritual growth of a divine human from conception and birth through maturity, to death, decay and resurrection.

Each individual's life course recapitulated humanity's evolution from "savagery" to "barbarian" to "civilized." The Ipet at Waset/Grand Lodge at Luxor was built using the mental and spiritual growth of the Divine human simultaneously comparing it to the physical human body. According to the writings of ancient African scientists in Kush-Kemet (Egypt), the human soul was divided into seven (7) sections.

The Soul (Ba) was believed to be the sum total of each human. The heart (Ab) was the vibration of the soul. While the spirit (Ka) of each person was the same in everyone and unified the human family with nature. The soul differentiated one person from another. Like the drops of water in the Great Ocean. All drops are in the same body of water (Universal Ka), but each drop is different (Individual Ka) from each other. Each characteristic of the soul (Ka, Ba, Kaba, Akhu, Seb, Putah and Atmu), described the varying natures within the human being. By combining the seven (7) levels of the soul, the ancient African scientists realized and taught that the power of the soul manifested itself through the transmutation of transformation.

The construction of this temple called, "The Temple of Man." measures the growth of Human Spirituality through seven (7) levels. Dr. Wade Nobles defined these seven (7) specific characteristics,

1) **Ka (From Conception and Birth to 2 years) – The Ages of Enhancing the Senses**

The Ka is the principle spiritual essence. It is the animating force within the human, that connects all living things with each other; from plants to animals to humans. The individual Ka is a microcosm of the universe which is the macrocosm. The Ka demonstrates that the human being is of heavenly energy, as well as earthly matter. The Ka acts as the glue that keeps all aspects of the soul united. The Ka is the force that gives the soul its wings allowing it to resurrect at death and fly (vibrate) into the next phase of life in the Eternal Temple of Immortality.

2) Ba (Ages 2 Through 6) –The Ages of Acquiring Foundational Knowledge

The Ba is the sum total of each human. It is the essence of breath, the living force within each human that gives each person his/her own individual personality. On a biological level, the Ba flows within the circulatory (blood) system and is the imprint of DNA. It is the unseen energy that creates all seen functions that exists in all and everything. When the Ka is fused with the Ba, a unique being is created that has its own divine character. Some call this period, "The Terrific Twos." The operative aspect of the child is questioning everything.

3) Kaba (Ages 7 through 9) – The Ages of Pre-Reasoning

The Kaba is the "Spirit of the Soul." It is the unseen protector of the auras that emanate from the Djet (Human Body). There is a natural connection from this outer protection with the inner auras we call "Chakras." It unites emotion with motion. It nurtures and sustains the senses with the ability to perceive light, heat and sound energy that creates the color spectrum. The Kaba is the seat of temptation and plays a part in the diseases of the human body. It is the cosmic library that contains all the information that has ever existed, exists now and will ever exist. It is the place that humans go to access universal wisdom. Humans, at their will, can reach into the recesses of their own consciousness and retrieve valuable knowledge he/she did not recognize they knew. It assures us that all wisdom we need resides within each person. The Kaba acts as a protective shield. During this period, children begin to compare and contrast their life's experiences.

4) Akhu (Ages 10 through 11) – The Ages of Reasoning

The Akhu is the center of the intellect, reason and language. It houses emotional wisdom and mental perception. The characteristics of the Akhu is judgment, analysis, and emotional and mental reflection. These characteristics are skills that need to be developed over time and dedicated to the ascension of the Divine Mind within each person. The Akhu is the soul of knowledge, understanding and wisdom.

5) Seb (Ages 12 through 14) – The Ages of the Sense of Self-Concept

The Seb is the ancestral soul within each person. It is the collected lineage of each human being. The Seb is the collected unconscious Soul of the Creator in unity with the ancestors. The Seb is the parents, grandparents, great-grandparents, and the entire past lines of descent (If you go back 20 generations [400 years], each of us has 1,046,576 ancestors). This soul manifests itself in human beings during adolescence and puberty. This soul is evoked during the Rite to Pass celebrations at the age of twelve (12) through fourteen (14). These ceremonies awakened, greeted and were welcomed by the community; while joining the initiate's Ka, Ba, Kaba and Akhu souls. The evidence of the presence of the Seb is the ability of the adolescent to reproduce him/herself. The Seb reminds the individual that the act of reproduction is the ultimate sacred act to be respected that also has regenerative and rejuvenative properties. The community realizes that it is his/her duty to teach these sacred lessons to their children. The Seb is that part of the Soul that remains on the earth after their physical life, in the form of offspring. The Seb expresses how humanity will remember your presence on earth. How will you be remembered? Seb tells this story of your earth-soul.

6)   Ptah (Ages 15 through 19) – The Ages of Connecting Higher Order Thinking Skills with Mental Ascension
7)

Ptah is the Soul of the original Creator of Creators, our first Mother and Father that is in each of us. The Ptah is our original ancestor, the Creator. Ptah is the cosmic memory that matures each individual. It governs and directs self-discipline that initiates and maintains respectful and ethical conduct. Ptah, as a level of the human soul, can be compared to Ptah of Shabaka's Stone, the Primeval Hill, rising from the Waters of Nun, bringing forward Atum who names all things and gives each thing its place in the cosmic universe. Ptah makes possible Atum, the "Divine Voice of Deep Thought." Ptah in harmony with the Akhu conceives cosmic wisdom which requires self-knowledge, self-discipline and self-mastery in the service of one's higher being in order to be considered a worthy citizen of the beloved cosmic community.

8)   Atmu (Ages 20 through Eldership) – The Ages of Uniting the Seven Souls
The Atmu is the Divine, eternal soul. It is represented by Parenthood. Atmu contains the presence of full creative powers and the ability to create the future. It is the diplomatic ambassador that defines the personality of the individual. Atmu unifies and synthesizes the Ka, Ba, Kaba, Akhu, Seb and Ptah."68
*See Appendix # 11 - Seven-Fold Soul

Ontogeny Recapitulates Phylogeny repeats the pattern in many different living systems. It demonstrates how organic life is related no matter if they belong to the bacteria, plant, fish, amphibian, reptile and mammal life. This comparative analysis can also be compared to the similarities on the spiritual, physical, mental and soulful realms.

Chapter 8 - SHTYT NT FND
The Sacred Sanctuary in the Nose that Leads to the Ascension of Cosmic Consciousness

The Place – The Covered Temple in the Southern most section in The Ipet at Waset (Grand Lodge of Luxor), Middle Kemet (Middle Egypt)
The Time – 17th/18th/19th Dynasty – The New Kingdom - 1500-1070 Before the Common Era
(about 3,521 years ago). All dates are subject to change.

There is scientific knowledge contained within the southern temple of the Ipet at Waset called the "Covered Temple." The Medu Neter (hieroglyphics) carved on the walls of the rooms in the covered temple represent the parts and functions of the human skull, brain and glands. The southeastern wall of room 5 and the northwestern wall of room 12 in the temple are built next to each other. When the writing on both walls is read simultaneously (as if the 2 hemispheres of the human brain were merged together), they reenact the process of breathing, by using ingenious and very unique writing methods called "Transparency," and "Transposition". Both concepts are a metaphor for holistic (whole brain) thinking.

Breathing air (Shu) is one of the most important functions organic life performs. Breathing in cooperation with sounds vibrates a particular part of the brain behind the olfactory area of brain that is responsible for smelling. Kush-Kemet called this section the **Shtyt Nt Fnd** (Shh-tite-ent-fnd), the Sacred Sanctuary. It was located where all six (6) senses intersect. The letter "M" when invoked from the human mouth creates a vibration that resonates in the **Shtyt Nt Fnd**, and takes the evoker to higher levels of peace, tranquility and consciousness. The letter "M" is the only sound made that requires the mouth to be closed and the lips firm.

This sound wave is directed inward passing the olfactory system to this sacred sensual meeting place, the **Shtyt Nt Fnd**. This area just behind our olfactory bulb, behind our nose is where our six (6) senses; thinking, seeing, hearing, smelling, tasting and feeling, join their six (6) spiritual senses. We have three (3) eyes, three (3) ears, three (3) nostrils, two (2) brains, two (2) tongues and two (2) skins. Deep within each conscious human there is knowledge of the spiritual senses. We have two (2) physical eyes, ears and nostrils, and one (1) skin, brain and tongue. We have one (1) spiritual sense for each physical sense. When all twelve (12) senses vibrate in the Shtyt Nt Fnd this area vibrates in a thick, rich clear black liquid. This resonating vibration initiates a heightened consciousness in the evoker of these chants allowing for the transcendence into a realm of blissful existence called, "The Cosmic Enrapture."

The artistic metaphors used to depict this energy is called Transposition and Transparency. Transposition requires the reader to superimpose the head of a human over the covered temple and identify the rooms associated with different parts of the brain. The symbols illustrate the process of breathing. From the air (Shu) entering the temple, the inhalation in the nostrils to the point of contact in rooms 5 and 12. When interpreted these rooms reenact the process of air (Shu) passing through the front of the face traveling to the sacred sanctuary. This allegory uses Medu Neter (hieroglyphics) symbols on the 2 joining walls of rooms 5 and 12 together, reading the writing as if they were on one wall. To do this, the 2 solid brick walls must be viewed as transparently joined in order that the entire message be interpreted correctly. This action suggests the use of both hemispheres of the brain, joined in the interpretation of the writing. Transparency allows the reader to manifest possibilities of spiritual ascension leading to intellectual illumination.

The Covered Temple in the Ipet at Waset is a natural divine image of the human brain, reflected in and designed by the image of the universe. The spiritual aspect of the cosmic reflection is scientifically described in the function of smelling, breathing, and the meditative vibrations created by the sound made by vocalizing the letter "M" in the Shtyt Nt Fnd. This dynamic tone harmonizes the evoker with Ma'at's resonance. The cosmic frequency. External life begins for the human infant when she/he inhales their first breath of H_2O into the nose.

Room 5 and 12 – The Atumic Ascendance to Cosmic Consciousness
Smell- The Nose Knows

The smells of a rose, perfume, freshly baked bread and cookies are made possible because of your nose and brain. The sense of smell, called olfaction, involves the detection and perception of chemicals floating in the air. Chemical molecules enter the nose and dissolve in mucous within a membrane called the olfactory epithelium. In humans, the olfactory epithelium is located about 2.8 inches up and into the nose from the nostrils.

The Art of Smell

The nostrils carry air towards specialized cells located just below the front of the skull. These cells are able to detect thousands of different types of odors at very low concentrations. The sense of smell is in many ways similar to the sense of taste. This is because both taste and smell rely on the ability of specialized cells to detect and respond to the presence of many different chemicals. The olfactory (smell) receptors in the nose convert these chemical signals into electrical signals which travel along nerve fibers to the brain. This process of breathing and smelling was depicted in the transposed and transparent walls in rooms 5 and 12 in the covered Temple in the Ipet at Waset.

144

The Olfactory System

Hair cells are the receptors in the olfactory epithelium that respond to particular chemicals. These cells have small hairs called cilia. In humans, there are about forty (40) million olfactory receptors, and in a dog, there are about two (2) billion olfactory receptors.

What causes olfactory receptors to react could be a chemical molecule's shape or size or electrical charge. The electrical energy produced in these hair cells is transmitted to the olfactory bulb. The information is then passed on to mitral cells in the olfactory bulb.

The olfactory tract sends the signals to the brain to areas such as the olfactory cortex, hippocampus, amygdala and hypothalamus. Many of these brain areas are part of the limbic system. The limbic system is involved with emotional behavior and memory. That's why when something is smelled, it often brings back memories associated with a person, place or object.

The papyrus that the 3rd Dynasty sage "Imhotep" compiled from medical records is today called, "The Edwin Smith Papyrus." It dates back before 3,000 years BCE (Before the Common Era). This document demonstrates that ancient Kush-Kemet had a remarkable knowledge of the inside of the skull. The nose was depicted in Medu Neter (Meh-doo Ne-cher) as "FND".

Another part of the nose, called the, **"SHTYT NT FND,"** (Shh-tite-ent-fnd) by the Kush-Kemet, refers to the nose bones and the areas they protect, which is the space at the very back of the nose where the cribriform plate is located; the very thin boney partition which separates the olfactory epithelium from the olfactory bulb and the frontal lobe of the brain.
See Appendix #12 - The Nose with Cribriform

Throughout the literature of ancient Kush-Kemet (Egypt), Shtyt is used to denote a spiritual concept, a sacred room or chamber in the human head. The Shtyt was always applied to the dwelling place of the Creator and ancestors. This idea of the Shtyt sanctuary behind the human nose is crucial to understanding the corresponding sanctuary in the Ipet at Waset (Temple at Luxor). Schwaller DeLubicz says,

"After reviewing the architecture of the nose, if the longitudinal section of the head is overlaid on the ground plan of the temple, it is apparent that the olfactory sensors are in room V (5) and the olfactory bulb and frontal lobe of the brain are in room XII (12). The temple wall which separates these two rooms corresponds to the cribriform bony plate of the ethmoid, through which the olfactory nerves flow to the olfactory bulb. The Egyptians (Kush-Kemet) knowledge of the brain is also indicated by their preparation for embalming. The brain was removed

through the nose by breaking through the thin cribriform bony plate with a surgical instrument. The olfactory sanctuary, is where the "Neset Bity," (Pharaoh) received the sacred function of the perfumed ointments." **69**
See Appendix # 13 - Nose and Cribriform

Oils and perfumes were applied on the forehead of the "Neset Bity," (Divine Human/Pharaoh) twice. At this precise location on the forehead, the cobra (Irta), also known as the Uraeus, is located on the pharaonic crown. The raised cobra is the pharaonic symbol of the ascension of cosmic consciousness.

Room five (5/V) and twelve (12/XII) in the Covered Temple, memorialized this supreme wisdom in its architecture; and symbolically explained the physical and spiritual function of the olfactory system in the human brain. This meeting place for the 12 senses was called the "Shtyt Nt Fnd."
See Appendix #14 – Transparency - Room 5 and 12

Rooms 5 and 12 represent the symbiotic function of two very important glands, the pituitary and pineal bodies. Schwaller DeLubicz notes,
"The organs of the direct intellect – principally, the pituitary gland (hypophysis) and the pineal "eye" (epiphysis) are located in the southern area of this secret sanctuary."**70**

The scientists applied a concept in the construction of the Ipet at Waset called transparency. The message of these two 2 rooms, 5 and 12 express the process of breathing. Metaphorically, the air passes through room 5 and enters through the walls to room 12. Transparency creates the concept of the connected walls of rooms 5 and 12 reenacting the "Breath of Life." In order to understand the message, the reader has to merge together the Medu Neter carved on both sides of the walls. In other words, the writing on the wall of room 5 that joins the wall on room 12 has to be read as if the stone was invisible and the writings could be read fluently as if they were written on one wall.
See Appendix # 15 - Transparency of Rooms 5 and 12.

By carving on the two sides of the walls of these rooms, the scribes encouraged the reader to holistically join the two hemispheres of the brain in order to act in the manner of a person inhaling air and traveling through the olfactory system, while thinking holistically.

The reading of a partition (image and text) remains absolutely incomplete without its complement given on the other surface of the same wall, just like in breathing. This same instance of transparency is found on the wall separating room 12 from room 5. This wall represents the "lamina cribrosa of the ethmoid bone" and the olfactory bulb is found in room 5, and the zone of olfactory sensation in room 12. The olfactory ramifications pass through the lamina cribrosa. However, on the side of the wall in room 12 we find the symbols for fabrics, and, in transparency in room 5, the "boxes for cloths". **71**
See Appendix # 16 - Transparency

This inscription of the "cloths" and "box for cloths" placed transparently is proof of the Kush-Kemet knowledge of the most secret functions of the human organism expressed using metaphor.

"Among the cerebral organs, the olfactory organ is the oldest; that is to say, it is the earliest (like the sun at the eastern horizon). It is in room 5, at the point where the hieroglyph (Medu Neter) for the "box for cloths" is located. This room is located exactly at the height at which the Uraeus (the figure of the sacred serpent) should be placed on the forehead (that is, the eastern external wall of room 5). **72**

The olfactory bulb resembles the box for cloths, Dr. deLubicz said,

Among animals, the serpent has the most primitive brain, which is typically an olfactory brain. The wall's characteristic of transparency, placing the hieroglyph for cloths in room 12 as the symbol "box for cloths" represented in room 5, would suffice to establish a relationship between the symbol for cloths and the olfactory bulb. To this concept was added the characteristic of what weaving represents as a symbol, the interlacing of threads, just as the nerves are interlaced so as to make perceptible the contact of the individual with the environment. **73**

The nose and olfactory bulb were physically represented in the Medu Neter carved on the walls of these two rooms (5 and 12). The internal chambers in the brain were depicted as a row of upside-down "Ys". Dr. deLubicz noted that,

"The olfactory bulb, with the olfactory tract splitting in two constitutes an organ whose image is identical to the symbol for Egyptian (Kush-Kemet) cloth. Since we are dealing with a primitive organ, which is extremely important for all primitive (sense perception) life, it merits using as a model." **74**
See Appendix # 17 - Olfactory and Box of Cloths Medu Neter

The manner in which the cloth is designed corresponds with the way the Olfactory fibers are intertwined in the nose section in the brain. Dr. deLubicz said,

"One can follow the olfactory fibers, some of which pass into the white commissure, where they interlace. Then the olfactory fibers proceed toward four centers. It is entirely probable that the hieroglyphic (Medu Neter) symbol for fabric is derived from the actual act of weaving, when the heddle separates the threads of the warp so as to enable the shuttle to pass with the thread of the weft. But the image of the olfactory bulb corresponds too well, and the choice of the site in the temple in which it is inscribed is too significant, not to suggest a desire to emphasize an esoteric intention." **75**
See Appendix # 18 – Olfaction and the Cloth

There was a sacred place in the limbic system of the brain. This specific area was known as the "Vault of Initiation." It housed the "Royal Three;" the three major glands that are responsible for the fundamental growth of the spiritual, physical and emotional ascension of the human being. The resonating sound of the letter "M" in the Shtyt Nt Fnd assisted the chanter to ascend into the higher realm, Atumic consciousness. Dr. deLubicz theorized,

"The Pharaonic teaching shows us Man composed of three beings: the sensual being (optic thalami gland), the corporeal being (pituitary gland), and the spiritual being (pineal gland). Each has its own body, glands and organs. These three beings are interdependent, in the flux of juices and the nervous influx; the spinal marrow is the column of "fire" that connects the whole. The being properly called "corporeal" is the body; the chest and abdomen, where the organs for the assimilation of solids, liquids, and air are located. The head is the container of the spiritual being, where the blood, built up in the body comes to be spiritualized in order to nourish the nervous flux and prepare the "ferments" of the blood and the "seed." **76**

The human voice is the vocalization of the divine frequency that exists within the body's sacred temple. The voice expresses our deepest feelings, our spiritual involution, our hope, happiness, joy, fear, expectation, and personal truth. Singing expresses our own unique, personal vocal frequency that includes the symbiotic relationship and cooperation of the diaphragm, chest, heart, lungs, throat, tongue, face, and the parts of our bodies where our deepest emotions reside. When we sing, we become a vibrating frequency. The voice is an instrument resonating with the power and beauty of tone and temper. When tuned into the specific frequency, a singer can feel the song vibrate through their entire body. The phonons (sound energy) link the body, mind, emotion, soul and spirit to the cosmos' frequency.

The voice is a spiritual instrument. Internal rooms in the Ipet at Waset's architectural structure were built representing the inside of the mouth. Singing words and blending vocal sounds create phonetic (sound) energy which allow harmony and balance to stimulate the natural environment.

In adjoining sections of the mouth and throat, resonating chambers are created that resemble sacred rooms in a cathedral or temple. Kush-Kemet's physical structures provide the inspiration for this sacred architectural science. In Luxor, the Holy of Holies in the covered temple at the Ipet (Grand Lodge at Luxor) also corresponds to the nasal cavity. These rooms in the Temple of Man are connected to the sympathetic and vagus nerves in the brain, centered near the olfactory bulb, responsible for breathing and smell. The vibrational stimulation of the nasal cavity by chanting the letters M, N and mantras such as Om, or humming; can result in ascended levels of consciousness.

Behind the nose and between the eyes, when chanting these sounds, magnetic mineral magnetite is deposited close to the pineal, optic thalami and pituitary glands of the spongy bone in the center of the head. However, the sound made when the "M" is evoked vibrates the Shtyt Nt Fnd in a pool of neuromelanin and cerebral spinal fluids. This vibration energizes all 12 senses, and the human becomes divinely conscious of consciousness, attaining the ultimate thought; "I am the Creator having a human experience". Kush-Kemet imaged and chose an owl to represent the sound "M". Mmmmmm. It was the symbol of great wisdom that initiates a series of actions that vibrates the seven (7) chakras.

Ancient African scholars along Hapi (Nile) depicted their pictographic language using plant, animal and mineral representatives. They chose their linguistical symbols utilizing complex neuro-linguistical vibrations to create their vocalized language. Once this frequency was achieved, the harmonic sound transcended from the original click sounds to vocalized sounds with vowels separating the quick click consonants. Over thousands of years these frequencies were metaphorically written as Medu Neter (Sacred Script).

Research has shown that by the time the first (1st) Dynasty existed in Kemet, Medu Neter (hieroglyphics) was already in use in Kush. Writing was not created in Kemet, it was improved and brought to other levels; but its grammar, syntax and general sentence and spoken structure was introduced from Kush, Inner Africa. The originators of this language were a short statured people called the Twa/Mbuti, the original humans from Central and South Africa. The Twa/Mbuti introduced rigorous curricula to their descendants, the Kush Nation of Northern Kenya, Ethiopia, Somalia, Eritrea, Djibouti, Sudan and Chad. The Kushites would eventually establish cities in Qustal, Edfu and finally Heka Ptah (Memphis) and establish what is called the "First (1st) Dynasty of the Old Kingdom." What is called the first (1st) Dynasty of Kemet (Egypt) is really an extension of the Kushite dynasty originating from Nubia (today this African country is called Sudan).

Symbolic language expressed in metaphor reveals that the owl came to be a sacred symbol because it possessed very special abilities. In studying the physical properties of the owl, ancient Kush-Kemet came to realize that owls could see in the dark. This was a very impressive attribute to possess as a human being. Upon further observation, they noticed that the owl could turn its head completely around its body. They recognized that the owl could observe its environment from every angle, 360 degrees.

Kush-Kemet enshrined the owl as a symbol of wisdom because they respected its ability to,
1) See light (intelligence) in the dark (ignorance)
2) See things from every perspective (holistic thinking)

Even today, owls are symbols of student graduations and even potato chips. However, when compared to other birds, owls are not necessarily the most intelligent birds. To Kush-Kemet, the metaphor was not always direct, sometimes the comparison was symbolically connected to the function of the representative chosen, in this case, it was the attributes of the owl, not necessarily its intelligence.

The structure of language was designed to evoke in those using it, an understanding of functional consciousness. The word "Shtyt," is used to describe the innermost sanctuary in the human being's temple called the "Holy of Holies." Its evocation creates the image of something hidden, secret, sacred, wise, moral and intelligent, but what is sacred within the nasal passage?

The name is based upon more than an abstract physical resemblance for this chamber. The letter and sound evoked with "M" has a special significance in the spiritual aspirations for perfection. This area corresponds to the sixth (6th) Chakra (pineal gland).

The chakras are not specific anatomical organs. Chakras are sites, centers and seats of complex sets of energetic activities that are simultaneously physical, emotional, psychological and spiritual.

These areas are connected to the sympathetic and vagus nerves, and when resonated in the nose, particularly by the sound of the letter, "M," a state of consciousness is achieved. Letters and sounds include, Mama, Om, etc.

The resonance transcends the sense of smell. This experience in meditation consists of exhaling a humming utterance that vibrates the olfactory area. The letter "M" is the only sound we make that our lips are completely closed. This creates the deep resonance in the mouth that ignites the vibration within the Shtyt Nt Fnd that takes the creator of this invocation into earthly Amenta, "The Hidden Land."

The thirteenth letter, "M" is the only letter in the English alphabet that is vocalized internally. "M" is a nourishing sound made with the lips closed which keeps tones circulating inside the mouth and into the body cavity, feeding the brain and quieting and stabilizing the nervous system. Humming helps clean the brain by bringing the skull into vibration which helps waste particles move through the blood/brain barrier.

These resonating exercises suggest that knowledge of the spiritual properties of this physical realm are evident in various initiatic spiritual disciplines. In Kush-Kemet, the sound uttered, invoked a physical reaction in the area that reflected consciousness. The owl demonstrates the origin of the scriptic symbol for the letter "M".

"M" is a primal sound from whence all other sounds are generated. Humming is one of our first sounds. It is the sound of nourishment, of bonding with our mother. This sound is universal to humans and animals alike. Humming is a universal sound, one of the first sounds we make while breastfeeding.

"M" is a sound related to the Cosmic Mother. There are many different words for mother around the world: Mama, Amma, Madre, Matter, Mater, Ma, Mut, Ma'at and even mathematics and meter. "Mmm," is a sound of bonding that transcends species. Cows and sheep bellow or bleat a deep low "Mmm" after giving birth to signal that it is time to nurse. "M" is the automatic sound of satisfaction. A good therapist knows this instinctively and has a variety of ways to say "Um Hmmm" to let their clients know that they are understood. When food tastes good, we say "mmmm". When we get a good idea, we say hmmmm. When something goes wrong, we say mmm...mmm...mmm. When we are in fear, we say hm...mmmm

See Appendix # 19 - Owl and Letter "M"

Humming while changing the position of the tongue inside the mouth generates harmonics, which many sound healers believe to be necessary for healing. Harmony is the desirable middle ground between two extremes, called Ma'at. We create relationships through our voices to others and to space itself. Through vowel harmonics, magic and mystery is created. When heard reverberating through our bodies they join a sacred place, be it a chamber or a cathedral.

The voice is a portable instrument that can create vowels. Vowels are vocal spaces that separate consonants. The emotional and spiritual content of speech is also the earliest speech in babies and in early humans. Singing vowels in sacred places create mystical and metaphysical experiences. Vowels are the only parts of the alphabet that are created by breath, the spiritual activating principle of life. In Kush-Kemet, Medu Nefer meant "Good Speech/Sound". In the sacred language of the Kush-Kemet (Egyptians), vowels were intoned, manifesting their existence through harmony, balance and frequency specific, Ma'at.

One of humanity's earliest sounds as an infant may be the sound "M" associated with the mother. Vowels are also our earliest sounds conveying both pleasure, surprise and pain. Instinctively we express ourselves through vowels. In Medu Nefer, (Sacred Speech) the heart is pronounced "Ahb." For example, we express awe, reverence and compassion through an "AH," the sound seed that resonates the heart; Allelujah, Amen, Allah and Algebra.

The entire human language is born in us. Every possible musical combination exists in the mouth, jaw, palate, tongue and throat. What we hear becomes what we speak as the same neural pathways are used over and over. The word "language," derives from the Latin "lingua," meaning, "tongue". Because we practice and select the sounds of our Mother's tongue, eventually we lose our ability to make vocal sounds from other languages easily. Infinite variations of sound and pitch exist within us.

Sound is spherical and each vowel and tone has its own sacred shape. We shape the air (Shu) when we speak or sing. Though we can't see this with the naked eye, the sonic energy we create through our voices infuses the air with our animated breath and is sent out into our immediate environment.

The sounds we make matter! The sounds the voice makes are phenomenal instruments used to create cosmic frequencies. When sung, sounds create pathways to the heavens. Ma'at, the patron of harmony and balance provides humanity the ability to live in tune with nature.

Our nervous system, and indeed the nervous system of the planet, are also related. Humming and singing during the day, renews the vitality in our world and creates opportunities for attaining cosmic consciousness and deeper connections with nature and the world around and within us.

Atum verbally modulates the coming into being of all and everything in the cosmic universe. Atum's role in these divine utterances located in the Covered Temple in the Ipet at Waset (Grand Loge of Luxor), were represented in various rooms and explained the development of psychological and functional consciousness in the human mind. This sacred room enhanced and embellished the four (4) stages of Intellectual Growth leading to the ascension through the four (4) Grades of Consciousness. Transposing the human head over the southernmost section of the Ipet, the covered temple, taught the process of breathing, speaking and thinking insightful thoughts. The philosophy of Shabaka's Stone is enshrined in Kush-Kemet architecture. Its use of transparency requires the student to merge the two hemispheres of the brain in order to come to an accurate holistic conclusion by using the correct method of interpretation. The Shtyt Nt Fnd was the sacred place bringing forward an Atumic Consciousness, that created the Kheperarian process of becoming divine.

Chapter 9 – Shabaka's Stone and the Grand Unified Theory

IF the Theories of Relativity + the Quantum Theory = Grand Unified Theory and
The Grand Unified Theory = The Waters of Nun then
The Waters of Nun = the Theories of Relativity + the Quantum Theory

The Unified Field theory consists of one series of consistent equations, this theory compares the,

- **Theory of Relativity (Special and General)** – This theory measures the limits of outer space. From human skin out

  Electromagnetism – Magnetism is the Law of Attraction-Electricity is the Law of
  Repulsion

- **Quantum Theory** - Measures the inner limits of the Human Body. From human skin in

  Gravity - Balance and Harmony

Almost all phenomena of nature are produced by these two primordial forces. The Unified Field Theory harmonizes the Relativity and Quantum theories with the strong and weak forces of the Nun (universe). It is the place where all and everything is in balance in the waters of the Nun. This Grand Unified Theory demonstrates the uniformity of the heavens with earth, by developing a relationship (mathematical equation) between outer cosmic space and Atumic inner space.

Electro-Magnetic Force

The electro-magnetic force is a force that exists between two charges, electrical and magnetic. Mathematicians and physicists created the concept of the electrical charge and magnetic field to determine the electro-magnetic force on an electrical charge and magnetic field at any point in time and space.
The magnetic field exerts a force on all magnets including those used in compasses. The fact that the Earth's magnetic field is aligned closely with the orientation of the Earth's axis causes compass magnets to become oriented because of the magnetic force pulling on the needle.

The connection between electricity and magnetism allows for the description of a unified electromagnetic force that acts on a charge. This force can be expressed as a sum of the electrical force (due to the electrical charge) and the magnetic force (due to the magnetic field). The natural law suggests,
1) The electro-magnetic force is the magnitude of the charge of the particle; the electrical charge is the velocity of the particle that is crossing over to the magnetic field.

2) The origin of electric and magnetic fields could be "self-generating" through a wave that traveled at a speed calculated to be the speed of light. This unites the fields of electromagnetic theory with optics and led directly to a complete description of the electro-magnetic spectrum.

A new theory of electromagnetism was developed using quantum mechanics. This final modification to electro-magnetic theory ultimately led to Quantum Electro-Dynamics or QED, which describes electromagnetic phenomena as being mediated by waveicles known as photons. In QED, photons are the fundamental exchange particle, which describe all interactions relating to electro-magnetism including the electromagnetic force.

There are two "nuclear forces", which today are usually described as interactions that take place in quantum theories of particle physics.

Strong Nuclear Force

The strong nuclear force is the force responsible for keeping the nucleus of the atom together. The strong nuclear force is the "strongest" of the four fundamental forces.

Weak Nuclear Force

The word "weak" derives from the fact that the field strength is much less than the strong nuclear force. The weak nuclear force is responsible for the decay of certain atomic nuclei.

The Atum (Atom) is a miniature solar system composed of a central nucleus (proton/neutron), surrounded by varying numbers of electrons, revolving in elliptical orbits. Humanity is the mediator between the Macrocosm (universe) and the world of the Microcosm (Atum/atom).

Special and General Law of Relativity

These two theories have shaped the Western mind's concepts of space, time, gravity and the realities that are very vast to be perceived. Relativity theories provide a comprehensive picture of an incredibly complex universe where the simple mechanical events of our earthly experience are the exceptions. There are two (2) Theories of Relativity,
1) General - 1905
2) Special - 1915

The Study of the Big World, Galaxies, Stars, Planets, etc.
The Outer World-The Cosmic World
From the Skin (Integumentary System) going outward

The Special Law of Relativity

Special Relativity experimentally confirmed the physical theory regarding the relationship between space (geography) and time (history). Special relativity was originally proposed by Albert Einstein in a paper published on 26 September 1905 titled, "On the Electrodynamics of Moving Bodies." This led to Einstein's development of special relativity, involving all motions and especially those at a speed close to that of light. Electromagnetism makes the laws of motion the basis of the principles of the relationship among distance, time, mass and all of their implications and results.

A defining feature of special relativity suggests that time and space cannot be defined separately from each other. Space and time are intrawoven into a single continuum known as "space-time." An event that occurs at the same time for one observer can occur at a different time for another person. Soon after publishing the special theory of relativity in 1905, Einstein started thinking about how to incorporate gravity into his new relativity framework. Physicists began to understand the concept of black holes and identified quasars as an objects' astrophysical manifestations.

The General Law of Relativity

General relativity is the geometric theory of gravitation published by Albert Einstein in 1915. It was the description of gravitation in modern physics. General relativity provides a unified definition of gravity as a geometric property of space and time. In particular, it studies the curvature of space-time in direct relationship to the energy and momentum of whatever matter and energy (radiation) are present.

Einstein's theory implies the existence of black holes, regions of absolute black space located in the center of galaxies where space and time are united in such a way that nothing, not even light, can escape. There is ample evidence that the intense radiation emitted by certain kinds of astronomical objects is due to black holes. Micro-quasars and active galactic nuclei result from the presence of stellar black holes and supermassive black holes, respectively. In addition, general relativity is the basis of current cosmological models of a consistently expanding universe.

The General theory deals with the systematic laws of nature, regardless of their state of motion. The theory focuses on the laws of gravity.
Gravity is the force which a body attracts another body increases with the mass of the object it attracts.

General relativity has been acknowledged as the theory that best explains gravity. Gravitation is not viewed as a force, but rather, an object moving freely in gravitational fields traveling under their own inertia in straight lines through curved space-time (4th dimension). Gravity measures the imprint that organic life leaves behind. For humans, it is like their footprint in the space-time continuum.

Gravity – The Centering Force

Gravity is always exerted in the precise degree necessary to overcome the inertia of any object. The distinction between gravitational force and electro-magnetic force, matter and energy, electrical charge and magnetic field, space and time; all fade in the light of their revealed relationship and resolve into configuration of the dimensional continuum, which is the space-time continuum in the universe. The continuum being Khepera, the process of becoming. All human perceptions of the world and all her/his abstract intuitions of reality merge finally into one deep, united underlying principle within the Universe, the waters of the Nun is the Unified Field Theory.

Gravitational attraction is stronger than the energy which makes it flee, but the two forces are of the same nature. It is the dualization of one single energy;
1) Expansion - Explosion – A Pushing Out while Pulling In – Centrifugal Force
2) Contraction - Implosion - Pulling In while Pushing Out - Centripetal Force

In the end, if the contracting force prevails, then inertia has the upper hand. If the expanding force overcomes the contracting force, the return to the origin prevails. Inertia is a property of all matter. It makes an object that is not moving, continue motionless unless some force puts it into motion. Inertia also makes a moving object continue to move at a constant speed and in the same direction, unless some outside force changes the object's motion. Only such a force can make a moving object slow down, speed up, stop, or turn.

The force required to change an object's motion depends on the mass of the object.

The acceleration of every object in free-fall was constant and independent of the mass of the object. The force of gravity on an object at the Earth's surface is directly proportional to the object's mass.

The Science of Cosmic Harmony

The Study of the Small World, Atoms, Neutrons, Protons, Electrons
The Inner World – The Atomic/Atumic World
From the Skin (Integumentary System) Going Inward.

Quantum Theory is Quantum Mechanics

The Quantum theory deals with the fundamental units of matter and energy. The Quantum demonstrates that elementary "trons" of matter do not behave like the larger trons we discern in the coarse-grained world of our perceptions. The Quantum theory defines more accurately than any mechanical model, the fundamental phenomena beyond the range of human vision. It is the calculation which brought Atumic power into being.

The aim of physics is to reproduce the laws of nature in even more precise mathematical terms. The nineteenth (19th) century physicists envisioned electricity using the metaphor of a fluid (juice), that evolved into the laws that generated our present electrical age. The Quantum theory shaped many of today's scientific ideas towards Atum (atoms), the basic units of matter and energy, and the realities that are too elusive and too small to be perceived.

Shabaka's Stone outlines, defines and theorizes the foundational principles of the Grand Unified Theory, also called The Theory of Everything.

The waters of Nun is the only place and time where all and everything rests in potential energy. They exist in the eternal realm of equality, balance, and harmony.

"Ma'at," is the righteous, true, moral path where justice, order, arrangement, reciprocity, integrity and harmony reign supreme.

At a specific cosmic time, "Ptah" began the process of becoming for the first time "Khepera Sep Tepy." Ptah converted energy at rest, into energy in motion. It was Ma'at within the Nun who provided her path for this conversion.

Ma'at's complement, Tehuti, representing knowledge, understanding and wisdom, joined his mate, Ma'at and assisted this process of becoming and intelligently ordered and arranged the cosmos within the universe, called "The Nun." This process merged the outer world (macro-cosmos/universe) with the inner world (micro-cosmos/organic life), on the same frequency of the vibrational pattern in the sacred sanctuary in the cosmic temple.

The word "quantum" derives from Latin, meaning "how great" or "how much". In quantum mechanics, it refers to a specific unit assigned to certain physical quantities such as the energy of an atom at rest. The discovery that particles are packets of energy with wave-like properties led to the branch of physics dealing with atomic and subatomic systems which is today called quantum mechanics.

Quantum Mechanics is also known as quantum physics, quantum theory, the wave mechanical model, or matrix mechanics, including the quantum field theory. The quantum field is a fundamental theory in physics which describes nature at the smallest scales of energy levels of atoms and subatomic particles. Subatomic particles and electromagnetic waves are neither particle nor wave, but, have certain properties of each. This originated the concept of wave-particle duality, also called "waveicles."

The function of the wave provides information about the physical properties of a particle. Dr. Max Planck's hypothesis suggests that energy is radiated and absorbed in small "quanta" (energy packets).

Quantum mechanics was constructed to describe the world of the very small. Quantum mechanics is essential to understanding the behavior of systems at atomic length scales and smaller, Atum (Atoms) measured from the integumentary system everything from the human skin, hair and nails inward.

The Grand Unified Theory

The variables in the Theory of Everything also called the Grand Unified Theory reveal the unification of the outer world with the inner world. Matter, space, infinity, finity, darkness, light, the hidden and revealed rest within the waters of the Nun. The place where everything exists in potentiality, awaiting awakening. Then, at an anointed time, Ptah rises energetically out of the immortal waters and starts the movement of Atum, the voice of the Creator. The word was in the water, the word was the Creator, and the Creator was the word.

This original Trinity started the Cosmic Universe's process of becoming, Khepera. The uncreated creations that followed, came two by two, in complimentary pairs, male and female energies within the waters of the Nun. They lived for and because of each other in symbiotic harmony. Shabaka's Stone tells of the continuing creation of essences one after the other, another from the other knowing that one day they would evolve into the masterpieces of the universe, the human family.

In their very distant future, they foresaw a race of humane humans who would continue producing Creators on Earth. As above the skin, so below the skin. Above is expressed by the Special and General Laws of Relativity. Below is reflected in Quantum Mechanics. Just as the electrons circle around the nucleus of an atom in the small world, the planets revolve around the Sun in the big world.

There are laws that govern the outer world (Laws of Relativity) and laws that regulate the inner world (Laws of Quantum Mechanics). However, both Relativity and Quantum laws are based in the one Ma'atian law that satisfies the equation for both worlds simultaneously, at the same time (time) in the same place (space). The Grand Unified Theory, the Theory of Everything is the waters of Nun, where all and everything rest in their potential equilibrium, balance and harmony. As above, So below. They anxiously await awakening to fulfil their Divine destiny.

Review

Shabaka's Stone explores and explains many scientific theories on multi-dimensional levels. In DNA, the four (4) amino acids that come in two (2) pairs can be compared to the Essences of Pre-Existing Order and Arrangement and the Essences of Order and Arrangement. The pattern in the tabernacle can be seen in the relationship that human evolution had with human embryology as humans in gestation go through in ten (10) months what it took organic life on earth to do over billions of years.

Medu Neter carved on that walls of the Ipet at Waset described the structure and function of the human brain where breathing and the sense of smell is explained. The Shtyt Nt Fnd located behind the Olfactory bulb was considered to be the vault of initiation. This sacred sanctuary is found in the limbic system of the brain.

Astronomy, physics and chemistry are defined in the Nun through the conception and birth of the masterpiece of the universe, the humane human being. The unification of the stellar universe and the earthly and organic world is theorized in the Grand Unified Theory.

Shabaka's Stone tells us that we are born with everything we need to solve all of our life's challenges. Every human is born with a Messiah (Asar/Heru) and a Judas (Seten). Judas' job is to stop us from achieving our divine purpose. The Messiah's responsibility is to make sure that Judas is not successful. Life is the result of the balance of this relationship. The Messiah may fall down nine (9) times, but rises ten (10) times. The metaphor of the Asarian Drama. We are the Creator having a human experience.

Worksheet - The Coming into Being and the Process of Becoming
How the Cosmic Universe Came into Being is Directly Related to How the Masterpiece Can Accomplish Their Goals

The Nun wanted to come into being. He/She tried countless times. Finally, one of her/his attempts succeeded and Ptah came forward and created Atum. Atum was consciousness and named all and every thing. This trinity began the beginning of time and continues to become to this day. Every day, when you wake up is like Ptah rising out of the Nun (state of unconscious). This energy conversion, waking you up initiates your simple and self-conscious state of thinking, realizing who you are coming up out of your sleep. The Nun had a goal to accomplish. He/She was successful. What are your goals. There is a pattern in the Cosmic Tabernacle.

We reenact the Coming into Being every day. Choose a goal you want to accomplish, but always find ways not to complete it. Make sure the GOAL you choose is "DO-ABLE". Begin with easy GOALS, then increase the challenge.

Step 1 – GOAL-The Waters of Nun
Identify a GOAL you want to accomplish

Step 2 - Things That Will Accomplish GOAL-Ptah
List 3 things you can do that will accomplish your GOAL

1)
2)
3)

Step 3 - Things That Stop You from Accomplishing GOAL-Seten

List 3 things that stop you from accomplishing your GOAL

1)
2)
3)

Step 4 - Things That Will Neutralize What Stops You from Accomplishing GOAL-Khepera Sep Tepy
List 3 things that you can do that will neutralize the things that stop you from accomplishing your GOAL

1)
2)
3)

Step 5 - Do STEP 4 to Neutralize STEP 3 – Ptah- The Conversion of Energy
Implement the 3 things that will neutralize what stops you from accomplishing your GOAL.

Conclusion- Atum-Khepera-The Process of Becoming
DO STEP 2 – ACCOMPLISH YOUR GOAL

Next Step – STEP 1 - Identify another GOAL to Accomplish
Accomplish your next GOAL. You started the Kheperarian Process of Becoming

Shabaka's Stone: An African Theory Concerning the Origin and Continuing Development of the Cosmic Universe
Endnotes, Bibliography and Booklist

Endnotes

1) **Wonderful Ethiopians of the Ancient Cushite Empire <u>Book II, Origin of Civilization from the Cushites,</u>** written by Drusilla Dunjee Houston, edited by Peggy Brooks-Bertram, Peggy Bertram Publishing, Buffalo, NY, 2007, p xxv.

2) **Stolen Legacy,** James, George, G. M., (Julian Richardson: CA), 1954, Chapter 8, "The Memphite Theology," p 139-151.

3) **The Book of the Tep Heseb: An Afrikological Research Methodology,** A. Dukuzumurenyi

4) **Mathematics in the Time of the Pharaohs,** Richard J. Gillings, Dover Publications, NY, 1972, p 45.

5) **The Rhind Mathematical Papyrus, British Museum 10057 and 10058. V1,** Arnold Buffum Chace and Raymond Clare Archibald, Mathematical Association of America, Oberlin, Ohio, 1927, p 1.

6) **The Book of the Tep Heseb: An Afrikological Research Methodology,** A. Dukuzumurenyi

7) **The Egyptian Book of The Dead: and The Ancient Mysteries of Amenta,** Gerald Massey, A and B Books, NY, 1907/1994, p 2.

8) **The Integration Trap: The Generation Gap: caused by a choice Between Two Cultures,** Oba T'Shaka, PH.D., Pan African Publishers and Distributors, Oakland, CA., 2005, p 82.

9) **Ibid.,** p 83.

10) **Ibid.,** p 83/84.

11) **Ibid.,** p 90.

12) ***African Power Notes: Affirming African Indigenous Socialization in the Face* of *the Culture Wars,*** Dr. Asa G. Hilliard III, Makare Publishing Company, Gainesville, Florida, 2002, p 22.

13) **Undated Essay, Hansberry's Private Papers** "African Religions: Worship of the Sun in Tropical Africa Today," Hansberry, William, Leo.

14) **Egypt Revisited,** Ed. Ivan Van Sertima, Journal of African Civilization, Vol 10, Summer, 1989, NJ, "African Philosophy of the Pharaonic Period," p 286-324.

15) **The Egypt Code,** Robert Bauval, and Consortium Book Sales: MN, 2008, p 135.

16) **Stolen Legacy,** James, George, G. M., (Julian Richardson: CA), 1954, Chapter 8, "The Memphite Theology," p 139-151.

17) **Why Darkness Matters: The Power of Melanin in the Brain,** Ed., Dr. Bruce Bynum, African American Images: Chicago, 2005, Chapter 4, "Neuromelanin: A Black Gate Threshold; The I33 Tissue of Heru: Historical, Neurophysiological, and Clinical Psychological Issues," Dr. Richard D. King, M.D., p137.

18) Ibid., **Stolen Legacy,** p 141.

19) **The Rhind Mathematical Papyrus, British Museum 10057 and 10058. V1,** Arnold Buffum Chace and Raymond Clare Archibald, Mathematical Association of America, Oberlin, Ohio, 1927, p 49.

The Book of the Tep Heseb: An Afrikological Research Methodology, A. Dukuzumurenyi, Google.

20) **Spirituality Before Religions-Spirituality is Unseen Science: Science is Seen Spirituality**, Kaba Hiawatha Kamene, Amazon Publishing, WA, 2019, p 9.

21) **Why Darkness Matters: The Power of Melanin in the Brain**, Ed., Dr. Bruce Bynum, African American Images: Chicago, 2005. Dr. Richard D. King, M.D., Chapter 4, "Neuromelanin: A Black Gate Threshold; The I33 Tissue of Heru, Historical, Neurophysiological, and Clinical Psychological Issues," p 129.

22) Ibid, **Why Darkness Matters: The Power of Melanin in the Brain**, p 130.

23) Ibid, **Why Darkness Matters: The Power of Melanin in the Brain**, p 130.

24) Ibid, **Why Darkness Matters: The Power of Melanin in the Brain**, p 130.

25) @ancestralfootprints.com

26) Ibid, **Why Darkness Matters: The Power of Melanin in the Brain**, p 132.

27) **Origins: Fourteen Billion Years of Cosmic Evolution**, Neil deGrasse Tyson and Donald Goldsmith,
    WW Norton and Co: NY/London, 2004, p 25.

28) Ibid, **Origins: Fourteen Billion Years of Cosmic Evolution**, p 73.

29) Ibid, **Origins: Fourteen Billion Years of Cosmic Evolution**, p 29.

30) Ibid, **Origins: Fourteen Billion Years of Cosmic Evolution**, p 33.

31) Ibid, **Origins: Fourteen Billion Years of Cosmic Evolution**, p 27.

32) **Origins: Fourteen Billion Years of Cosmic Evolution**, Neil deGrasse Tyson and Donald Goldsmith,
    WW Norton and Co: NY/London, 2004, p 53.

33) Ibid, **Origins: Fourteen Billion Years of Cosmic Evolution**, p 61.

34) Ibid, **Origins: Fourteen Billion Years of Cosmic Evolution**, p 26.

35) Ibid, **Origins: Fourteen Billion Years of Cosmic Evolution**, p 132.

36) Ibid, **Origins: Fourteen Billion Years of Cosmic Evolution**, p 133-134.

37) Ibid, **Origins: Fourteen Billion Years of Cosmic Evolution**, p 71.

38) Ibid, **Origins: Fourteen Billion Years of Cosmic Evolution**, p 78.

39) Ibid, **Origins: Fourteen Billion Years of Cosmic Evolution**, p 78.

40) Ibid, **Origins: Fourteen Billion Years of Cosmic Evolution**, p 117.

41) Ibid, **Origins: Fourteen Billion Years of Cosmic Evolution**, p 128.

42) **Stolen Legacy**, George G. M. James, (Julian Richardson: CA), 1954, Chapter 8, "The Memphite Theology," p 139-151.

43) **The Ethiopian Book of Life – The Lefafa Sedek,** Dr. E. A. Wallis Budge, Frontline Books, Chicago, 1929/2003, P 3-4.

44) **Selections from The Husia: Sacred Wisdom of Ancient Egypt**, Selected and Retranslated by Dr. Maulana Karenga, Kawaida Publications, Los Angeles, 1984, p 5/6.

45) Ibid, **Selections from The Husia: Sacred Wisdom of Ancient Egypt**, p 6/7.

46) **GAGUT G i j , j = 0: Radically Unifies Mathematics and solves Riemann Hypothesis, A Clay Mathematics Millennium Problem**, Professor Gabriel A. Oyibo, OFAPPIT Institute of Technology Press, Dix Hills, NY, 2010, p 294.

47) **Origins: Fourteen Billion Years of Cosmic Evolution**, Neil deGrasse Tyson and Donald Goldsmith, WW Norton and Co: NY/London, 2004, p 136.

48) Ibid, **Origins: Fourteen Billion Years of Cosmic Evolution**, p 138-139.

49) Ibid, **Origins: Fourteen Billion Years of Cosmic Evolution**, p 152.

50) Ibid, **Origins: Fourteen Billion Years of Cosmic Evolution**, p 159.

51) Ibid, **Origins: Fourteen Billion Years of Cosmic Evolution**, p 27.

52) Ibid, **Origins: Fourteen Billion Years of Cosmic Evolution**, p 28.

53) **Man, God and Civilization,** John G. Jackson, (Citadel Press Book: NY),
1993, p 5.

54) **The Elements: What You Really Want to Know**, Ron Miller, Twenty-First Century Books: 2006, 61.

55) **Universe Down To Earth**, Neil de Grasse Tyson, Columbia University: 1994, p 171

56) Ibid, **Origins: Fourteen Billion Years of Cosmic Evolution**, p 225.

57) Ibid, **Origins: Fourteen Billion Years of Cosmic Evolution**, p 234.

58) Ibid, **Origins: Fourteen Billion Years of Cosmic Evolution**, p 237.

59) Ibid, **Origins: Fourteen Billion Years of Cosmic Evolution**, p 237.

60) **The Paleo-American: A Primer on Ancient American History,** Neser Em Neheh Ali, Chicago, Il. 2009, p 10/11.

61) **Ibid, The Paleo-American: A Primer on Ancient American History,** p 11. **Spirituality Before Religions-Spirituality is Unseen Science: Science is Seen Spirituality**, Kaba Hiawatha Kamene, Amazon Publishing, WA, 2019, p 9.

62) **Why Darkness Matters: The Power of Melanin in the Brain**, Ed., Dr. Bruce Bynum, African American Images: Chicago, 2005. Dr. Richard D. King, M.D., Chapter 4, "Neuromelanin: A Black Gate Threshold; The I33 Tissue of Heru Historical, Neurophysiological, and Clinical Psychological Issues," p 129

63) Ibid, **Why Darkness Matters: The Power of Melanin in the Brain**, p 130.

64) Ibid, **Why Darkness Matters: The Power of Melanin in the Brain,** p 130.

65) Ibid, **Why Darkness Matters: The Power of Melanin in the Brain**, p 130

66) Ibid, **Why Darkness Matters: The Power of Melanin in the Brain**, p 132.

67) Ibid, **Why Darkness Matters: The Power of Melanin in the Brain**, p 132.

68) **Kemet and the African Worldview**, ed. Drs. Maulana Karenga and Jacob Carruthers, "Ancient Egyptian Thought and the Development of African (Black) Psychology, Dr. Wade Nobles, (University of Sankore Press: Los Angeles), p 108-110.

69) Ibid, **Temple in Man**, by R.A. Schwaller DeLubicz, Inner Traditions, Rochester, VT, 1949, p 99.

70) Ibid, **Temple in Man**, p 102.

71) Ibid, **Temple in Man**, p 99.

72) Ibid, **Temple in Man**, p 102.

73) Ibid, **Temple in Man**, p 103.

74) Ibid, **Temple in Man**, p 103.

75) Ibid, **Temple in Man**, p 104.

76) Ibid, **Temple in Man**, p 107.

BIBLIOGRAPHY

Libation

1. **Wonderful Ethiopians of the Ancient Cushite Empire,** Dr. Drusilla Dunjee Houston, Black Classic Press: Baltimore, MD, 1926/1985.

2. **Wonderful Ethiopians of the Ancient Cushite Empire Book II, Origin of Civilization from the Cushites,** written by Drusilla Dunjee Houston, edited by Peggy Brooks-Bertram, Peggy Bertram Publishing, Buffalo, NY, 2007.

3. **Stolen Legacy,** James, George, G. M., (Julian Richardson: CA), 1954, Chapter 8, "The Memphite Theology," p 139-151.

4. **Mathematics in the Time of the Pharaohs**, Richard J. Gillings, Dover Publications, NY, 1972

5. **The Rhind Mathematical Papyrus, British Museum 10057 and 10058. V1,** Arnold Buffum Chace and Raymond Clare Archibald, Mathematical Association of America, Oberlin, Ohio, 1927,

6. **The Egyptian Book of The Dead: and The Ancient Mysteries of Amenta**, Gerald Massey, A and B Books, NY, 1907/1994.

Chapter 1 - Introduction

- *African Power Notes: Affirming African Indigenous Socialization in the Face of the Culture Wars,* Dr. Asa G. Hilliard III, Makare Publishing Company, Gainesville, Florida, 2002, p 22.

- **Egypt Revisited**, Ed. Ivan Van Sertima, Journal of African Civilization, Vol 10, Summer, 1989, NJ, "African Philosophy of the Pharaonic Period," p 286-324.

- **Undated Essay, Hansberry's Private Papers** "African Religions: Worship of the Sun in Tropical Africa Today," Hansberry, William, Leo.

- **The Egypt Code**, Robert Bauval, and Consortium Book Sales: MN,

- 2008, p 135.

- **Stolen Legacy**, James, George, G. M., (Julian Richardson: CA), 1954,

- Chapter 8, "The Memphite Theology," p 139-151.

- **Why Darkness Matters: The Power of Melanin in the Brain**, Ed., Dr. Bruce Bynum, African American Images: Chicago, 2005, Chapter 4, "Neuromelanin: A Black Gate Threshold; The I33 Tissue of Heru: Historical, Neurophysiological, and Clinical Psychological Issues," Dr. Richard D. King, M.D., p137.

- **The Book of the Tep Heseb: An Afrikological Research Methodology**, A. Dukuzumurenyi, Google.

- **The Integration Trap: The Generation Gap: caused by a choice Between Two Cultures,**

Oba T'Shaka, PH.D., Pan African Publishers and Distributors, Oakland, CA., 2005.

Chapter 2 - Shabaka's Stone - Philosophy #1 - Primate of the Essences

- **Spirituality Before Religions-Spirituality is Unseen Science: Science is Seen Spirituality**, Kaba Hiawatha Kamene, Amazon Publishing, WA, 2019.
- **Why Darkness Matters: The Power of Melanin in the Brain**, Ed., Dr. Bruce Bynum, African American Images: Chicago, 2005.Dr. Richard D. King, M.D., Chapter 4, "Neuromelanin: A Black Gate Threshold; The I33 Tissue of Heru, Historical, Neurophysiological, and Clinical Psychological Issues."
- **Dark Light**, Edward Bruce Bynum, Inner Traditions, Rochester, Vermont, 2012.
- **Origins: Fourteen Billion Years of Cosmic Evolution**, Neil deGrasse Tyson and Donald Goldsmith, WW Norton and Co: NY/London, 2004.
- **Online,** @ancestralfootprints.com

Chapter 3 - Shabaka's Stone - Philosophy #2 – Essences of Pre-Existing Order and Arrangement

- **Stolen Legacy**, George G. M. James, (Julian Richardson: CA), Chapter 8, "The Memphite Theology," 1954.
- **The Ethiopian Book of Life – The Lefafa Sedek,** Dr. E. A. Wallis Budge, Frontline Books, Chicago, 1929/2003.
- **Selections from The Husia: Sacred Wisdom of Ancient Egypt**, Selected and Retranslated by Dr. Maulana Karenga, Kawaida Publications, Los Angeles, 1984.
- **GAGUT G i j, j = 0: Radically Unifies Mathematics and solves Riemann Hypothesis, A Clay Mathematics Millennium Problem**, Professor Gabriel A. Oyibo, OFAPPIT Institute of Technology Press, Dix Hills, NY, 2010.
- **Origins: Fourteen Billion Years of Cosmic Evolution**, Neil deGrasse Tyson and Donald Goldsmith, WW Norton and Co: NY/London, 2004.
- **Universe Down To Earth**, Neil de Grasse Tyson, Columbia University: 1994.
- **The Elements: What You Really Want to Know**, Ron Miller, Twenty-First Century Books: 2006.

Chapter 4 - Shabaka's Stone - Philosophy # 3 – Essences of Order and Arrangement

- **Why Darkness Matters: The Power of Melanin in the Brain**, Ed., Dr. Bruce Bynum, African American Images: Chicago, 2005, Dr. Richard D. King, M.D., Chapter 4, "Neuromelanin: A Black Gate Threshold; The I33

Tissue of Heru, Historical, Neurophysiological, and Clinical Psychological Issues," p 127-160.
- **Dark Light**, Edward Bruce Bynum, Inner Traditions, Rochester, Vermont, 2012.
- **The Paleo-American: A Primer on Ancient American History,** Neser Em Neheh Ali, Chicago, Il. 2009.

Chapter 5 – Atumic Consciousness
- **The African Unconscious: Roots of Ancient Mysticism and Modern Psychology**, Bynum, Edward, Bruce, Teachers College Press, NY, 1998.
- **Dark Light, Consciousness: Melanin, Serpent Power, and the Luminous Matrix of Reality**, Bynum, Edward, Bruce, Inner Traditions, Rochester, Vermont, 2012.
- **African Origins of Biological Psychiatry**, Dr. Richard King, (Seymour-Smith, Inc: Tn), 1990.

Chapter 6 - DNA-RNA
- **The Paleo-American: A Primer on Ancient American History,** Neser Em Neheh Ali, Chicago, Il. 2009.
- **Spirituality Before Religions-Spirituality is Unseen Science: Science is Seen Spirituality**, Kaba Hiawatha Kamene, Amazon Publishing, WA, 2019, p 9.
- **Why Darkness Matters: The Power of Melanin in the Brain**, Ed., Dr. Bruce, Bynum, African American Images: Chicago, 2005. Dr. Richard D. King, M.D., Chapter 4, "Neuromelanin: A Black Gate Threshold; The I33 Tissue of Heru, Historical, Neurophysiological, and Clinical Psychological Issues," p 129.

Chapter 7 - Ontogeny Recapitulates Phylogeny
- **Kemet and the African Worldview**, ed. Drs. Maulana Karenga and Jacob Carruthers,
  "Ancient Egyptian Thought and the Development of African (Black) Psychology, Dr. Wade Nobles,
  (University of Sankore Press: Los Angeles), p 108-109.
- **Ontogeny Recapitulates Phylogeny**, Stephen Jay Gould, Belnap Press of Harvard University Press, MA, 1977.
- **The African Unconscious: Roots of Ancient Mysticism and Modern Psychology**, Bynum, Edward, Bruce, Teachers College Press, NY, 1998.
- **Melanin-A Key to Freedom**, Dr. Richard King, U.B. and Us Books, VA, 1994.

- **The African Unconscious: Roots of Ancient Mysticism and Modern Psychology**, Bynum, Edward, Bruce, Teachers College Press, NY, 1998.
- **Dark Light**, Edward Bruce Bynum, Inner Traditions, Rochester, Vermont, 2012, p 6.
- **The Spirit of Intimacy: Ancient African Teachings in the Ways of Relationships**, Sobunfu Some, Harper Press, NY, 1997.
- **Ritual: Power, Healing and Community**, Malidoma Patrice Some, (Swan/Raven & Company: Portland, Oregon) 1993.

Chapter 8 - Shtyt Nt Fnd

- **Temple in Man**, by R.A. Schwaller DeLubicz, Inner Traditions, Rochester, VT, 1949.
- **Sacred Space, Sacred Sound: The Acoustic Mysteries of Holy Places**, Susan E. Hale, M.A., Quest Books, Illinois, 2007.
- **Egypt Revisited**, ed., Ivan Van Sertima, Transaction Publishers, New Brunswick, 1991, "Waset, The Eye of Ra and the Abode of Ma'at: The Pinnacle of Black Leadership in The Ancient World," Asa G. Hilliard III.

Chapter 9 – Grand Unified Theory

- **The African Unconscious: Roots of Ancient Mysticism and Modern Psychology**, Bynum, Edward, Bruce, Teachers College Press, NY, 1998.
- **Dark Light, Consciousness: Melanin, Serpent Power, and the Luminous Matrix of Reality**, Bynum, Edward, Bruce, Inner Traditions, Rochester, Vermont, 2012.
- **African Origins of Biological Psychiatry**, Dr. Richard King, (Seymour-Smith, Inc: Tn), 1990.
- **The Physics of the Future,** Michio Kaku, Anchor Books, New York, 2012.
- **GAGUT Gij,j = 0: Radically Unifies Mathematics and solves Riemann Hypothesis, A Clay Mathematics Millennium Problem**, Professor Gabriel A. Oyibo, OFAPPIT Institute of Technology Press, Dix Hills, NY, 2010.
- **Origins: Fourteen Billion Years of Cosmic Evolution**, Neil deGrasse Tyson and Donald Goldsmith, WW Norton and Co: NY/London, 2004.
- **Universe Down To Earth**, Neil de Grasse Tyson, Columbia University: 1994.

- **Stolen Legacy,** James, George, G. M., (Julian Richardson: CA), 1954, Chapter 8, "The Memphite Theology," p 139-151.

- **Egypt Revisited,** Van Sertima, Ivan, (Transaction Pub: NJ), Vol. 10, Summer 1989, Journal of African Civilization, Habib Sy, Jacques, "Theophile Obenga: At the Forefront of the African Renaissance in Philosophy," p 227-285.

- **Egypt Revisited,** Van Sertima, Ivan, (Transaction Pub: NJ), Vol. 10, Summer 1989, Journal of African Civilization, Obenga, Theophile, "African Philosophy of the Pharaonic Period," p 286-324.

- **Civilization or Barbarism,** Diop, Cheikh, Anta, (Lawrence Hill: NY), 1991, Chapter 17, "Does an African Philosophy Exist?" p 309-376.

- **Ancient Egypt and Black Africa**, Obenga, Theophile, (Karnak House: London), 1992.

- **African Philosophy: The Pharaonic Period: 2780-330 BCE**, Obenga, Theophile, Per Ankh, Paris, 2004, p 74-90.

- **Essays in Ancient Egyptian Studies,** Carruthers, Jacob, (University of Sankore Press: LA), 1984, "Ma'at: The African Universe."

- **Kemet and the African Worldview**, Carruthers, Jacob, and Karenga, Maulana, (University of Sankore Press: LA), 1986.

- **Intellectual Warrior**, Jacob H. Carruthers, Third World Press: Chicago, 1999.

- **Mdw Ntr: Divine Speech – A Historiographical Reflection of African Deep thought From the Time of the Pharaohs to the Present,** Carruthers, Jacob, (Karnak House: London), 1995, p 20-35, 40-47, 51-53, 58-62, 80-81, 116-119,

- **African Genesis: Amazing Stories of Man's Beginnings, Vol 1,** Barashango, Ishakamusa, (Fourth Dynasty Publishing Co.: MD), 1991.
    - Chapter 11, "An Introduction to the Memphite Theology – The Original Cosmic Science of Divine Balance, the

Memphite Drama: An Original Afrikan Genesis," p 153-162.

- Chapter 12, "The Memphite Drama and the Ptah Principle of Rational
  Intelligence in Earth's Creative Process – The Science of the Primeval Waters,"
  p 163-182,
- Chapter 13, "The Memphite Theology and the Unmoved Mover, Principle in Ancient Afrikan Atomic Science, Atum: The All and not yet being," p 183-194.
- Chapter 14, "Description and Function of the None Powers of Ancient Afrikan Astro-Atomic Science," p 195-202.
- Epilogue, "Awakening the Sleeping Giant Within," p 203-206.

- **Memphite Theology: Ancient Egyptian Mystic Wisdom of Ptah and the Metaphysics of Creation, Mind and the Path of Self-Mastery**, Ashby, Muata, (Cruzian Mystic Books: FL), 1996.

- **Mysteries of Mind: Memphite Theology-Philosophy of Ptah-Path to Immortality,** Ashby, Muata, (Cruzian Mystic Books: FL), 1996, 86-177.

- **Anunian Theology,** Ashby, Muata, Cruzian Books: FL, p 158-161.

- **The Egyptian Book Of The Dead: The Ancient Egyptian Book Of Enlightenment**, Ashby, Muata, Cruzian Mystic Books, FL, 2000, p 49, 83, 144.

- **The Egyptian Book Of Life: Symbolism of Ancient Egyptian Temple and Tomb Art**, Applegate, Melissa, Littlefield, Health Communications, Inc., FL, p xv-xix, 1-6. 7-38.

- **Foundation of African Thought**, Kamalu, Chukwunyere, (Karnak: London), 1990.

- **egyptian mysteries**, Lamy, Lucy, (Thames and Hudson, Inc: NY), 1981, p 8-23, 33-65.

- **Ancient Egyptian Literature: The Old and Middle Kingdoms, Vol 1**, Lichtheim, Miriam, University of California Press, LA, 1914/1975, p 51-57.

- **The Husia**, Karenga, Maulana, Kawaida Publications, Los Angeles, 1984, p 3-9.

- **The African Unconscious: Roots of Ancient Mysticism and Modern Psychology**, Bynum, Bruce, Edward, Teachers College Press, NY, 1998, p 121-122, 124, 163, 174.

- **Dark Light, Consciousness: Melanin, Serpent Power, and the Luminous Matrix of Reality**, Bynum, Edward, Bruce, Inner Traditions, Rochester, Vermont, 2012, p 34, 35-36.

- **The Egypt Code**, Robert Bauval, Consortium Book Sales: MN, p 135-137, 2008.

- **Why Darkness Matters: The Power of Melanin in the Brain**, Ed., Dr. Bruce Bynum, African American Images: Chicago, 2000.

- **GAGUT G i j,j=0: Radically Unifies Mathematics and Solves Riemann Hypothesis, A Clay Mathematics Millennium Problem**, Professor Gabriel A. Oyibo, OFAPPIT Institute of Technology Press, Dix Hills, NY, 2010.

- **The Festival Songs of Aset and Neb-Het-Tet:** A Litany to the Sun-God, is a work of ancient Kemetic (Egyptian) literature whose author is unknown. The songs form part of the funeral hieratic papyrus of Nesi Ámsu (No. 10158 in the British Museum). It has been translated by M. de Horrack and is titled *"Les Lamentations d'Isis et Nephthys."*

Appendices

1) Shabaka's Stone

THE PRIMATE OF THE
ESSENCES

NUN

PTAH

ATUM *hpr*

3) Philosophy # 2 – Essences of Pre-Existing Order and Arrangement

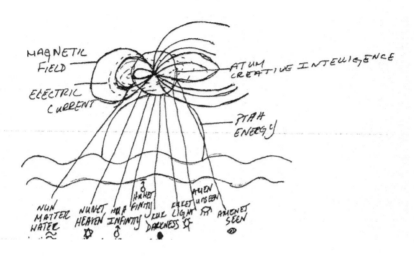

ATUM   SHU   TEFNUT   GEB   NUT   AUSAR   ASET   SETESH   NEB-HET-TET

5)   Cosmic Panspermia

6) Human Panspermia – Egg with Spermatozoa

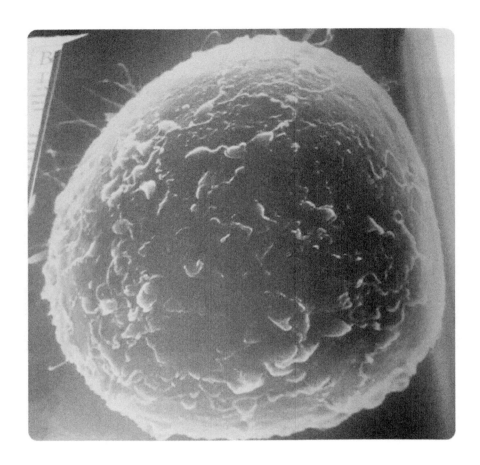

7) Atumic Consciousness – Stages/Intellect-Grades/Consciousness

KEY

Stages of Intellectual Development
```
Percept              =Per
Recept               =Rec
Concept              =Con
Intuition            =Int
```

Grades of Consciousness
```
Unconsciousness      =UnC=Per
Simple Conscious     =SiC=Per+Rec
Self Conscious       =SeC=Per+Rec+Con
Cosmic Conscious     =CoC=Per+Rec+Con+Int
```

` NUN = Female Womb...PTAH = Male Sperm...ATUM = Zygote

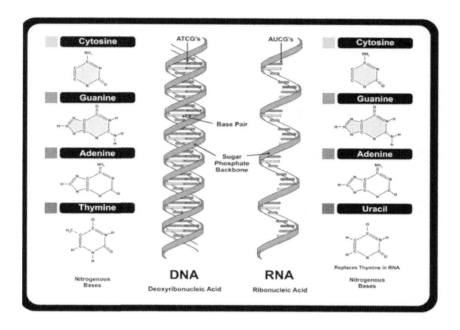

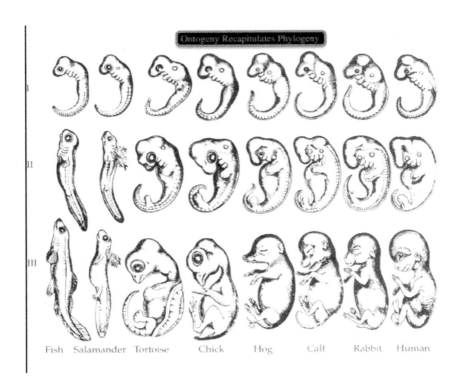

Ontogeny Recapitulates Phylogeny

Fish   Salamander Tortoise   Chick   Hog   Calf   Rabbit   Human

Appendix 8 - The Ipet at Waset and the 7 Levels of the Soul's Transformation

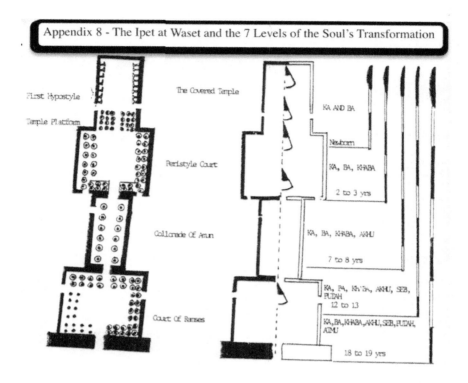

First Hypostyle

Temple Platform

The Covered Temple

Peristyle Court

Collonade Of Amun

Court Of Ramses

KA AND BA

Newborn

KA, BA, KHABA

2 to 3 yrs

KA, BA, KHABA, AKHU

7 to 8 yrs

KA, BA, Kh'ba, AKHU, SEB, PUTAH

12 to 13

KA, BA, KHABA, AKHU, SEB, PUTAH, ATMU

18 to 19 yrs

The Ipet at Wa'at (Grand Lodge at Luxor) was built depicting the different ages of the human being. By combining the seven (7) levels of spirituality, we see that the ancient Africans also realized and taught that spirituality manifested itself through TRANSMUTATION. Each level grew out of the preceding one. The ancients believed that humans had to nurture the soul by obeying the laws of MA'AT.

12) Olfactory System

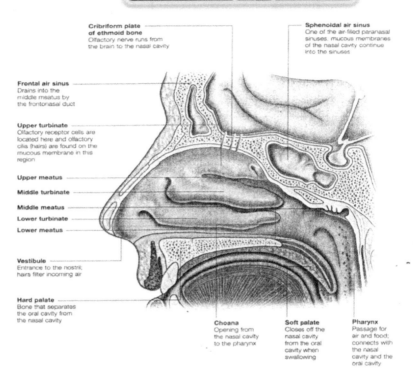

Olfactory System

**Cribriform plate
of ethmoid bone**
Olfactory nerve runs from
the brain to the nasal cavity

Sphenoidal air sinus
One of the air-filled paranasal
sinuses; mucous membranes
of the nasal cavity continue
into the sinuses

Frontal air sinus
Drains into the
middle meatus by
the frontonasal duct

Upper turbinate
Olfactory receptor cells are
located here and olfactory
cilia (hairs) are found on the
mucous membrane in this
region

Upper meatus

Middle turbinate

Middle meatus

Lower turbinate

Lower meatus

Vestibule
Entrance to the nostril;
hairs filter incoming air

Hard palate
Bone that separates
the oral cavity from
the nasal cavity

Choana
Opening from
the nasal cavity
to the pharynx

Soft palate
Closes off the
nasal cavity
from the oral
cavity when
swallowing

Pharynx
Passage for
air and food;
connects with
the nasal
cavity and the
oral cavity

Olfactory
bulb

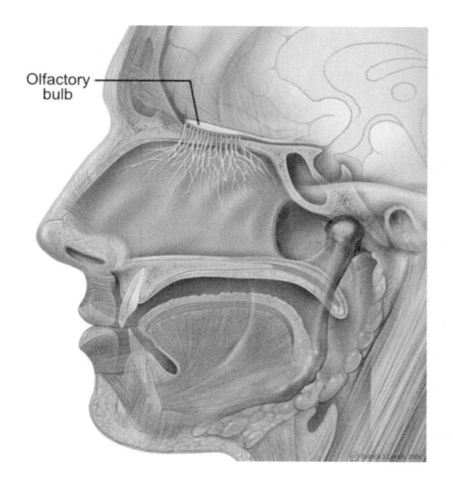

14) Room 5 and 12 in Covered Temple – Ipet at Waset

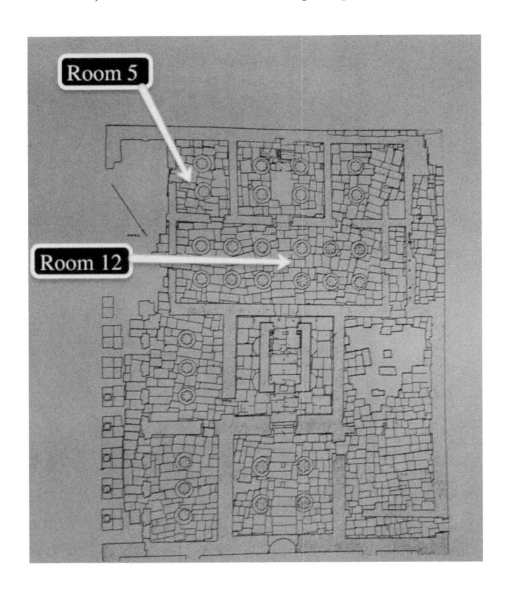

15) Room 5 and 12 – Transposition in the Covered Temple, Ipet at Waset

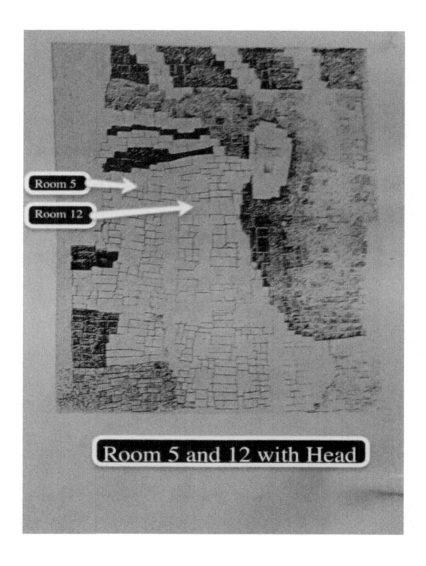

Room 5 and 12 with Head

16) Example of Transparency in Room 5 and 12 – Covered Temple – Ipet at Waset

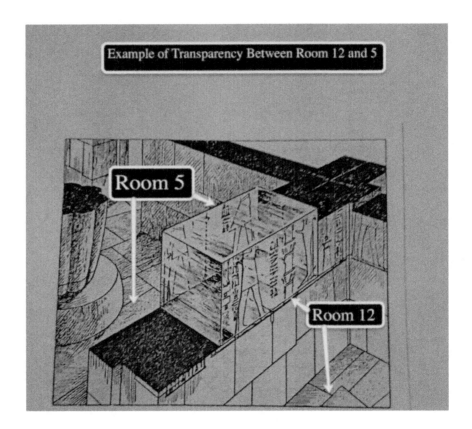

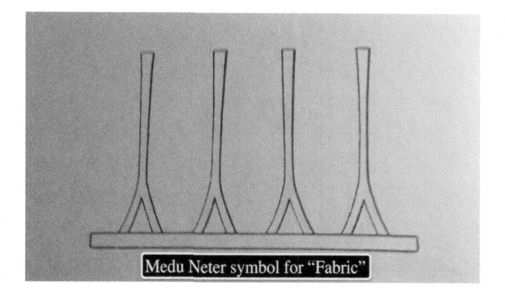

Medu Neter symbol for "Fabric"

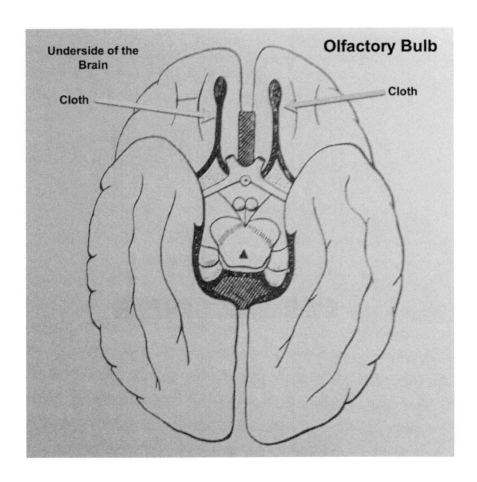

The M's in Owl

About the Author

Professor Kaba Hiawatha Kamene is an international, 40-year plus, Pan African and African Centered Conscious teacher, consultant, administrator, staff developer, and curriculum writer who has taught every grade level in the New York Department of Education and State University of New York at New Paltz.

Over Kaba Hiawatha's long career in Education, he has consulted many Boards of Education, Schools, Community, Parent, and Student groups. He has visited many classrooms around the country and implemented successful strategies in the teaching/learning process. He is firmly dedicated to the belief that culture plays a vitally important role in education and proudly credits many of his academic views to his teacher world-renowned educator, Professor John Henrik Clarke.

Professor Kaba Hiawatha Kamene is the former Principal Facilitator and Chief Executive Officer of the African-Centered Science Academy, "Per Ankh (Temple/House Of Life)".

He is the co-author of "Mi aMoor" and author of "Honoring William Leo Hansberry" and has starred in several African Science Centered, critically acclaimed, educational documentaries such as Tariq Nasheed's, Hidden Colors 1-5 and 1804: The Hidden History of the Haitian Revolution, Buck Breaking.

Additionally, he is the featured narrator in the hit documentary, "Out of Darkness" and "Heavy is the Crown" by Amadeuz Christ as well as starring in "Elementary Genocide", "Black Friday 1-2" and Dame Dash's, "The Secret to Ballin" with Snoop Dogg, Ice T, Rev. Dr. Michael Beckwith, and other community icons.

Professor Kaba Hiawatha Kamene's voice, speeches, writing, and narration have been performed in independent productions, "NeruvianDoom" by Nehru and Doom, "Om", "From Kaos to Order" and "Mi aMoor". He is also the feature writer and performer on Wu-Tang Clan's EP, "The Saga Continues" track, "Message"

His motto to the African conscious community is *"Keep on Keepin' on; cause it ain't over 'til we win!"* Professor Kaba Hiawatha Kamene lives in New York with the love of his life, Sharen of 37 years and they have two daughters and one son, Sasha Madeline, Candace Coleman and his son, Heru who have all followed in their parent's footsteps to serve humanity and the African American community.

# # #

Professor Kaba Hiawatha Kamene's Educational Library

1. (Video Stream) - The InnerGround Railroad: Freeing Your Mind
2. (DVD) - The InnerGround Railroad: Freeing Your Mind
3. 3 Video Stream Bundle of Origin of the Human Family
4. (Video Stream) - The Dogon (Part 1) (Stages of Intellectual Growth & Grades of Consciousness)
5. (Video Stream) - The Dogon (Part 3) (Dogon History) (Duration: 76 minutes)
6. (Video Stream) - The Dogon (Part 2) (Dogon Geography)
7. Free - DVD (Video Stream) - The African Family Unity Forum - Mt. Vernon, NY - Doles Community Center (Duration: 36 minutes)
8. DVD (2 SET) - Hopkinsville, Kentucky
9. DVD (Video Stream) - Harlem Liberation School - Harlem, NY
10. DVD (Video Stream - 2 SET) - [Hopkinsville, Kentucky
11. DVD (Video Stream): Spirituality - It's Origins and Success
12. DVD (2 SET) - West Africa - Ancient To 1492 - Part 1 - Origin Human Migration in Africa
13. 2 DVD Set - The Dogon Nation of Mali, West Africa
14. (3 DVD Set) - Bringing the Brilliance of Malcolm X Into the 21st Century
15. New DVD from Professor Kaba Hiawatha Kamene - Ma'at: The Feathered WombedMan
16. DVD - Hidden Wisdom of Black Holes in the African Woman's Womb
17. FREE DOWNLOAD: Notes on Essential Notions of Black Skin (32-page special report)
18. DVD - Introduction and Overview of the Moors in World History http://bit.ly/2kymZAN
19. CD - Mi aMoor
20. HARDCOVER BOOK - Mi aMoor (Full Color Photographs - 123 pages)

RACE WAR WEBINAR SERIES:

Race War Webinar Series with Professor Kaba Hiawatha Kamene

SBR WEBINAR SERIES:

Spirituality Before Religions Webinar Series with Professor Kaba Hiawatha Kamene

Printed in Great Britain
by Amazon

46622364R00111